T0183660

Lecture Notes in Artificial Intelligence 12298

Subseries of Lecture Notes in Computer Science

More information about this subseries at http://www.springer.com/series/1244

Andrea Aler Tubella · Stephen Cranefield ·
Christopher Frantz · Felipe Meneguzzi ·
Wamberto Vasconcelos (Eds.)

Coordination, Organizations, Institutions, Norms, and Ethics for Governance of Multi-Agent Systems XIII

International Workshops COIN 2017 and COINE 2020
Sao Paulo, Brazil, May 8–9, 2017 and Virtual Event, May 9, 2020
Revised Selected Papers

Editors
Andrea Aler Tubella
Umeå University
Umeå, Sweden

Stephen Cranefield
University of Otago
Dunedin, New Zealand

Christopher Frantz
Norwegian University of Science
and Technology (NTNU)
Gjøvik, Norway

Felipe Meneguzzi
Pontifical Catholic University of Rio
Grande do Sul
Porto Alegre, Brazil

Wamberto Vasconcelos
University of Aberdeen
Aberdeen, UK

ISSN 0302-9743 ISSN 1611-3349 (electronic)
Lecture Notes in Artificial Intelligence
ISBN 978-3-030-72375-0 ISBN 978-3-030-72376-7 (eBook)
https://doi.org/10.1007/978-3-030-72376-7

LNCS Sublibrary: SL7 – Artificial Intelligence

This Springer imprint is published by the registered company Springer Nature Switzerland AG
The registered company address is: Gewerbestrasse 11, 6330 Cham, Switzerland

Preface

This volume collates selected revised papers presented at the 2017 edition of the Coordination, Organization, Institutions, and Norms Workshop (COIN), co-located with the International Conference on Autonomous Agents and Multiagent Systems (AAMAS) in Sao Paulo, Brazil, as well as papers from the 2020 edition of the workshop, likewise co-located with AAMAS in Auckland, New Zealand – held virtually due to the pandemic situation. Reflecting novel topic foci of researchers and scholars interested in the theoretical and empirical evaluation of technologies for the presentation and analysis of the coordination of social behaviour, the workshop has been relabelled as Coordination, Organization, Institutions, Norms, and Ethics for Governance of Multi-Agent Systems (COINE). This modification specifically responds to the focus on governance of social systems as the overarching theme of the COINE workshop series, and therein the explicit consideration of ethical aspects.

Submissions to both the 2017 and 2020 editions of the workshop underwent two rounds of blind peer review. Full versions of all papers underwent reviews by at least three reviewers, with an initial assessment as part of the admission to the presentation, and a second round in which the authors had the opportunity to refine and extend the previously submitted version based on feedback received as part of the reviews and the presentations.

The 2017 edition of the COIN workshop received ten submissions, of which five were accepted for presentation and three as posters. Out of those, two papers were refined and submitted as part of this volume. The 2020 edition of the COINE workshop received ten submissions, out of which eight were accepted for presentation, subsequently refined, and included in this post-proceedings volume.

While distributed over two editions of the workshop, the proceedings organise the workshop papers into three themes, namely empirical applications of COINE technologies, followed by papers with a focus on convention emergence, as well as establishment and optimisation of social metrics. The final theme focuses on conceptual frameworks and architectures that embed behaviour coordination from a socio-normative perspective as well as the characterisation of social constructs more generally.

Empirical Applications of COINE Technologies

The papers in this section address the application of COINE-related technology with specific focus on normative behaviour. Doing so, the papers draw on real-world datasets and selectively focus on the detection of norms, as well as detecting their violation or conflicts.

- *Norm Conflict Identification using a Convolutional Neural Network* by Aires and Meneguzzi applies a combination of traditional machine learning techniques and convolutional neural networks in order to automate conflict detection in legal text, with specific focus on a large-scale contract dataset – for which the authors showcase promising results.

- *Norm violation in online communities – A study of Stack Overflow comments* by Cheriyan et al. proposes an approach to automate the detection of intentional or unintentional norm violation in Stack Overflow comments in order to automatically identify and flag comments for moderation, or to indicate potential violations to authors themselves – thereby alleviating the spread of hate speech and other forms of inappropriate expression.
- *Mining International Political Norms from the GDELT Database* by Murali et al. applies Bayesian norm mining to identify political norms as expressed by linked international events documented in the GDELT news database – showcasing the potential of norm mining techniques over conventional probabilistic discrete-event models in institutional settings.
- *Developers' responses to app review feedback — A study of communication norms in app development* by Savarimuthu et al. describes a large-scale study of developer responses to app reviews for popular applications in the Android app ecosystem. The authors identify a set of norms distributed over three general categories that can serve as a basis to develop recommendation systems to support developers when interacting with users or by automating the generation of responses.

Emergence & Social Metrics

The second group of papers focuses on the themes of emergence as well as estimation and optimisation of COINE concepts, including values, norms and general social metrics.

- *Convention Emergence in Partially Observable Topologies* by Marchant and Griffiths explores approaches to promoting efficient norm emergence by strategic placement of influencing agents in topologies. As a central contribution, the authors propose a learning algorithm that is able to identify preferable locations in a topology based on a finite number of observations.
- *Improving Confidence in the Estimation of Values and Norms* by Calvacante Siebert et al. proposes an approach to improve the confidence of artificial agents to estimate values and norms of human agents in the context of an ultimatum game setting. The work identifies two promising methods that can be variably applied in a scenario-dependent manner.
- *Should I tear down this wall? Optimizing social metrics by evaluating novel actions* by Kramar et al. investigates the potential of learning linkages between behavioural trajectories and environmental circumstances in order to assess the impact of modifications in an agent society's physical environment on social metrics at large.

Conceptual Frameworks & Architectures

The final section of the proceedings is dedicated to approaches that emphasise the architectural dimension of normative agents, as well as laying out the fundamental relationships between different social coordination concepts.

- *Impact of different belief facets on agents' decisions – a refined cognitive architecture to model the interaction between organisations' institutional characteristics and agents' behaviour* by Afshar Sedigh et al. draws linkages between the Belief-Desire-Intentions agent architecture and social-psychological theories, with specific focus on the Theory of Planned Behaviour. The paper explores the impact of individual weightings based on different personal characteristics on behavioural outcomes, making theoretically discussed concepts, such as cognitive dissonance, overt.
- *A Norm Emergence Framework for Normative MAS – Position Paper* by Martin-Morris et al. discusses directions toward a novel norm synthesis process that drives norm emergence based on dedicated synthesiser agents that further accommodate intentional norm change based on participant agreement as well as validation by an artificial external authority.
- *Social rules for agent systems* by Mellema et al. provides an overview of social concepts, such as social practices, norms and conventions – as relevant for COINE technologies – and identifies their conceptual relationships. This work aims at providing a basis for the integrated discussion and analysis of associated dynamics.

In addition to the contributions by the authors of the 2017 and 2020 editions of (now) COINE, we gratefully acknowledge the programme committee members for both workshops, who are listed after this preface, and the guidance offered by the COIN(E) Champions.

February 2021

Andrea Aler Tubella
Stephen Cranefield
Christopher Frantz
Felipe Meneguzzi
Wamberto Vasconcelos

Organization

Program Chairs

Andrea Aler Tubella	Umeå University, Sweden
Stephen Cranefield	University of Otago, New Zealand
Christopher Frantz	Norwegian University of Science and Technology (NTNU), Norway
Felipe Meneguzzi	Pontifícia Universidade Católica do Rio Grande do Sul, Brazil
Wamberto Vasconcelos	University of Aberdeen, UK

Program Committee

Mohsen Afsharchi	University of Zanjan, Iran
João Paulo Aires	Charles University, Czech Republic
Huib Aldewereld	HU University of Applied Sciences Utrecht, The Netherlands
Leonardo Rosa Amado	Pontifícia Universidade Católica do Rio Grande do Sul, Brazil
Estefania Argente	Universidad Politécnica de Valencia, Spain
Alexander Artikis	NCSR "Demokritos", Greece
Olivier Boissier	Mines Saint-Étienne/Institut Mines-Télécom, France
Patrice Caire	University of Luxembourg, Luxemburg
Daniel Castro Silva	University of Porto, Portugal
Amit Chopra	Lancaster University, UK
Rob Christiaanse	EFCO BV, The Netherlands
Luciano Coutinho	Universidade Federal do Maranhão, Brazil
Natalia Criado	King's College London, UK
Mehdi Dastani	Utrecht University, The Netherlands
Dave de Jonge	Western Sydney University, Australia
Frank Dignum	Umeå University, Sweden
Nicoletta Fornara	Università della Svizzera italiana (USI), Switzerland
Amineh Ghorbani	Delft University of Technology, The Netherlands
Aditya Ghose	University of Wollongong, Australia
Nathan Griffiths	University of Warwick, UK
Jomi Fred Hübner	Federal University of Santa Catarina, Brazil
Jie Jiang	University of Surrey, UK
Özgür Kafali	University of Kent, UK
Anup Kalia	IBM T. J. Watson Research Center, USA
Martin Kollingbaum	University of Aberdeen, UK
JeeHang Lee	Sangmyung University, South Korea
Henrique Lopes Cardoso	FEUP/LIACC, Portugal

Emiliano Lorini	IRIT, France
Samhar Mahmoud	King's College London, UK
Eric T. Matson	Purdue University, USA
John-Jules Meyer	Utrecht University, The Netherlands
Daniel Moldt	University of Hamburg, Germany
Martin Neumann	Johannes Gutenberg-Universität Mainz, Germany
Pablo Noriega	IIIA-CSIC, Spain
Timothy Norman	University of Southampton, UK
Nir Oren	University of Aberdeen, UK
Julian Padget	University of Bath, UK
Simon Parsons	University of Liverpool, UK
Jeremy Pitt	Imperial College London, UK
Alessandro Ricci	University of Bologna, Italy
Ana Paula Rocha	University of Porto, Portugal
Antônio Carlos da Rocha Costa	Universidade Federal do Rio Grande do Sul, Brazil
Juan Antonio Rodríguez Aguilar	IIIA-CSIC, Spain
Bastin Tony Roy Savarimuthu	University of Otago, New Zealand
Brian Scassellati	Yale University, USA
Jaime Sichman	Universidade de São Paulo, Brazil
Liz Sonenberg	Melbourne University, Australia
Pankaj Telang	SAS, USA
Myrthe Tielman	Delft University of Technology, The Netherlands
Luca Tummolini	ISTC-CNR, Italy
Javier Vázquez-Salceda	Universitat Politècnica de Catalunya · BarcelonaTech, Spain
Harko Verhagen	Stockholm University, Sweden
George Vouros	University of Piraeus, Greece
Marina De Vos	University of Bath, UK
M. Birna van Riemsdijk	University of Twente, The Netherlands
Leon van der Torre	University of Luxembourg, Luxemburg

Contents

Empirical Applications of COINE Technologies

Norm Conflict Identification Using a Convolutional Neural Network

João Paulo Aires(✉) and Felipe Meneguzzi(✉)

Pontifical Catholic University of Rio Grande do Sul, Porto Alegre, RS, Brazil
joao.aires.001@acad.pucrs.br, felipe.meneguzzi@pucrs.br

Abstract. Contracts formally represent agreements between two or more parties as deontic statements or norms within their clauses. Norms may conflict between each other if not carefully designed, which may invalidate entire contracts. Human reviewers invest great effort to write conflict-free contracts that, for complex and long contracts, can be time-consuming and error-prone. In this work, we develop an approach to automate the identification of potential conflicts between norms in contracts. We build a two-phase approach that uses traditional machine learning together with a convolutional neural network to extract and compare norms in order to identify conflicts between them. Using a manually annotated and artificially generated set of conflicts as train and test set, our approach obtains 84% accuracy.

Keywords: Norms · Contracts · Deep learning · Natural language

1 Introduction

Society imposes regulations to its members in order to minimize conflicting behaviors [20]. Such regulations also known as social norms, define expected behaviors accepted for society members and that ensure that individuals act according to a socially acceptable behavior. Besides regulating entire societies, social norms are also used to regulate interactions in smaller groups, and are often present in social relationships involving agreements over products and services. A common way to formalize a set of norms applied to an agreement is through contracts. In human societies, contracts are semi-structured documents written in natural language, which are used in almost every existing formal agreement. Contracts define the parties involved in the agreement, their relations, and the behavior expected of each party within clauses. When written in natural language, contracts may use imprecise and possibly vague language to define parties, obligations and objects of its clauses, leading to inconsistencies. Such inconsistencies may create, in the long run, unforeseen legal problems for one or more of the involved parties. To identify and solve such conflicts and inconsistencies, the contract maker needs to read the entire contract and identify each conflicting pair of norms. As contracts tend to have a large number of

A. Aler Tubella et al. (Eds.): COIN 2017/COINE 2020, LNAI 12298, pp. 3–19, 2021.
https://doi.org/10.1007/978-3-030-72376-7_1

norms, the task of identifying norm conflicts is quite difficult for human beings, which makes it error-prone and takes substantial human effort.

Our main contributions in this work are four: Regarding the identification of norms in contracts, we (1) manually annotated a dataset containing sentences as norms and non-norms[1] and (2) developed a model to address the identification of norm sentences in contracts. Regarding the norm conflict identification, we (3) manually annotated a corpus containing artificially generated normative conflicts[2]; and (4) trained a model to identify potential normative conflicts between natural language contract clauses. We process raw text from contracts and identify their norms. Then, we train a convolutional neural network to classify norm pairs as conflict or non-conflict. We evaluate our approach using a dataset of contracts in which conflicts have been deliberately but randomly introduced between the norms, obtaining an accuracy around 84% in conflict identification for a 10-fold cross validation.

2 Norms and Contracts

Norms ensure that individuals act according to a defined set of behaviors and are punished when they are perceived not to be complying with them given a social setting [3]. Norms provide a powerful mechanism for regulating conflict in groups, governing much of our political and social lives. They are often represented using deontic logic, which has its origins in philosophical logic, applied modal logic, and ethical and legal theory. The aim of deontic logic is to describe ideal worlds, allowing the representation of deviations from the ideal (i.e. violations) [30]. Thus, deontic logic and the theory of normative positions are very relevant to legal knowledge representation, and consequently they are applied to the analysis and representation of normative systems [18]. Norms often use deontic concepts to describe permissions, obligations, and prohibitions. A prohibition indicates an action that must not be performed, and, if such action is carried out, a violation occurs. Conversely, a permission indicates an action that can either be performed or not, and no violation occurs in either case. In most deontic systems, a prohibition is considered to be equivalent to the negation of a permission, thus, an action that is not permitted comprises a prohibition. Whereas in permissive societies, an action not prohibited becomes a permitted one. Although these two modalities are sufficient to represent most norms, obligations are also commonly employed in norm representation. An obligation represents an action that must be performed, and it is equivalent either to the negation of a permission not to act or a prohibition not to act.

In contracts, norms are defined within clauses and are often directed to one or more parties of the contract. A contract is an agreement that two or more parties enter voluntarily when it is useful to formalize that a certain duty comes into existence by a promise made by at least one of the parties. The creation of a contract formalizes what each party expects from the other, creating a

[1] https://bit.ly/30oKcgU.

[2] https://goo.gl/3Hbl1r.

warranty that each party will fulfill their duties [25] and legally enforceable obligations between these parties. These enforceable obligations are defined by a set of norms, which are responsible for describing any expected behavior from the parties.

With the use of the Internet, electronic contracts arise as a new way to represent formal agreements and are increasingly explored for commercial services. An electronic contract is very similar to a traditional paper-based commercial contract, following the same rules and structure [23]. Almost all types of contract can be represented electronically, leading to the need of managing such contracts, dealing with the representation and evaluation of agreements. In this work, we deal with contracts written in natural language, thus, the task of analyzing and evaluating norms is traditionally done by human readers. As more contracts are required to codify an increasing number of online services which span over multiple countries and different legal systems, the tasks of writing and verifying contracts by humans become more laborious, taking substantial time [12].

2.1 Norm Conflicts

Sadat-Akhavi [26] describes four causes for a norm conflict to arise. The first cause is when the same act is subject to different types of norms. Thus, two norms are in conflict "if two different types of norms regulate the same act, i.e., if the same act is both obligatory and prohibited, permitted and prohibited, or permitted and obligatory". For example, consider a norm n1 that states that company X must pay product Z taxes, and a norm n2 that states that company X may pay product Z taxes. The second cause is when one norm requires an act, while another norm requires or permits a 'contrary' act. In this case, there is a normative conflict if "two contrary acts, or if one norm permits an act while the other norm requires a contrary act" [26]. For example, consider a norm n1 that states that Company X shall deliver product Z on location W, whereas norm n2 states that company X must deliver product Z on location Q. The conflict arises when an agent tries to comply with one norm and, at the same time, violates the other. The third case defines a cause of conflict when a norm prohibits a precondition of another norm. For example, norm 1 obliges company X to perform α in location θ, whereas norm 2 prohibits company X to be in location θ. In this case, company X cannot comply with norm 1 since been in location θ implies in a violation of norm 2. Finally, Sadat-Akhavi defines a cause of conflict when one norm prohibits a necessary consequence from another norm. For example, norm 1 states that company X shall/may replace its material supplier each year and the process shall not last more than two weeks, whereas norm 2 states that company X cannot be without a material supplier. In this case, the process of replacing the material supplier (norm 1) implies to company X an amount of time without a material supplier, complying with such norm makes company X violate norm 2.

3 Deep Learning

Deep learning is a branch of machine learning that tries to solve problems by automatically finding an internal representation based on hierarchical layers [14]. Such layers can extract complex features from data as they get deeper, which makes feature design from human engineers unnecessary [5]. There are multiple architectures of deep neural networks that achieve this type of learning, such as, convolutional neural networks (CNN) [6], recurrent neural networks (RNN) [17], and autoencoders [29].

3.1 Convolutional Neural Networks

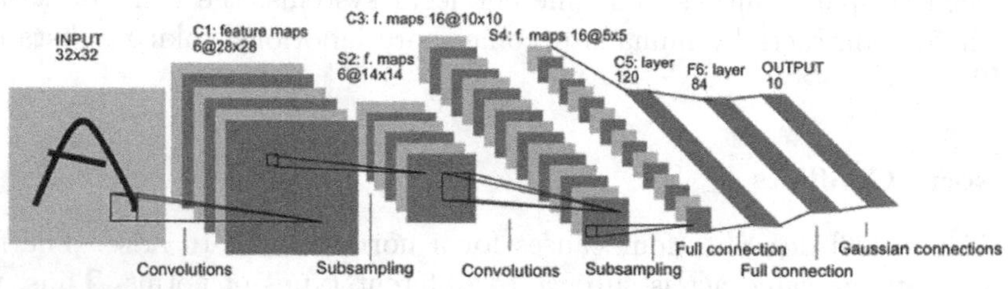

Fig. 1. Abstract representation of a CNN (extracted from LeCun *et al.* [6])

Convolutional neural networks were first introduced by LeCun *et al.* [6]. They modify the usual neural network by adding successive convolutional layers before the fully connected neural network output layer, as illustrated in Fig. 1. A convolutional layer uses the convolution mathematical operator to modify specific regions of input data using a set of kernels, substantially diminishing the number of neural connection weighs a learning algorithm must adjust close to the input features. A convolution can be viewed as an operation between two functions that produces a third one. Each kernel of a convolutional layer has a defined size and contains a value for each cell; these values, called weights, multiply the values from the input features resulting in a new feature map. The kernel goes through the input multiplying every matrix cell, as illustrated in Fig. 2. The result of applying multiple convolutions to an input is a set of feature maps with specific information from the input.

In order to reduce the dimensionality of features resulting from convolutions, convolutional networks often contain pooling layers between successive convolutional layers. These layers have a single kernel without weights that goes through the input aiming to down-sample the size of the image, much in the same way resizing an image reduces its dimensions, as illustrated in Fig. 3. They can be either a max pooling or a mean pooling, the former outputs the highest value among the ones in the kernel size and the later outputs the mean value among the ones in the kernel. LeCun *et al.* use this type of neural network to identify handwritten numbers from zip codes in real U.S. mail. From then on, convolutional neural networks have been used extensively to solve image processing problems. More recently, researchers have used CNNs to solve classical natural language processing problems [13,31], such as part-of-speech tagging, named entity recognition, and sentiment analysis. In most cases, approaches using CNNs have matched and surpassed previous approaches using rule-based and probabilistic approaches. The key challenge in applying CNNs to text processing is finding a suitable matrix representation for the input text.

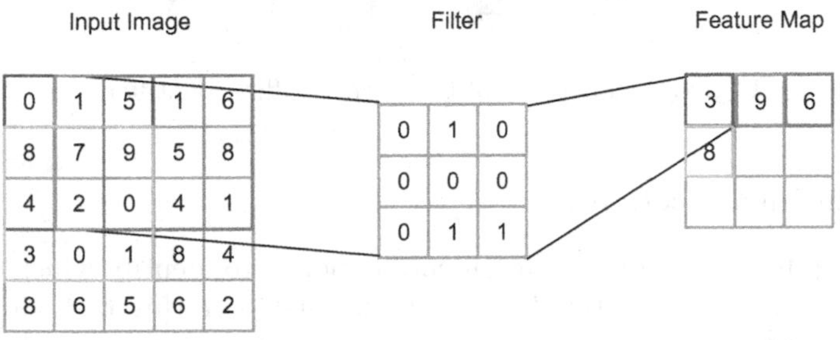

Fig. 2. Convolution example

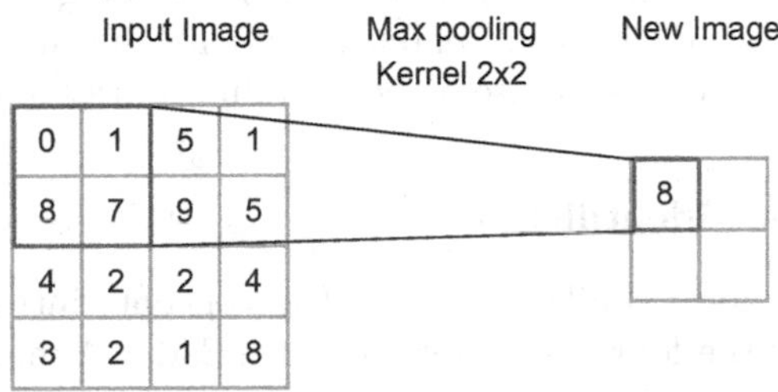

Fig. 3. Pooling example

4 Conflict Detection Approach

Our approach to identifying potential conflicts between norms in contracts is divided into two phases. In the first one, we identify norms within contractual sentences by training a Support Vector classifier using a manually annotated dataset. In the second part, we classify norm pairs as conflicting or non-conflicting using a CNN. Figure 4 illustrates the architecture of our approach.

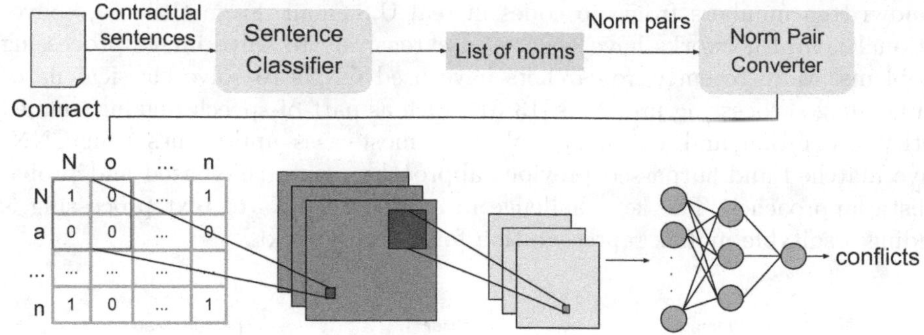

Fig. 4. Architecture of the norm conflict identifier

4.1 Norm Identification

The first step towards norm conflict identification is to identify which sentences in a contract contain deontic statements (norms). For this task we consider contract sentences to be of two exclusive types: norm sentences and non-norm sentences. In order to separate norm sentences from the rest of the contract text, we train a classifier based on Support Vector Machines (SVM) using a manually annotated dataset. We created the dataset using real contracts extracted from the *onecle* website[3], specifically contracts of the manufacturing domain[4]. We manually annotated the sentences in each contract as being either norm or non-norm, resulting in a set of 699 norm sentences and 494 non-norm sentences from a total of 22 contracts, which we use as both train and test sets.

4.2 Norm Conflict Identification

In order to identify norm conflicts, we use the concepts introduced by Sadat-Akhavi [26]. Besides the four causes for conflicts, Sadat-Akhavi identifies three main types of conflicts, which are:

- Permission x Obligation;
- Permission x Prohibition; and
- Obligation x Prohibition.

We base our conflict identification on these three conflict types in addition to the first and second causes of norm conflict defined by Sadat-Akhavi. Thus, in this work, we consider norm conflicts to be:

- Pairs of norms with different deontic concepts applied to the same actions and the same parties; and

[3] http://contracts.onecle.com/.
[4] http://contracts.onecle.com/type/47.shtml.

– Pairs of norms where the obliged action of one clause is either prohibited or permitted in another clause.

The key challenge in processing text using CNNs is to generate a representation suitable for the matrix-format input required for the convolutional layers. Here, we take inspiration from recent work that deals with natural language. The first sentence representation, created by Zhang and LeCun [31], in which they use a CNN to deal with natural language processing problems. Their approach aims to, among other tasks, classify the sentiment (positive, negative, and neutral) of product reviews from Amazon. Since CNNs are designed to process images, the solution they propose to translate a sentence into an image is to create a matrix representation with the review characters as lines and the alphabet as columns. Thus, given a cell $\{i, j\}$, they assign 1 when the *ith* character is equal to the *jth*, otherwise, they assign 0. Figure 5 illustrates their sentence representation using as example a sentence that begins with 'above'. The resulting matrix has 1 where letters are equal (such as cell $1, 1$ and $2, 2$) and 0 otherwise.

	a	b	...	x	y	z
a	1	0	...	0	0	0
b	0	1	...	0	0	0
o	0	0	...	0	0	0
...	...	...	...	...	...	...
e	0	0	...	0	0	0

Fig. 5. Sentence representation by Zhang and LeCun

The second work is from Kim [19], which uses a sentence representation to classify sentences in different natural language processing problems. Here, the representation is a matrix in which the lines are the words of a sentence and columns are the word embedding of each word. An embedding is a representation that turns words into vectors of floating point numbers. Such representation may have a variable size and carries semantic information from each word. In Kim's approach, the resulting matrix is a group of word embedding lines. Figure 6 illustrates this sentence representation.

One of the key aspects in norm conflicts is that both norms tend to be very similar as they usually refer to the same party/parties with similar actions, and conflicting deontic modalities. Therefore, the similarity distance between two sentences often indicates how norm pairs are likely to conflict. Consequently, we rely on training examples that consist of binary images created from each pair of norms

Embedding

Sentence						
I	0.9	0.5	...	0.6	0.1	0.2
like	0.1	0.2	...	0.5	0.5	0.6
the	0.1	0.3	...	0.2	0.9	0.1
new	0.7	0.3	...	0.4	0.1	0.2
device	0.6	0.4	...	0.8	0.3	0.7

Fig. 6. Sentence representation by Kim

denoting the distance between these norms. We created a pair-of-norms representation using a matrix to denote similar characters in each norm. Given two norms α and β, our matrix consists of the characters from α in its lines and the characters from β in its columns, as Fig. 7 illustrates. Given a cell {i, j}, we assign 1 to it when the ith character of α is equal to the jth character of β and 0 otherwise. For this work, we limit the lengths of both norms to 200 characters, which is the mean length of norms from our dataset and truncate overlong sentences. We performed tests using different norm lengths, which demonstrate that using more than 200 characters does not improve the final result. Using this representation, we train a CNN to generate a model to classify norm pairs as conflicting and non-conflicting. Here, we rely on the power of CNN to connect information from different regions of the input matrix to extract features that indicate conflicting aspects. Thus, we consider that a CNN is able to identify patterns that relate to deontic meaning, subject, and object between norms.

5 Experiments

In this section, we discuss our experiments using our different models over our manually annotated datasets for both identification of norms and norm conflicts.

Norm 2

Norm 1	T	h	...	n	o	w
I	0	0	...	0	0	0
t	1	0	...	0	0	0
...	...	...	...	...	...	...
o	0	0	...	1	0	0
n	0	0	...	0	0	0

Fig. 7. Norm pair representation in our approach

5.1 Norm Identification Dataset

We identify norms in contracts by classifying contract sentences as norms and non-norms. Our classifier trains over a manually annotated dataset containing 1193 sentences. We randomly selected sentences from contracts of a public contract repository[5]. Then, a human annotator classifies the sentence as norm or non-norm. As result, we obtained 699 norms and 494 non-norm sentences.

5.2 Norm Conflict Dataset Annotation

To evaluate our approach to detect potential conflicts between norms, we required a corpus with contracts containing real conflicts. However, since we found no such corpus available, we created a dataset with semi-automatically generated norm conflicts using a set of real non-conflicting norms as a basis. To assist in the creation of conflicts, we developed a system to assist human users to insert conflicts randomly in a contract, while still maintaining language syntactic correctness. In order to create such conflicts, we relied on the assistance of two volunteers each of which was responsible for inserting two different types of conflict. Each volunteer was asked to create one of the two causes of conflict. We asked the first volunteer to insert conflicts that have only differences in the modal verb, e.g. changing an obligation modal verb ('must') for a permission one ('may'). This volunteer created 94 conflicts in 10 different contracts, totaling 13 conflicts between Permission x Prohibition, 36 conflicts between Permission x Obligation, and 46 conflicts between Obligation x Prohibition. We asked the second volunteer to insert conflicts that contain deontic conflicts and modifications in the norm actions. This volunteer created 17 conflicts in 6 different contracts, totaling 4 conflicts between Permission x Prohibition, 8 conflicts between Permission x Obligation, and 5 conflicts between Obligation x Prohibition.

We developed a semi-automatic process conflict creation within a system that, when prompted, selects a random norm from a random contract, makes a copy of it, and asks the user to modify it. After user modification, the system creates a new contract containing both the original norm and the modified copy, ensuring that a semantically similar, but conflicting, clause is present in the resulting contract. Thus, we use these new contracts to identify the inserted conflicts.

From the contracts we used to create conflicts, we selected all sentences not used in the conflict creation to produce a set for the non-conflicting norm class. This set has a total of 204,443 norm pairs.

[5] https://www.onecle.com/.

5.3 SVM

To create the sentence classifier, we trained an SVM classifier using the dataset described in Sect. 4.1. SVM is often used to classify datasets with few training examples with multiple features and a binary classification task since it creates a hyperplane that tries to find the best division between two classes [16]. In order to train the SVM, we turn each sentence into a bag-of-words representation [15], which represents the frequency of words from a fixed dictionary in sentence. Using this representation, the SVM learns from the frequency each word appears in a class.

5.4 CNN

To create the norm conflict identifier, we train a CNN using norm pairs from the dataset described in Sect. 5.2. In this work, we use the classical *LeNet* CNN, developed by LeCun *et al.* [6]. The network architecture consists of two convolutional layers followed by a max pooling layer and two fully-connected neural networks. Each convolutional layer has 32 kernels that are responsible for extracting features from the input image. The network receives as input an image representation of each norm pair.

6 Results

6.1 Sentence Classifier

To evaluate our sentence classifier, we divided our manually annotated dataset into train and test set. We use a 80/20 division, which results in 954 sentences in the train set and 239 sentences in the test set. Both sets are balanced according to the number of elements in each class, i.e., 559 norm sentences and 395 non-norm sentences in the train set, and 140 norm sentences and 99 non-norm sentences in the test set. To compare the SVM with other linear models, we test the same dataset with two other classifiers: Perceptron and Passive Aggressive. Perceptron is a well-known linear model, which can be better explained as a neuron in a neural network [21]. It processes the input by multiplying it using a set of weights. The result goes to an activation function, which defines the input class. Passive Aggressive [4] is a linear model that has its name based on its weight update rule that, in each round, can be passive, when the hinge-loss result of its update is zero, and aggressive, when it is a positive number. In our evaluation, we consider four metrics: accuracy, precision, recall, and f-score. We obtain them by extracting the true and false positives (tp and fp, respectively), and the true and false negatives (tn and fn, respectively) from the confusion matrix resulted running the model over the test set. Table 1 shows the results for each classifier. The "Classifier" column indicates which learning algorithm corresponds to the results in the following columns. Column "Prec." corresponds to the precision metric as the result of the following equation: $\frac{tp}{tp+fp}$. "Rec." corresponds to the recall metric calculated using the following equation: $\frac{tp}{tp+fn}$. Column "F-Score" corresponds to the harmonic mean between precision (*prec*) and recall (*rec*), calculated by the equation: $2 \times \frac{prec \times rec}{prec + rec}$. Finally, the "Acc" column corresponds to the accuracy calculated by: $\frac{tp+tn}{tp+tn+fp+fn}$.

Table 1. Results for sentence classifier

Classifier	Prec.	Rec.	F-Score	Acc.
Perceptron	0.89	0.88	0.88	0.87
Pass. Agr.	**0.92**	0.88	0.90	0.89
SVM	0.88	**0.94**	**0.91**	**0.90**

All models obtain similar results in all metrics. However, since we are dealing with a large feature space and few training examples, we decided to use SVM as our main training model.

6.2 Norm Conflict Identifier

To train and evaluate the norm conflict identifier, we used a 10-fold cross-validation step dividing our dataset into train, validation, and test. Since we have a total of 104 norm pairs with conflicting norms and 204,443 conflict-free norm pairs, the first step is to create a balanced dataset. Thus, we reduced the number of non-conflicting norm pairs to 104, which gives us a total of 208 samples. Each fold has 10% of the data, which is around twenty samples, ten of each class. In each round, we use eight folds to train, one to validate, and one to test. To prevent overfitting, we use the early stopping technique that monitors the accuracy in the train and validation set. When the accuracy in the validation set starts to decrease and the train accuracy keeps increasing, an overfitting is detected, resulting in the termination of the training phase.

In order to understand how our CNN is learning the patterns from the input matrix, we captured the activation values from the first convolutional layer. Thus, given the trained model, we passed as input two norm pairs: one containing a conflict between norms and the other conflict free. Figure 8 shows the activation for the conflicting pair. As we can see, only part of the feature map is activated. In this small region, the main diagonal, which corresponds to the similarity between norms, is fully activated. Such behavior indicates that the CNN is using the similarity to classify norm pairs as conflicting. Figure 9 shows the activation for the non-conflicting norm pair. Unlike the activation from the conflicting pair, here the activation covers a bigger part of the feature map. This indicates that the CNN looks for different kind of patterns when dealing with non-conflicting norm pairs.

We show the accuracy results for each fold and the mean accuracy overall in Table 2. Here, each fold represents the test set, whereas the other correspond to the train and validation sets. For instance, the accuracy in column "0" is the result from a model trained with folds 1 to 8 and validated using fold 9.

Fig. 8. Activation from the first convolution when identifying a conflicting norm pair

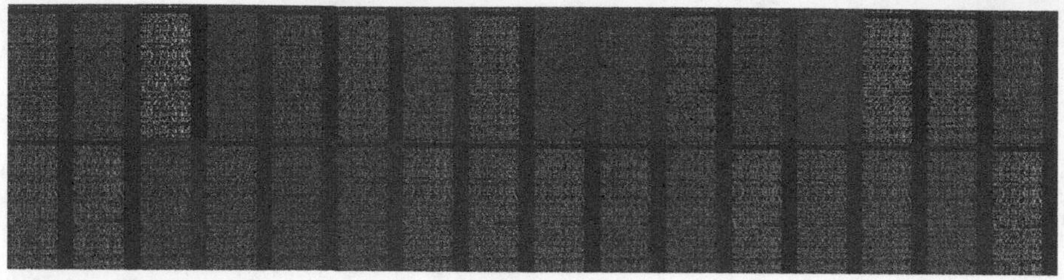

Fig. 9. Activation from the first convolution when identifying a non-conflicting norm pair

Recent work [1,2] (see Sect. 7) consider the use of sentence embeddings to represent norms and identify norm conflicts. We compare our results against their work in Table 3. As we can see, Aires *et al.* [2] obtain a better accuracy when compared to our approach. However, we consider our result a competitive one as our approach relies solely on the characters of norms. Their approach uses a pre-trained model to create dense vector representations of norms, and relies on a manual selection of a threshold to indicate a conflict between norms.

Table 2. Results for the norm conflict identifier

Fold	0	1	2	3	4	5	6	7	8	9	Mean
Accuracy	0.85	0.85	0.76	0.95	0.85	0.76	0.71	0.95	0.95	0.80	0.84

Table 3. Accuracy comparison between our approach and existing work.

Approach	Accuracy
Our	0.84
Aires *et al.* [2]	**0.95**
Aires *et al.* [1]	0.78

7 Related Work

Our approach mixes information retrieval (norm identification) with contract reasoning (norm conflict identification). Thus, in this section, we describe how existing work compare to our approach considering the manipulation of contracts.

Rosso *et al.* [24] propose an approach to retrieve information from legal texts. Their approach uses JIRS[6] (Java Information Retrieval System), a system that measures distances between sentences using n-grams, to develop a solution for three problems: passage retrieval in treaties, patents, and contracts. In the first problem, they want to answer questions from treaty documents. Given a question about the content of the treaty, they use JIRS to measure the distance between the question and the text in the treaty, thus, they can rank the best answers to each question by their similarity. To the second problem, they develop an approach to help patent creators identify similar patents. As in the first problem, given a set of patents and a new one, they use JIRS to measure how similar the new patent is to existing ones. To the third problem, they develop an approach to identify conflicts between norms in contracts. To do so, they create a contract example between an airline and a ground operations company with a defined set of norms applied to both parties. They divide the process of conflict identification into three steps, first, they translate every norm in contract to a formal contract language ($\mathcal{CL}$ [9]), which they call Contract Language clauses. Second, they analyze the clauses using a model checker performed by the contract analysis tool *CLAN* [10]. From the identified conflicts, they use JIRS to translate the sentences from $\mathcal{CL}$ to natural language. Although this work also tries to identify norm conflicts, it differs from ours in two points. First, our work tries to identify normative conflicts dealing directly with natural language, whereas in their work they use the approach proposed by Fenech *et al.* [10], which uses a single contract that has its norms *manually translated* into the controlled language $\mathcal{CL}$. Second, to identify norm conflicts, *CLAN* uses a series of predefined rules, whereas in our approach we rely on a convolution neural network that processes matrix of distances between pairs of norms automatically extracting the information needed to classify them.

Aires *et al.* [2] propose the use of sentence embeddings to represent norm sentences as dense vectors and use them to identify norm conflicts. Their approach consists of creating a single embedding vector that corresponds to the norm conflict concept. They create such conflict vector by obtaining the average of the offset between the representations of conflicting norm pairs. Once calculated, they use this conflict vector as a reference to identify norm conflicts. Thus, given two norms, they convert them into sentence embeddings, subtract them and measure the distance to the conflict embedding. Finally, they indicate as conflicting norm pairs with distances equal or smaller than a manually defined threshold. As result, they obtain 95% of accuracy on norm conflict identification.

[6] http://sourceforge.net/projects/jirs/.

More recently, Aires *et al.* [1] expanded Aires *et al.* [2] approach to identify and classify norm conflicts in contracts written in natural language. They define four norm conflict types, which can be assigned to norm conflicts according to their configuration. To manipulate norms, they convert them into dense vectors using the Sent2Vec algorithm [22]. In order to classify a norm pair, they subtract the representations and use the result as input to a Support Vector Machine model that defines the conflicting type. As a result, they obtain 78% of accuracy on norm conflict identification and 77% on norm conflict classification.

These two work give a step further on norm conflict identification. The main difference between our work and theirs is that they rely on pre-trained models to generate norm representations. Our approach uses only the characters from the norm pair, which makes it simpler and cheap to process. Although Aires *et al.* [2] obtain a higher accuracy on norm identification, they rely on the manual definition a threshold to classify norm pairs as conflicts, which may not generalize well on a scenario with diverse norms.

Curtotti and McCreath [7] propose an approach to annotate contracts using machine learning and rule-based techniques. They aim to classify each component of contractual sentences based on their structure. To extract data for machine learning, they create a hand-coded tagger and manually correct its outcome. As data, they use the Australian Contract Corpus [8] with 256 contracts, containing 42910 sentences and a vocabulary of 14217 words. In their experiments, they randomly select 30 contracts and divide them into three sets, one for train and two for test. Using different classifiers to compare the results, they obtain 0.86 of F-score. Instead of classifying each clause structure with a different class, in this work we want to identify norm clauses. However, we can use Curtotti and McCreath annotation for a further work with a deeper contract analysis.

Gao and Singh propose two different solutions for problems concerning information extraction from contracts. In the first one, they propose an approach to extract exceptions within norms in contracts [12]. They use a corpus with 2,647 contracts from the Onecle repository[7] as data for processing. As result, Enlil obtains an F-score of 0.9 in classifying contracts using a manually annotated corpus. Although Gao and Singh work is similar to ours by dealing with contractual norms, we have different ends. In our work, we use norms to find potential conflicts, whereas they use them to identify exceptions within a contract. However, we can use their concept of exception in a new approach to identify conflicts with a high-level of detail, since exceptions in norms may induce to new types of conflicts.

In their second work, Gao and Singh [11] develop a hybrid approach for extracting business events and their temporal constraints from contracts. Using different machine learning algorithms they obtain an F-score of 0.89 for event extraction and 0.9 for temporal constraints. This, similar to the first work, is an approach to extract information from contracts. The main difference between their work and ours is that they try to identify temporal elements from norms. This is also an improvement we can apply to the norm conflict identification process.

[7] http://contracts.onecle.com.

Vasconcelos *et al.* [28] propose an approach to deal with normative conflicts in multi-agent systems. They develop mechanisms for detection and resolution of normative conflicts. To resolve conflicts they manipulate the constraints associated to the norms' variables, removing any overlap in their values. In norm adoption, they use a set of auxiliary norms to exchange by the ones applied to the agent. In norm removal, they remove a certain norm and all curtailments it caused, bringing back a previous form of the normative state. Figueiredo and Silva's work [27] consist of an algorithm for normative conflict detection using first-order logic. They use the Z language to formalize the conflict types and then identify them between norms. Both approaches from Vasconcelos *et al.* and Figueiredo and Silva propose a solution for norm conflicts applied to normative multi-agent systems. The main difference between their work and ours is that we make the identification of potential conflicts between norms from contracts written in natural language. It creates the need for a different approach since natural language is not structured. However, an alternative approach would be the translation of natural language to first-order-logic and use one of these approaches to identify conflicts.

8 Conclusion and Future Work

In this work, we developed a two-phase approach to identify potential conflicts between norms in contracts. Our main contributions are: (1) a dataset with manually annotated normative and non-normative sentences from real contracts; (2) a machine learning model to classify contractual sentences as normative and non-normative; (3) a manually annotated dataset with contracts containing artificially generated conflicts between norms; and (4) a deep learning model to classify norm pairs as conflicting and non-conflicting. We evaluate both models and we obtain an accuracy of 90% for the sentence classifier and around 84% for the norm conflict identifier.

Our approach has clear limitations regarding the small dataset used for training. Although our CNN obtains a high accuracy using the text from scratch, we must improve the dataset to contain more challenging examples. The model focus mainly on the similarity between the beginning of both norms to indicate a conflict. By providing negative cases with similar norms, we can improve the model generalization. Thus, besides improving our dataset, as future work, we aim to develop two different approaches. First, we aim to develop a pre-processing step in the norm conflict identification to identify elements that may improve the detection of conflicts, such as temporal information. Second, to fairly compare our results with the work proposed by Fenech *et al.* [10], we aim to create an approach to translate natural language to $\mathcal{CL}$ (contract language) and use *CLAN* to discover conflicts.

Acknowledgements. We gratefully thank Google Research Awards for Latin America for funding our project.

References

1. Aires, J.P., Granada, R., Monteiro, J., Barros, R.C., Meneguzzi, F.: Classification of contractual conflicts via learning of semantic representations. In: Elkind, E., Veloso, M., Agmon, N., Taylor, M.E. (eds.) Proceedings of the 18th International Conference on Autonomous Agents and MultiAgent Systems, AAMAS 2019, Montreal, QC, Canada, May 13–17, 2019, pp. 1764–1766. International Foundation for Autonomous Agents and Multiagent Systems (2019)
2. Aires, J.P., Granada, R., Monteiro, J., Meneguzzi, F.: Norm conflict identification using vector space offsets. In: Proceedings of the 2018 International Joint Conference on Neural Networks, pp. 337–344. IJCNN 2018, IEEE, Washington, DC, USA, July 2018 (2018)
3. Axelrod, R.: An evolutionary approach to norms. Am. Political Sci. Rev. **80**(4), 1095–1111 (1986)
4. Crammer, K., Dekel, O., Keshet, J., Shalev-Shwartz, S., Singer, Y.: Online passive-aggressive algorithms. J. Machine Learn. Res. **7**, 551–585 (2006)
5. Cun, L., Bengio, Y., Hinton, G.: Deep learning. Nature **521**(7553), 436–444 (2015)
6. Cun, L., et al.: Handwritten digit recognition with a back-propagation network. In: Advances in Neural Information Processing Systems, pp. 396–404. Morgan Kaufmann (1990)
7. Curtotti, M., Mccreath, E.: Corpus based classification of text in australian contracts. In: Proceedings of the Australasian Language Technology Association Workshop, Melbourne, Australia, pp. 18–26 (2010)
8. Curtotti, M., McCreath, E.C.: A corpus of australian contract language: description, profiling and analysis. In: Proceedings of the 13th International Conference on Artificial Intelligence and Law, pp. 199–208. ICAIL 2011, ACM, New York, NY, USA (2011). https://doi.org/10.1145/2018358.2018387
9. Fenech, S., Pace, G.J., Schneider, G.: Automatic conflict detection on contracts. In: Leucker, M., Morgan, C. (eds.) ICTAC 2009. LNCS, vol. 5684, pp. 200–214. Springer, Heidelberg (2009). https://doi.org/10.1007/978-3-642-03466-4_13
10. Fenech, S., Pace, G.J., Schneider, G.: CLAN: a tool for contract analysis and conflict discovery. In: Automated Technology for Verification and Analysis, 7th International Symposium, ATVA 2009, Macao, China, October 14–16, 2009. Proceedings, pp. 90–96 (2009). https://doi.org/10.1007/978-3-642-04761-9_8
11. Gao, X., Singh, M.P.: Mining contracts for business events and temporal constraints in service engagements. Services Computing, IEEE Trans. PP(99), 1 (2013). https://doi.org/10.1109/TSC.2013.21
12. Gao, X., Singh, M.P., Mehra, P.: Mining business contracts for service exceptions. IEEE Trans. Serv. Comput. **5**(3), 333–344 (2012)
13. Gillick, D., Brunk, C., Vinyals, O., Subramanya, A.: Multilingual language processing from bytes. arXiv preprint arXiv:1512.00103 (2015)
14. Goodfellow, I., Bengio, Y., Courville, A.: Deep learning, book in preparation for MIT Press (2016)
15. Harris, Z.S.: Distributional Structure, pp. 775–794. Springer, Dordrecht (1970). https://doi.org/10.1007/978-94-017-6059-1_36
16. Hearst, M.A., Dumais, S.T., Osman, E., Platt, J., Scholkopf, B.: Support vector machines. IEEE Intell. Syst. Appl. **13**(4), 18–28 (1998)
17. Jain, L.C., Medsker, L.R.: Recurrent Neural Networks: Design and Applications, 1st edn. CRC Press Inc., Boca Raton (1999)

18. Jones, A.J.I., Sergot, M.J.: Deontic logic in the representation of law: towards a methodology. Artif. Intell. Law **1**(1), 45–64 (1992)
19. Kim, Y.: Convolutional neural networks for sentence classification. In: Moschitti, A., Pang, B., Daelemans, W. (eds.) Proceedings of the 2014 Conference on Empirical Methods in Natural Language Processing, EMNLP 2014, 25–29 October 2014, Doha, Qatar, A meeting of SIGDAT, a Special Interest Group of the ACL, pp. 1746–1751. ACL (2014)
20. Meneguzzi, F., Rodrigues, O., Oren, N., Vasconcelos, W.W., Luck, M.: BDI reasoning with normative considerations. Eng. Appl. Artif. Intell. **43**, 127 – 146 (2015). https://doi.org/10.1016/j.engappai.2015.04.011
21. Minsky, M., Papert, S.: Neurocomputing: foundations of research. In: Anderson, J.A., Rosenfeld, E. (eds.) Neurocomputing: Foundations of Research, Perceptrons, pp. 157–169. MIT Press, Cambridge, MA, USA (1988)
22. Pagliardini, M., Gupta, P., Jaggi, M.: Unsupervised learning of sentence embeddings using compositional n-gram features. In: NAACL 2018 - Conference of the North American Chapter of the Association for Computational Linguistics (2018)
23. Prisacariu, C., Schneider, G.: A formal language for electronic contracts. In: Bonsangue, M.M., Johnsen, E.B. (eds.) FMOODS 2007. LNCS, vol. 4468, pp. 174–189. Springer, Heidelberg (2007). https://doi.org/10.1007/978-3-540-72952-5_11
24. Rosso, P., Correa, S., Buscaldi, D.: Passage retrieval in legal texts. J. Logic and Algebraic Program. **80**(3–5), 139–153 (2011). https://doi.org/10.1016/j.jlap.2011.02.001
25. Rousseau, D.M., McLean Parks, J.: The contracts of individuals and organizations, vol. 15, JAI Press Ltd. (1993)
26. Sadat-Akhavi, A.: Methods of Resolving Conflicts Between Treaties. Graduate Institute of International Studies (Series), vol. 3, M. Nijhoff (2003)
27. da Silva Figueiredo, K., da Silva, V.T.: An algorithm to identify conflicts between norms and values. In: Coordination, Organisations, Institutions and Norms in Multi-Agent Systems, pp. 259–274 (2013)
28. Vasconcelos, W.W., Kollingbaum, M.J., Norman, T.J.: Normative conflict resolution in multi-agent systems. Autonomous Agents Multi-Agent Syst. **19**(2), 124–152 (2009). https://doi.org/10.1007/s10458-008-9070-9
29. Vincent, P., Larochelle, H., Bengio, Y., Manzagol, P.A.: Extracting and composing robust features with denoising autoencoders. In: Proceedings of the 25th International Conference on Machine Learning, pp. 1096–1103. ICML 2008, ACM, New York (2008). https://doi.org/10.1145/1390156.1390294
30. von Wright, G.H.: Deontic Logic, New Series, vol. 60. Oxford University Press on behalf of the Mind Association (1951)
31. Zhang, X., Cun, L.: Text understanding from scratch. CoRR abs/1502.01710 (2015)

Norm Violation in Online Communities – A Study of Stack Overflow Comments

Jithin Cheriyan(✉), Bastin Tony Roy Savarimuthu, and Stephen Cranefield

Department of Information Science, University of Otago, Dunedin, New Zealand
jithin.cheriyan@postgrad.otago.ac.nz,
{tony.savarimuthu,stephen.cranefield}@otago.ac.nz

Abstract. Norms are behavioral expectations in communities. Online communities are also expected to abide by the established practices that are expressed in the code of conduct of a system. Even though community authorities continuously prompt their users to follow the regulations, it is observed that hate speech and abusive language usage are on the rise. In this paper, we quantify and analyze the patterns of violations of normative behaviour among the users of Stack Overflow (SO) – a well-known technical question-answer site for professionals and enthusiast programmers, while posting a comment. Even though the site has been dedicated to technical problem solving and debugging, hate speech as well as posting offensive comments make the community "toxic". By identifying and minimising various patterns of norm violations in different SO communities, the community would become less toxic and thereby the community can engage more effectively in its goal of knowledge sharing. Moreover, through automatic detection of such comments, the authors can be warned by the moderators, so that it is less likely to be repeated, thereby the reputation of the site and community can be improved. Based on the comments extracted from two different data sources on SO, this work first presents a taxonomy of norms that are violated. Second, it demonstrates the sanctions for certain norm violations. Third, it proposes a recommendation system that can be used to warn users that they are about to violate a norm. This can help achieve norm adherence in online communities.

Keywords: Norms · Norm identification · Norm violation · Norm signalling · Sanctioning · Stack Overflow

1 Introduction

Online social media platforms have enabled users to express their viewpoints and hence have become a place for information sharing. Applications like Facebook and Twitter are the forerunners in this arena along with multitudes of other applications. Interactions among users of these applications are generally observed as positive, inclusive and creative. Stack Overflow (SO), a technological division of Stack Exchange – a network of question-answer websites on topics in diverse fields, is a platform for beginners to get free technical support from

A. Aler Tubella et al. (Eds.): COIN 2017/COINE 2020, LNAI 12298, pp. 20–34, 2021.
https://doi.org/10.1007/978-3-030-72376-7_2

professionals and well-versed programmers. Those who are interested can join the site for free and post questions they may have about programming to get the best possible answer. Anyone can ask questions in any joined communities and anyone can post answers or comments to that question, making the site dynamic and inclusive. The intent of SO is to give power back to the community [30] so that a new way of knowledge sharing can be created.

This work is inspired by the post by the Executive Vice President of SO, regarding the alarming transformation of SO as an unwelcoming place [9]. Even though millions of comments are generated by the users of various communities day-by-day, a considerable amount of them were found to violate the Code of Conduct (CoC) of the site [7], which advocates for friendliness and inclusiveness. This could be because the users may be ignorant of SO norms as indicated in CoC or the lack of effective monitoring and stronger punishments for norm violations. To monitor the proper usage of the site, site authorities have selected reputed community members as moderators to monitor and review all the posts [9]. The reputation score in SO decides a user's future as a moderator. Reputation score comes from a range of activities including the up-votes of all the answers that one makes and it reflects how much a person has been accepted as a valued resource in that community [29]. If a comment is found to breach the CoC of the site, moderators would either remove that comments or may contact the author to remove it. Some examples of comments that have been deleted by the moderator are given below.

"shut up sir....."
"I just hate this answer oh downvote you senseless clods <profanity>."
"Its called your brain. If you can't review your code ask someone else to do it."
"you can convert it into seconds, then compare. I think you learned that in your school."

In addition to these human moderators, SO brings into play an automatic bot [3] which helps to identify comments containing certain triggering keywords reflecting toxic contents, and will report that to the moderators if they exceed a certain threshold. These norm violating comments, bearing highly toxic contents, would be flagged 'red' and those will be censored by the human moderators immediately [12]. Moderators who are online will be sent a notification to deal with this. Thereby an important set of norms are enforced on the site. Figure 1 shows the process of moderation in SO. However, no prior work has investigated the types of norms and their violations pertaining to SO and this work bridges this gap.

Even though SO has been offered in myriads of languages like Spanish, Portuguese, Russian and Japanese [10], this work intends to study the norm violations in comment posting in English only [11]. In this proposed work, by analysing comments on SO, we address three objectives: 1) propose a classification of the types of norms and also quantify norm violations, 2) quantify the different types of punishments for norm violations and 3) propose a recommendation system to minimise norm violations in SO in terms of comment posting.

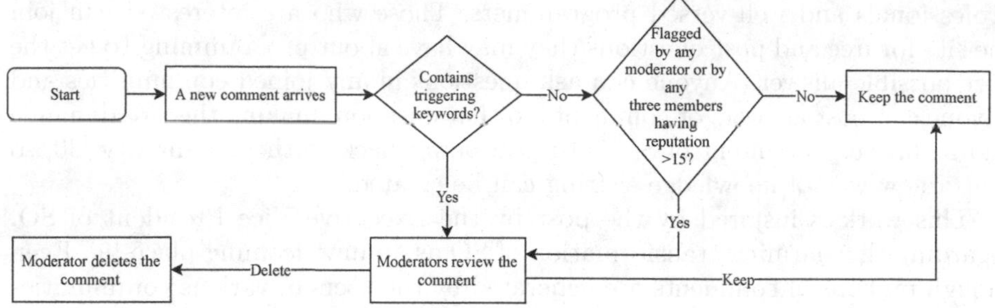

Fig. 1. A flowchart of comment moderation in Stack Overflow

The paper is structured as follows. Section 2 provides background and related work in norms, norm identification and norm violations. Also, this section establishes the purpose of identification of norm violation in online discussion forums. Section 3 describes the context of norm investigation process in this study. The methodology is explained in Sect. 4 and Sect. 5 presents our results. Section 6 discusses the results and also presents the implications of the study in the context of a normative recommendation system. Finally, Sect. 7 concludes the paper.

2 Background and Related Work

In many areas of human life, rules, conventions and norms play a vital role in the smooth functioning of the system [22,27]. Even though rules are enforced by law or authorities, norms are considered as the set of expected practices of interpersonal behaviour in societies, and may only be socially monitored [22]. While the breaching of rules results in punishment, usually norm violations may not get punished all the time [22,23]. As norms are not been imposed by those in power, it is the mindset of the people and the extent to which sanctions are perceived to be applied which make members of society follow or violate the norms. Since norms are specific to a society, identifying and following a certain norm in an unknown community is challenging for people [13,22,24,27,28]. A system that is able to recognise potential norm violations and warn users about them would be ideal. However, such a system must be able to identify what are the norms that exist in the society.

Many researchers have investigated the norm creation, norm learning and norm emergence processes in agent systems, especially in multi-agent systems (MAS) [22,25,27]. Other than research on agent based systems, many others have focused on norm adherence and violation by the members of various social media platforms like Facebook and Reddit [5]. For example, Chandrasekharan et al. have tried to identify and classify the macro and meso norms being violated in Reddit comments [6]. Nowadays, to identify and moderate online hate speech, for an example, a meaningful amalgamation of both these streams (works on norms and online communities) has been utilized by all leading social networking sites [18,21]. We examine both of these streams of norms identification in the following sub-sections.

2.1 Norms in Multi-agent Systems

MAS may contain both artificial and human agents. Therefore, it is expected that these communities also would follow certain behavioural norms inside the community. Usually, agents follow the norm life cycle—norm creation, spreading, learning, enforcement and emergence [13,22,26]. Norms are created by the norm-leaders and inferred by agents by observing the patterns of actions of other agents of the society. Thus, that predominant practice would become a norm to be followed by the community.

In a MAS, the learning process can be either offline or online [22,28]. In offline mode of learning, certain rules would be embodied into the agents and they would follow these regulations in a top-down model. However, in a MAS, the norms may be changed dynamically, requiring an ability of an agent to learn the updated norm from the behaviour of other agents. Therefore, in the online fashion of learning, multiple agents interact with others simultaneously and at the same time they would learn the etiquette through the interactions. This is a bottom-up approach and it is usually expected that the agents should learn from their own experiences to fit in a dynamic community. Like human beings, agents also may communicate to achieve coordination and cooperation [31]. Usually, as part of online learning, the agents may exchange information regarding their present state or the resources they hold, thereby gaining a better understanding of themselves and others' expectations of its behaviour [2].

Norm enforcement refers to the process of discouraging norm violation either by sanctions or punishments [22]. Punishment could be monetary or blacklisting an agent. As per Singh et al. [28] and Savarimuthu et al. [22], categories of norms are a) obligation norms 2) prohibition norms and 3) permission norms. Obligation norms are the set of patterns of actions which an agent is supposed to do like tipping in a restaurant. Likewise, an agent system is not expected to perform an action that has been prohibited by the society such as littering the park. Violating the above mentioned two classes of norms would invite sanctions or punishments while the third one, permission norms, usually may not get sanctioned as it refers to the set of actions an agent is permitted to do. This work concerns prohibition norms.

2.2 Mining Norms from Online Social Media Platforms

Online social networking sites like Facebook, Twitter and Reddit provide a digital world where interactions happen. Even though there are centralised rules regarding the effective and constructive usage of these applications, there exist some users who do not abide by these rules, resulting in abuse and hate speech. When people get upset, especially in online media, they are likely to overlook the norms and may start bullying others for even small mistakes, which has found a surge in last decade [1]. Also, it is observed that aggressive behaviour is more common in online spaces than face-to-face [16]. This hostile nature has long lasting detrimental effects, e.g., the CEO of Twitter has admitted that Twitter loses their users because of online hate speech [1]. The European Union has passed a law that all leading social media platforms must delete abusive contents within 24 h[1]. This justifies the requirement of a scalable computational system to systematically locate and remove online hate speech in social media platforms.

As a result of social and legislative pressure, all prominent social media applications are forced to employ human moderators from within the community to identify and moderate provoking, abusive and unnecessary contents [8]. These community moderators monitor the posts that have violated the norms of the community, and potentially delete these posts. Along with these human moderators, computational tools like chatbots (agents) are used to identify abusive or offensive terms and notify the human moderators for possible moderation. Abusive language detection is an interdisciplinary domain which integrates technical components like natural language processing and machine learning [14]. Even though the human moderation process has been found effective, this tedious task could be minimised if all the community members follow the norms. Unfortunately, norm violation in social media is becoming commonplace and there is an increased need for understanding the types of norms and their violations in online communications. In this work we investigate the norms of SO on a posted comment.

The goal of the paper is to identify the norms that a comment is expected to follow and the nature of violations. We provide the context of our study in the next section.

3 Norm Investigation in Stack Overflow

Having learned about the toxicity through the aforementioned blog post of SO top officials, we investigated the nature of comments by collecting the comments from one particular day with the goal of checking the number of comments that are deleted in subsequent days. We found that around 9.3% of total comments of that day disappeared within one month and this increased to 14% within two months, and this process still continues. Comments were collected between 2 December 2019 and 13 February 2020 for posts with tags 'Java' and 'Python'. Between these two dates, 3221 comments that originally appeared on 2 December were deleted. There are two possible reasons for a comment's disappearance: either voluntarily deleted by the author or removed by the moderator as part of moderation (i.e., deleted because it violates a norm). Therefore, the set of deleted comments comprise those that were voluntarily removed by the author and deleted by the moderator. The reason for moderation could be the possible violation of generic rules of a society or, some rules or norms specific to SO. Based on prior work [15] and a bottom-up analysis of deleted comments, in this work we investigate two major classifications of norms and patterns of norm violations that can be observed from textual comments: (1) Generic norms and (2) SO specific norms.

Generic Norms and Their Violations - Generally, it is expected that in the community we live in, we are not supposed to use rude or offensive words that may hurt others. So, the norm is to be polite, and also respect individuals and their unique attributes such as gender and ethnicity. While interacting in online communities we are also expected to follow these rules to keep the decorum. SO is such a forum where the CoC requires its users to respect fellow community members irrespective of their knowledge level, ethnicity or gender. Therefore, generic norms refer to a set of universally accepted norms pertaining to the use of refined language. These norms are likely to be similar across online communities. The norms under this category of prohibition norms are norm against a) personal harassment, b) use of racial slurs, c) use of swear words, and d) use of unwelcoming language. A fine grained description along with examples of these norms are given in Table 1.

SO Specific Norms and Their Violations - It is a common courtesy to express gratitude for any kind of help, especially in online media. People will acknowledge and apologize for small mistakes to keep the space amiable. However, as aforementioned, the CoC of SO has the policy of keeping the site useful to everyone by containing only relevant knowledge and reducing noise. As a part of that, even though users usually post acknowledging or apologising comments, these are usually removed by moderator as those comments may distract the users from gaining knowledge, or the newly joining members may consider the site to be too chatty [20]. Also, if someone asks an irrelevant question as a follow up of a posted question, this may also get removed. These norms of not accepting or not promoting pleasantries are unique to SO as these comments distract from the intended purpose of knowledge sharing. Therefore, the very specific norms of SO is to keep the site less noisy (free of clutter). Details about four SO-specific norms are shown in the lower half of Table 1.

4 Methodology

There are two parts of this study: identifying violations of *generic* and *specific* norms in SO. To study the pattern of generic norms, we collected the data from the SO Heat Detector bot [19] that identifies violations based on regular expressions and various machine learning algorithms. We collected all comments that were flagged by the bot between 16 May 2016 and 31 January 2020. There were a total of 56382 comments. Since these comments are related to violations of generic norms (norm type 1) and did not contain violations of SO specific norms (norm type 2), we created a deleted comments dataset, by collecting comments that were posted on a particular day (2 December 2019), and subsequently checking which of those were deleted from that set in the next two months. We discuss these in detail in the following sub-sections.

Identifying Generic Norms and Their Violations - In SO, a comment flagged by the bot may violate the abuse norms of SO. A sample entry from the bot is *"SCORE: 7 (Regex:(?i)/bullshit NaiveBayes:1.00 OpenNLP:0.75 Perspective:0.90)"*. Here the Regex (regular expression) attribute shows the nature

Table 1. Norm categorization

Norm violation type	Label	Description	Examples	Evidence
Violation of generic norms	Personal harassment	Personally targeting, name calling, intimidating, defaming or trolling one user	Can you please stop posting such unrelated rubbish	[7]
			Shut up sir.....	
	Racial	Treating a user unfavourably based on his/her skin tone, race or ethnicity	Somebody is blocking you, are you Chinese?	[7]
			Who the hell are you to talk? An Arabian terrorist?	
	Swearing	Usage of any swear words or profanities to abuse one.	That means you have fu***d-up the routers	[7]
			This community is moving to a**hole level	
	Other unwelcoming	Any other unfriendly comments or accusations which violates the inclusive policy of SO	You copied my idea	[7]
			This is spam	
Violation of SO specific norms	Gratitude	Expressing gratitude	Thanks for your response Thanks, works perfectly.	[17]
	Apologizing	Expressing apology for mistakes	Sorry I was offline	[17]
			My humble apologies sir	
	Welcoming	Welcoming a new member to SO or to the community	Welcome to Stack Overflow, Hamza	[17]
			Welcome to SO Kyle!	
	No longer needed	These are comments that were once useful but are not anymore. But the specific reason is unknown	I found your post valid	[17]
			That would be a nice idea	

of the violation (i.e., the use of the word bullshit). While the entry has other attributes such as the SCORE indicating the extent to which a comment might be a violation (i.e., 7 out of 10) and the output from other machine learning algorithms such as Naive Bayes, we consider only those comments that have Regex. Only these comments can be classified into one of the four groups, as the actual comments have been deleted by SO. After the bot flags a comment, the moderators review the nature of the violation. The outcome of the review process may be any one of the following: (1) the moderators may deem the comment to be appropriate and permit the comment to be available in the site, (2) the comment may be deleted from the site but the reason is not disclosed, (3) the author may remove the comment voluntarily, after the moderator contacts the author because of its inappropriateness, (4) the comment may be deleted by the moderator because of its inappropriateness. The classification of comments based on the outcome from the moderation process is shown in Table 2. Outcomes A and M can be considered as punishments for norm violation. These deletions are considered as punishments because the system may have a record of users' actions and this may impact their reputation in the future.

The dataset contained 56382 comments of which 673 comments do not have the links to locate the comment. In the remaining 55709 comments we found that only 19872 have Regex values to consider for norm classification. After collecting the set of Regex keywords used in SO from the GitHub repository of the

Table 2. Table describing outcomes of moderator review

Number	Type	Description
1	E	Contains matching keywords, but not deleted (i.e., they **E**xist in SO)
2	U	Deleted (**U**nknown reason)
3	A	Deleted voluntarily by the **A**uthor
4	M	Deleted by the **M**oderator

Heat Detector bot[1], we manually classified the Regex collection into four norm groups—personal harassment, racial, swearing and other unwelcoming comments as listed in Table 1. The full list of Regexs that correspond to each group can be found online[2]. A Python program was used to identify the outcome of each violation by selecting the link for each comment and extracting the nature of the outcome from the resulting page (e.g., moderator deleted the comment). This extracted data was then grouped based on different outcomes.

Identifying SO Specific Norms and Their Violations - To identify SO specific norm violations, we collected comments from one particular day - 2 December 2019, for two months. We identified that 3221 comments were deleted within that period. We examined the reason for moderation of the comments. The reasons fall under two major categories. The first one is pleasantries. The reason for moderation is that, being a technical question-answering site, SO discourages the formalities of expressing gratitude, apology and welcoming someone new to the site or community. The second measure is the scale of essentiality of the comment. The reason of moderation is that the moderators may find those comments no longer needed towards knowledge sharing goal of the site.

5 Results

This section presents results of norm violation for the two categories of norms. The discussion of these results is presented in the subsequent section.

Violation of Generic Norms - Figure 2 shows the occurrence of the top thirty Regexs in the dataset. Out of the top ten Regex keywords, both swearing and personal targeting keywords appear thrice each and unwelcoming keywords appear four times. This shows that even in SO, a technical discussion forum, people may violate the norms of politeness and may tend to use abusive words so frequently. Moreover, the presence of keywords representing other unwelcoming comments show that people may accuse others or others' comments as being a spam, sarcastic or rude, which has been traditionally been considered as the duty of moderators. Racial abuse related keywords are found in small numbers (i.e., 377 comments). Complete Regex occurrence details can be found online[3].

[1] https://github.com/SOBotics/HeatDetector.
[2] http://www.mediafire.com/file/o39ypolha0v0ik0/Regex_classification.pdf/file.
[3] http://www.mediafire.com/file/mez6z6lcszz6ybi/Regex_occurrence.pdf/file.

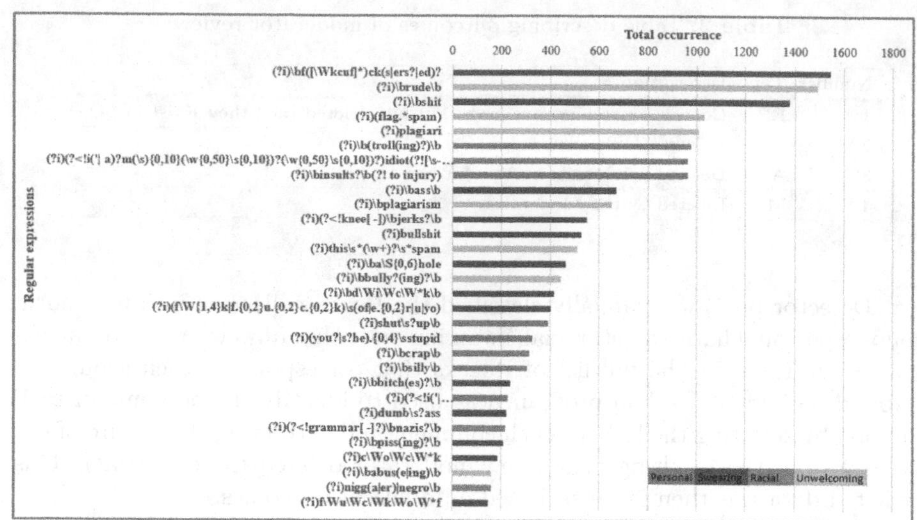

Fig. 2. Top 30 Regexs and their corresponding occurrence

Figure 3 shows the percentage of comments that violated norms belonging to the four categories. We have observed that personal harassment keywords and swearing terms are the two most common reasons for norm violation in the examined dataset (33.3% and 33.2% respectively). 66.5% of the total violations come from both these two groups. However, another 31.5% comes from other unwelcoming comments category. Only just 2% of the violations were found for racial norms.

Figure 4 shows the outcome of the flagging process of the bot. As presented earlier, the outcome is one of the four options shown in Table 2. We observed that in all four categories of norm violations, the type U outcome occurs the most, showing that the comments have been deleted from the site for an unknown reason. It is likely that the authors of the comments (without any prompting) realized the issue with their own posts and removed them. Out of 19872 comments evaluated, 45% of comments belong to this category. The next category of outcome is those comments deleted by the moderator (M) with 28%. Also, in 9% of comments, the author voluntarily removed them (type A). The rest of the comments (18%) are still present on the site (type E) showing that despite possessing certain objectionable words, the human tolerance for these comments have not been exceeded. On the other hand, strict punishments are imposed on norm-violating comments. This is evident from the moderation process which removed 37% of total comments which fell in categories A and M. Figure 5 shows the outcome of the flagging process by the bot for the four norm categories. It is evident that in all four categories, most of the comments are deleted from the site for an unknown reason (type U). Followed by this is type M where the moderator has deleted all these comments. Voluntary removal of the comment by the author (type A) is the outcome with the smallest count. It can be

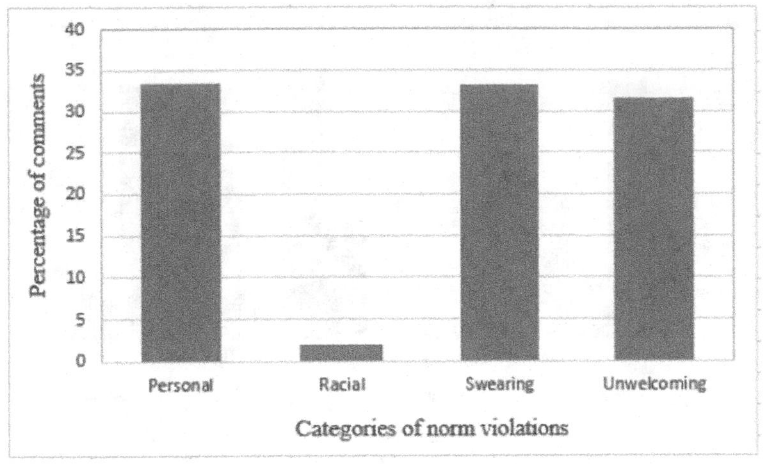

Fig. 3. Percentage of norm violations in four categories

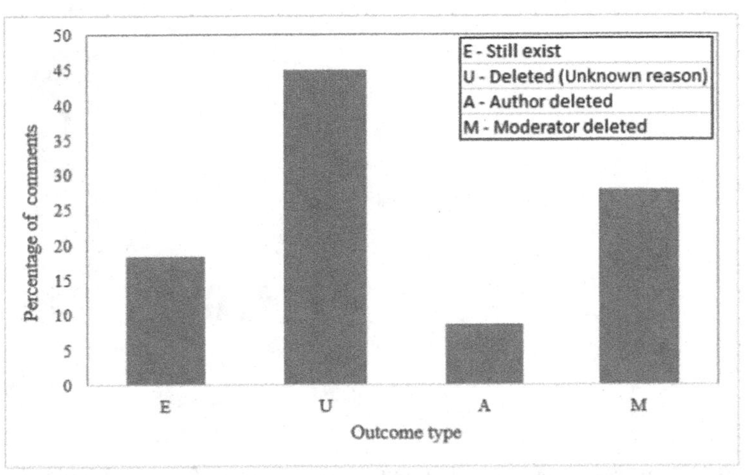

Fig. 4. Outcome statistics of moderator review after bot flagging

observed that the type E (comments still exist) outcome happens more than the type A outcome. Therefore, the general trend is U >M >E >A in all four norm categories.

Violation of SO Specific Norms - Figure 6 presents the percentage of various SO specific norm violations in the dataset. Out of 3221 comments evaluated, 84% of the comments were in the 'no longer needed' category. Since these are no longer needed for the site, those are deleted. 2% are apologies that were removed. 2% are welcome messages and 12% are gratitude messages. It is interesting that pleasantries (apologies, welcome and gratitude) account for 16% of the comments and these are in fact deemed to be not useful to the knowledge creation

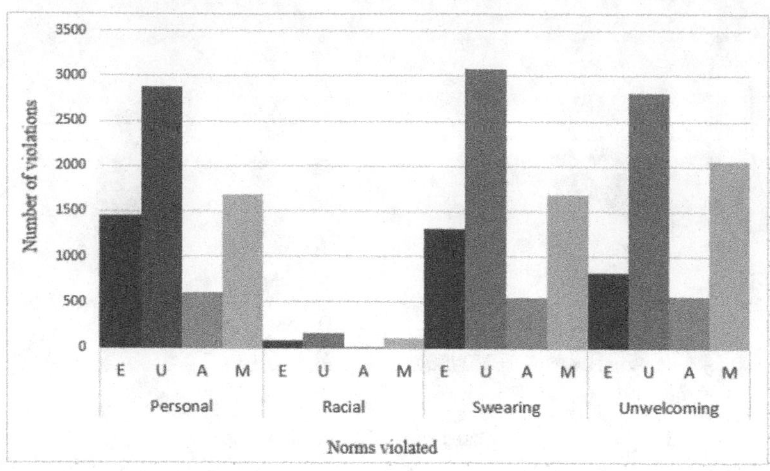

Fig. 5. Norm violations identified in bot flagging outcome

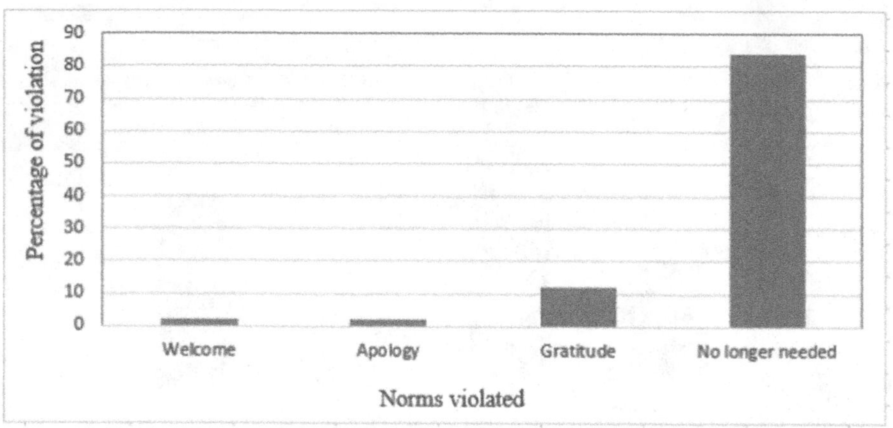

Fig. 6. Norm violations present in extracted dataset of one particular day

process. In addition to these, we also observed 9 comments in the dataset that were personal harassment messages indicating the violation of generic norms (not shown in Fig. 6). This shows that the moderation process is not instantaneous (i.e., removing harassment messages takes time) since these are possibly milder (borderline) offenses and may require multiple users flagging them before a decision could be made.

6 Discussion

In this section we provide a discussion of the results presented in Sect. 5, particularly discussing their implications for developing a recommendation system to prompt the users to follow the norms of SO when posting a comment.

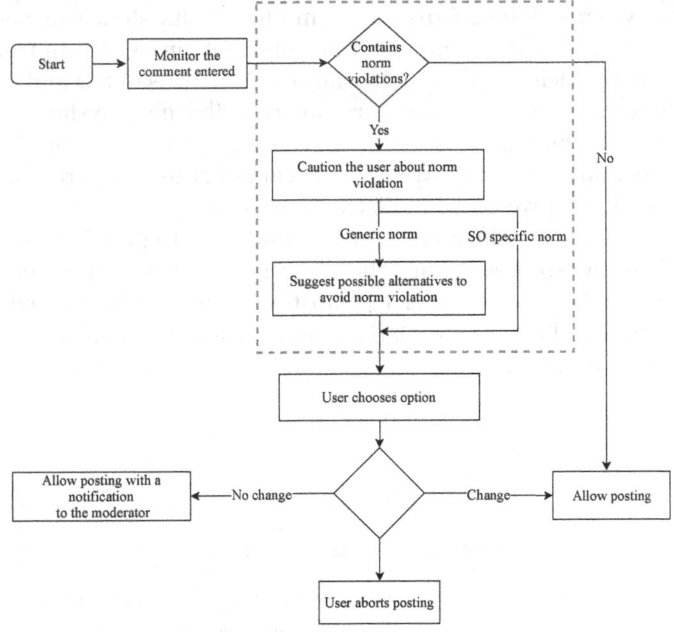

Fig. 7. The proposed norm adherence recommendation system

Generic Norms - From the results shown in Sect. 5, it can be inferred that nearly equal contribution for generic norms violation come from the three categories of personal, swearing and other unwelcoming comments. Also, these three together contribute substantially towards total generic norm violation of 98%. Therefore, if we can restrict the abusive language usage, we would be able to improve the quality of the system for everyone. This provides an opportunity to develop an online norm recommendation system for comments which may violate the generic norms of SO. Figure 7 displays the high level workflow of the application which provides norm recommendation.

In the recommendation system, when a new comment has been entered, the generic norm violations can be detected. If the comment violates norms, the system would alert the user regarding the abusive content and the nature of norm violation. Moreover, the system would provide certain rephrased options for the same comment using deep learning techniques. A good candidate for such an approach is GPT-3, that provides suggestions for auto-completion of text [4]. If the user accepts the proposal, the rephrased comment is posted. If the user does not rephrase or accept the options presented, the post would be allowed, however, a notification will be sent to the moderators regarding the norm violation. Then it would be the discretion of the moderator to review and decide the destiny of the comment. The user also has the option to abort the comment in which case the comment will not be posted. Figure 8 shows an example of the options available to the user for rephrasing a bad comment.

SO Specific Norms Violations - From the results shown in Sect. 5, it is evident that more than three-fourths of the comments in SO are in the category 'no longer needed' which are abiding by the specific norms of SO and are neutral in nature. However, these comments are not contributing anything productive to the community, which is likely to be the reason for moderation. In addition to these set of comments, pleasantries also became a substantial reason for norm violations. Therefore, if we could limit the usage of these two categories of comments, SO specific norm adherence can be enhanced. Figure 7 shows that if a comment violates SO specific norms, the system would notify the user about the nature of norm violation. The user can abstain from posting the comment. If not, the user will be allowed to post the comment and the moderator would be notified regarding norm violation.

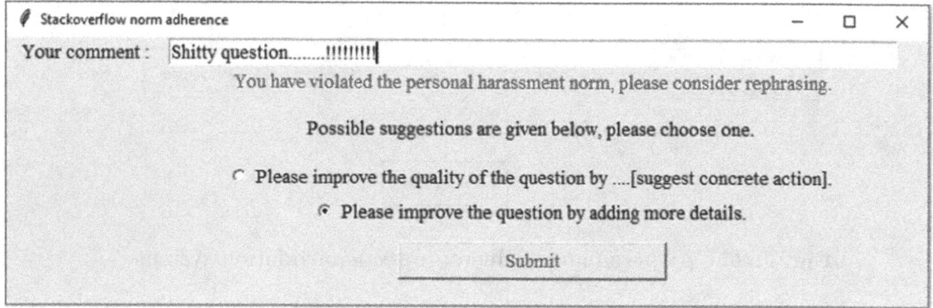

Fig. 8. Norm recommendation system

In the future, we intend to build the norm recommendation system proposed in Fig. 8 using deep learning techniques. Also, we plan to extend the proposed system to improve the reputation of users in SO community by abiding by the norms pertaining to the site. Thereby, better knowledge sharing without clutter can be facilitated, trust can be guaranteed and gentler treatment can be expected among community members.

7 Conclusion

The type of norms and their violations in SO are seldom addressed by prior work and that formed the focus of the current work. Our objectives are to identify and quantify the patterns of norm violations in SO comments and to propose a norm recommendation system for SO comments. We have identified two categories of norms, the generic norms and SO specific norms. We found that a significant proportion of violations in the first category has been contributed by the violation of three norms: personal harassment, swearing and other unwelcoming comments. In the second category, the main violations are 'no longer needed' and pleasantries. We have proposed an approach that can identify and alert the user regarding the presence of violations in comments which would potentially limit norm violations in SO.

References

1. 3rd Workshop on Abusive Language. https://sites.google.com/view/alw3/. Accessed 17 Feb 2020
2. Anastassacos, N., Hailes, S., Musolesi, M.: Understanding the impact of partner choice on cooperation and social norms by means of multi-agent reinforcement learning. arXiv: 1902.03185
3. app - Natty - Bringing 10k moderation to All. Stack Apps. http://stackapps.com/questions/7049/natty-bringing-10k-moderation-to-all. Accessed 17 Feb 2020
4. Brown, T.B., et al.: Language models are few-shot learners. arXiv preprint arXiv:2005.14165 (2020)
5. Chandrasekharan, E., Gilbert, E.: Hybrid approaches to detect comments violating macro norms on reddit. arXiv preprint arXiv:1904.03596 (2019)
6. Chandrasekharan, E., Samory, M., Jhaver, S.: The internet's hidden rules: an empirical study of reddit norm violations at micro, meso, and macro scales. In: Proceedings of the ACM on Human-Computer Interaction, vol. 2, pp. 1–25 (2018). https://doi.org/10.1145/3274301
7. Code of Conduct. Stack Overow. https://stackoverflow.com/conduct. Accessed 17 Feb 2020
8. Corr, R.: Legal studies: moderating the power of social media. Alternat. Law J. **43**(4), 313 (2018). https://doi.org/10.1177/1037969x18806713
9. Hanlon, J.: EVP of Culture and Experience. Stack Overow Isn't Very Welcoming. It's Time for That to Change. Stack Overow Blog, 26 April 2018. https://stackoverflow.blog/2018/04/26/stack-overflow-isnt-very-welcoming-its-time-for-that-to-change/
10. Do posts have to be in English on Stack Exchange? Meta Stack Exchange. https://meta.stackexchange.com/questions/13676/do-posts-have-to-be-in-english-on-stack-exchange. Accessed 17 Feb 2020
11. Atwood, J.: Non-English Question Policy. Stack Overow Blog, 23 July 2009. https://stackoverflow.blog/2009/07/23/non-english-question-policy/. Accessed 17 Feb 2020
12. Atwood, J.: Raising a Red Flag. Stack Overow Blog. https://stackoverflow.blog/2009/04/11/raising-a-red-flag/
13. Gao, X., Singh, M.P.: Extracting normative relationships from business contracts. In: 13th International Conference on Autonomous Agents and Multiagent Systems, AAMAS 2014, 1 January 2014, pp. 101–108 (2014). https://www.csc2.ncsu.edu/faculty/mpsingh/papers/others/AAMAS-14-Normative.pdf
14. Gupta, S., Gupta, S.K.: Natural language processing in mining unstructured data from software repositories: a review, vol. 12, p. 244. https://doi.org/10.1007/s12046-019-1223-9
15. Al-Hassan, A., Al-Dossari, H.: Detection of hate speech in social networks: a survey on multilingual corpus. In: 6th International Conference on Computer Science and Information Technology. https://doi.org/10.5121/csit.2019.90208
16. Jones, L.M., Mitchell, K.J., Finkelhor, D.: Online harassment in context: Trends from three Youth Internet Safety Surveys (2000, 2005, 2010). Psychol. Viol. **3**(1), 53–69 (2013). https://doi.org/10.1037/a0030309
17. No Thanks, Damn It! Meta Stack Overow. https://meta.stackoverflow.com/questions/288160/no-thanks-damn-it. Accessed 17 Feb 2020

18. Park, J.H., Fung, P.: One-step and two-step classification for abusive language detection on Twitter. In: Proceedings of the First Workshop on Abusive Language Online, vol. 3006 (2017). https://doi.org/10.18653/v1/W17-3006, http://aclweb.org/anthology/W17-3006
19. Queen bot - chat.stackoverow.com. https://chat.stackoverflow.com/search?q=heat&user=6294609&room=. Accessed 21 July 2020
20. Rahman, M., Rigby, P.: Cleaning stack overflow for machine translation. In: 2019 IEEE/ACM 16th International Conference on Mining Software Repositories (MSR). https://doi.org/10.1109/MSR.2019.00021
21. Razavi, A.H., Inkpen, D., Uritsky, S., Matwin, S.: Offensive language detection using multi-level classification. In: Farzindar, A., Kešelj, V. (eds.) AI 2010. LNCS (LNAI), vol. 6085, pp. 16–27. Springer, Heidelberg (2010). https://doi.org/10.1007/978-3-642-13059-5_5
22. Savarimuthu, B.T.R., Cranefield, S.: Norm creation, spreading and emergence: a survey of simulation models of norms in multiagent systems. Multiagent Grid Syst. **7**, 21–54 (2011). https://doi.org/10.3233/MGS-2011-0167
23. Savarimuthu, B.T.R., Cranefield, S., Purvis, M.: Identifying prohibition norms in agent societies. Artif. Intell. Law **21** (2012). https://doi.org/10.1007/s10506-012-9126-7
24. Savarimuthu, B.T.R., Licorish, S.A., Devananda, M.: Developers' responses to app review feedback-a study of communication norms in app development. In: Proceedings of the COIN 2017 workshop@ AAMAS (2017)
25. Savarimuthu, B.T.R., Padget, J., Purvis, M.A.: Social norm recommendation for virtual agent societies. In: Boella, G., Elkind, E., Savarimuthu, B.T.R., Dignum, F., Purvis, M.K. (eds.) PRIMA 2013. LNCS (LNAI), vol. 8291, pp. 308–323. Springer, Heidelberg (2013). https://doi.org/10.1007/978-3-642-44927-7_21
26. Savarimuthu, B.T.R., Purvis, M., Purvis, M., Cranefield, S.: Social norm emergence in virtual agent societies. In: Baldoni, M., Son, T.C., van Riemsdijk, M.B., Winikoff, M. (eds.) DALT 2008. LNCS (LNAI), vol. 5397, pp. 18–28. Springer, Heidelberg (2009). https://doi.org/10.1007/978-3-540-93920-7_2
27. Sen, S., Airiau, S.: Emergence of norms through social learning. In: IJCAI, vol. 1507, p. 1512 (2007). https://www.aaai.org/Papers/IJCAI/2007/IJCAI07-243.pdf
28. Singh, M.P., Arrott, M., Cranefield, S.: The uses of norms. In: Dagstuhl Follow-Ups, vol. 4. Schloss Dagstuhl-Leibniz-Zentrum fuer Informatik (2013). https://drops.dagstuhl.de/opus/volltexte/2013/4004/pdf/p191-ch07-singh-use-of-norms.pdf
29. What is reputation? How do I earn (and lose) it? - Help Center. Stack Overow. https://stackoverflow.com/help/whats-reputation. Accessed 17 Feb 2020
30. Who are the site moderators, and what is their role here? - Help Center. Stack Overow. https://stackoverflow.com/help/site-moderators. Accessed 17 Feb 2020
31. Xuan, P., Lesser, V., Zilberstein, S.: Communication decisions in multi-agent cooperation: model and experiments. In: Proceedings of the International Conference on Autonomous Agents (2001). https://doi.org/10.1145/375735.376469

Mining International Political Norms from the GDELT Database

Rohit Murali[1], Suravi Patnaik[2], and Stephen Cranefield[3(✉)]

[1] Indian Institute of Science, Bangalore, India
[2] Sponsa Limited, Wellington, New Zealand
suravi@sponsa.co
[3] University of Otago, Dunedin, New Zealand
stephen.cranefield@otago.ac.nz

Abstract. Researchers have long been interested in the role that norms can play in governing agent actions in multi-agent systems (MAS). Much work has been done on formalising normative concepts from human society and adapting them for the government of open software systems, and on the simulation of normative processes in human and artificial societies. However, there has been comparatively little work on applying normative MAS mechanisms to learn the norms existing in human society.

This work investigates this issue in the context of international politics. Using the GDELT dataset, containing machine-encoded records of international events mentioned in news reports, we extracted bilateral sequences of inter-country events and applied a Bayesian norm mining mechanism to identify norms that best explained the observed behaviour. A statistical evaluation showed that the normative model fitted the data significantly better than a probabilistic discrete event model.

Keywords: Norm mining · Bayesian inference · GDELT · Big data

1 Introduction

Norms are patterns of expected behaviour in human societies. In multi-agent systems, norms have been an active area of research where they have been used to facilitate desired agent-behaviour by constraining choices through prohibitions, obligations and permissions. Norms have been shown to facilitate social order [7] and improve cooperation and coordination among agents [29], and an active research community has investigated many theoretical and practical aspects of normative reasoning in multi-agent systems [1].

An emergent line of work considers how individual agents can use observations and experience to identify the norms that are prevalent in their society. Most work on observation-based norm learning has been limited to simulation-based studies. This work aims to extend the prior work by inferring norms from a real dataset in the domain of international politics. This is done by a novel approach combining a Bayesian norm learning mechanism [9] with a probabilistic language model fitted to the observed event sequence data.

A. Aler Tubella et al. (Eds.): COIN 2017/COINE 2020, LNAI 12298, pp. 35–56, 2021.
https://doi.org/10.1007/978-3-030-72376-7_3

The Global Database of Events, Language and Tone (GDELT) [20] is a geopolitical database that captures events recorded in broadcast, print and web news from all around the world using an automated text mining process. Events are encoded in terms of 61 attributes such as the date, event type and countries involved [15]. The database is continuously updated and has over half a billion records. It has been used for studies such as predicting future violence levels in Afghanistan [35], and detecting protest events in the world [23].

GDELT records event occurrences, with no information about the reasons underlying them. The objective of our research is to investigate the hypothesis that political interactions between countries, represented as sequences of events, are governed by norms, and to discover what these norms may be. We also aim to demonstrate the application of a Bayesian norm learning mechanism to real-world data.

We use the GDELT data to train a model of the probability of events occurring between a pair of countries, conditional on the event history and existence (or not) of a given norm. Given a set of candidate norms generated by a simple language, the odds of each norm holding are *latent variables* [4] that we wish to uncover via Bayesian inference. This involves encoding the semantics of norms as patterns of expected behaviour via a *likelihood function*: the probability of a given sequence of events under the assumption that a candidate norm holds.

We consider the following research question: *Can the GDELT event database be better explained by a model combining probabilities and norms than by a purely probabilistic model?* Our research comprised five stages: i) collecting and preprocessing data from the GDELT database; ii) fitting a probabilistic model to serve as the baseline model; iii) defining a model to calculate the likelihood of observed sequences of events, given an assumed norm; iv) using this model to mine norms from the GDELT database based on Bayesian learning; and v) comparing the fit of the two models with the data.

Note that we do *not* aim to build a model to *predict* future behaviour in international politics; instead we focus on adapting a Bayesian norm-learning technique to identify norms that may underlie the observed event data.

The rest of the paper is outlined as follows. In Sect. 2 we discuss prior work on analysis of GDELT data and on norm learning. Section 3 provides an overview of our approach to norm learning. Section 4 discusses how we pre-processed the GDELT data to extract bilateral sequences of mutually relevant events. Section 5 presents the probabilistic model used as a baseline for our work, and Sect. 6 discusses the Bayesian approach to norm learning, and our model for normative reasoning in the form of a likelihood function for event sequences given a candidate norm. Section 7 and 8 present the results of our experiments and a statistical evaluation of the increased explanatory power that our model gives for the data compared to the baseline probabilistic model. Finally, we present our conclusions and suggestions for future work.

2 Prior Work

2.1 Analysis of GDELT Data

The GDELT dataset has attracted researchers from various fields including history, political science and computer science [5,16,17,19,23]. Research using this dataset can be broadly classified into descriptive and predictive approaches. The *descriptive approaches* (e.g. [5,17]) explain how certain events unfolded through the narrative of political events as viewed from the data captured in GDELT. The *predictive approaches* present models that can be used to predict future outcomes (e.g. [16,35]). Relevant work employing these two approaches is discussed below.

Descriptive Approaches. The work of Keertipati et al. [17] explored the GDELT data associated with two specific events (the Sri Lankan civil war, and the 2006 Fijian coup d'état) and their work confirmed that the data extracted from news articles in fact captured these global events. De Cadenas-Santiago et al. [5] analysed social unrest dynamics in Eurasian countries. They built a model based on the GDELT data to analyse the "unrest cycle" involving social agents and state response. Using their model, they showed that unrest and government action are not homogeneous across the entire Eurasian region and certain areas are more prone to conflict escalation where the enforcing ability of the state is low. The work by Gao et al. [12] showed that global political revolutions such as the Arab Spring can be explained through abnormalities in previously observed long-range correlations in political events. Qiao et al. [23] developed an approach for detecting and monitoring protests that happen around the world.

Predictive Approaches. The work of Yonamine [35] was the first to demonstrate that the data from GDELT dataset can be used to predict violence levels (in various districts of Afghanistan). Subsequently, several researchers created prediction models that utilised GDELT data for various purposes. The work of Keneshloo et al. [19] showed how the GDELT data can be used for detecting and predicting domestic conflicts. The work of Jiang et al. [16] predicted future bilateral relationships between USA and other countries based on the past data. There has also been work in creating a model predicting required humanitarian logistics in violence-stricken regions using the GDELT data [24].

To the best of our knowledge, none of the prior research has analysed the GDELT dataset to identify international norms. This work applies a Bayesian approach to learn the norms that best explain behaviour recorded in the GDELT dataset, and thus falls under the descriptive category.

2.2 Norm Learning

Norm learning (also known as norm mining, identification or recognition) is an active area of research in multi-agent systems. Researchers have employed various techniques for learning norms including association rule mining [25,26], case-based reasoning [3,6], reinforcement learning [28], inductive logic programming [8,30] and Bayesian inference [9]. Most work in this area is limited to learning norms from simulated agent societies. For example, the work of Savarimuthu et al. [25,26] inferred prohibition and obligation norms in simulated park littering and restaurant scenarios, while Sen and Airiau [28] investigated social learning by simulating repeated encounters in an abstract model of a traffic intersection. While there is value in simulation studies that demonstrate the feasibility of an approach, there is a need for norm-learning techniques that can be demonstrated to apply successfully to real-world scenarios.

There has been some work on applying multi-agent system norm-learning techniques to infer norms from real-world datasets. Researchers have explored the identification of software development norms from open source software repositories [10] and to extract norms from a corpus of business contracts [13]. Norms in these domains are explicitly stated (e.g. "One must not do X") and use sentence features (e.g. deontic modalities such as *must* and *must not*) to infer norms. These works typically either use smaller datasets (e.g. 868 sentences in the work of Gao and Singh [13]) and/or the information about a norm is found in a single document [2]. In contrast, this paper deals with a very large dataset where norms are implicit in patterns of behavior and norm-related information pertaining to a norm (e.g. details about norm triggers, violations and sanctions) cannot be found in a single document, but is spread across different articles, potentially spanning a long period of time. For example, the statement by a particular country disallowing the United Nations team from assessing their nuclear facilities may be in one article, and the ensuing sanctions (from different countries) might be in subsequent articles. These events will appear as separate entries in the GDELT dataset. Thus, extracting the behaviour that may be subject to norms requires extracting chains of events across multiple news sources.

3 Overview of Our Approach

Figure 1 shows an overview of our approach, which is explained in more detail in subsequent sections. We begin by pre-processing the GDELT event data (top of the figure), which consists of a set of attribute values for each event extracted from news sources. We filter the data to retain the events occurring between government actors, and then partition these into bilateral event sequences (i.e. those involving a pair of country actors) in which the events are mutually relevant. We do not retain the country names, as we focus on identifying generic norms that apply to *all* bilateral interactions between countries, rather than specific countries, regions or cultures. We model events as having a type (provided by GDELT as an *event code* attribute), and a direction (from the first country to the second, or vice versa). Some events (shown as lightning bolts in the figure) are considered to be sanctions, based on their event codes. The figure depicts non-sanction events as circles that are coloured to indicate different event types, with

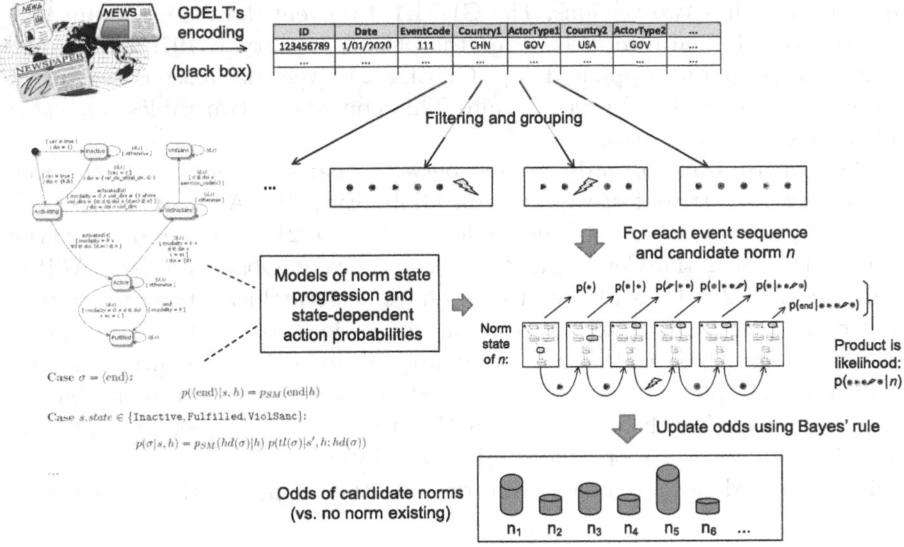

Fig. 1. Overview of our approach. The norm state machine and equations on the left are shown in full in Fig. 2 and Sect. 6.4, respectively.

embedded arrow heads to denote their direction. Sanctions also have directions, as shown in the figure.

For each sequence and candidate norm, the likelihood of the sequence occurring given that norm, and its likelihood if there is no norm, are calculated. Bayes' Rule is then used to update the odds of each candidate norm holding compared to the absence of a norm. Baseline conditional probabilities are obtained by fitting a probabilistic language model to the sequence data (not shown in the figure). We define a model that modifies these probabilities in the presence of a norm, which is sketched out on the left of the figure and presented in full in Sect. 6. This consists of two parts: (i) a state machine defining how a norm becomes activated, fulfilled or violated, and the subject of a sanction, together with (ii) a set of equations defining the conditional probabilities of events given an event history and a hypothesized norm that is in a particular state induced by the event history. Thus, a sequence's likelihood (given a norm) is decomposed into a product of event probabilites that are conditional on the prior events in the sequence and the current norm state.

4 Data Pre-processing

The GDELT project monitors the world's broadcast, print and web news from across the world and identifies people, locations, organizations, themes, sources, emotions, counts, quotes, images and events using natural language processing and data mining algorithms. We focus, in particular, on the GDELT *event database*. This has two versions. The GDELT 1.0 event database contains over a quarter of a billion records covering the period January 1, 1979 to February 17, 2014. It is no longer updated. The GDELT 2.0 event database is the current version which is updated every 15 min. This consists of two tables: an *events table* and a *mentions table*.

The events table records events between pairs of actors. Each event has 61 encoded attributes; we focus on GlobalEventID, Actor$N$CountryCode, Actor$N$Type1Code, Day, and EventCode (for $N \in \{1, 2\}$). Event and actor types are encoded using the Conflict and Mediation Event Observations (CAMEO) coding scheme [27]. CAMEO event codes have a hierarchical structure, with 20 "root codes" (in GDELT terminology) as shown in Table 1. These are further specialised into "base codes", and some are subdivided into a further level of detail. For example, "S. Korea joins US-led efforts to send astronauts back to moon" is encoded with base code 036 (Express intent to meet or negotiate), which is a subcode of root code 03 (Express Intent to Cooperate). The event attributes record the two actors' countries and their types: both *government*.

Table 1. CAMEO root event codes

01	Make public statement
02	Appeal
03	Express intent to cooperate
04	Consult
05	Engage in diplomatic cooperation
06	Engage in material cooperation
07	Provide aid
08	Yield
09	Investigate
10	Demand
11	Disapprove
12	Reject
13	Threaten
14	Protest
15	Exhibit military posture
16	Reduce relations
17	Coerce
18	Assault
19	Fight
20	Engage in unconventional mass violence

We considered events occurring from June 19, 2018 to June 20, 2019, recorded in 35039 data files, and retained only those involving two country actors (as opposed to other international organisations) with a primary role code of *government*. In our analysis, we used the CAMEO root codes only. We categorised the following root event codes as sanction events as they signal disapproval towards another country: 11 (Disapprove), 12 (Reject) and 16 (Reduce relations)[1].

Our data pre-processing phase involved extracting these events and partitioning them into sequences of related events. To do this, we introduced the notion of *mutual relevance* via a *co-mention* relation. We defined two events to be co-mentioned if they appear in the same news source as recorded in the GDELT *mentions table* [15]. This relation on the set of events is denoted by $\sim_{cm}$. This relation is symmetric and reflexive by definition. We define the mutual relevance relation $\sim_r$ as the transitive closure of $\sim_{cm}$. The mutual relevance relation is an equivalence relation and thus partitions the set of events. As we are interested in bilateral events, we divide each partition into sub-partitions containing events involving a distinct pair of country actors. These sub-partitions, when ordered by date, form sequences of mutually relevant bilateral events. When two events occur on the same day we order them randomly. Each event in a sequence is represented by its CAMEO event code and actor 1 and actor 2 country names.

Our initial generation of sequences resulted in some that seemed overly long[2] to comprise only mutually relevant events. We found two issues contributing to this problem. Many BBC news reports had non-unique mention identifiers, such as the string "as listed in Russian/BBC Monitoring/(c) BBC". These caused all events from the same BBC news source to be considered as mutually relevant. We therefore filtered out events with "BBC" in their mention identifiers before determining the mutually relevant event sets. We also found that some events were highly mentioned, possibly as the general background to news stories. These functioned as hubs linking many events together via the co-mention relationship. We resolved this problem by 'cloning' events with more than 250 mentions, i.e. for each mention of a highly mentioned event we generated a separate copy of that event with a unique mention identifier. After these two steps, our processed data consisted of 513,906 sequences with the maximum sequence length of 161. The resulting dataset is available online [21].

5 Baseline Probabilistic Model

We follow a Bayesian approach to norm learning [9], which we explain in detail in Sect. 6. This requires computing the likelihood of an observed sequence of events, given each norm hypothesis (including the hypothesis that there are no norms). Prior work on Bayesian learning of norms assumed knowledge of the plans that govern agents' public behaviour [9]—this provided a model of the possible agent behaviours in the absence of normative reasoning. In this work, as we do not have a plan-based model of international political interactions, we fit a probabilistic

[1] We omit conflict event types (such as Threaten, Assault and Fight) from this list, as we consider these to be events that are likely to be subject to norms, rather than reactions to norm violations.

[2] Some sequences contained as many as 20,000 events.

model to the set of event sequences resulting from our data pre-processing. This is used when defining the likelihood of observed sequences given norm hypotheses, and also serves as a baseline model for the evaluation of our normative model, as described in Sect. 8. We chose to use the libPLUMP implementation[3] of the *sequence memoizer* (SM) [34], due to Murphy's description of the SM as "the best-performing language model" [22, p.595]. The SM is a Bayesian non-parametric model that can be trained to learn a conditional distribution for the next symbol given all previous symbols [14], i.e. a set of conditional probability distributions of the form $p(x_{i+1}|x_1, \cdots, x_i)$. Here, $x_1, \cdots, x_i$ is a sequence of observed symbols (the *context*), and the distribution tells us the probability of symbol x_{i+1} being the next symbol to appear after the given context. The non-parametric nature of the SM means that there is no a priori limit on the length of context that can be modelled.

The SM's underlying mathematical model assumes that the symbols that can occur within sequences have a power-law distribution of probabilities, as occurs in many natural settings, e.g. the frequency of words in human languages. This smooths the fitted model to account for unseen data and avoids overestimating the probability of rare symbols that might be observed by chance. However, for our aim of discovering norms to help explain the data, rather than predicting new behaviour, we used an SM parameter setting that suppressed the power-law scaling.

The event sequences extracted from the GDELT dataset contained events represented as triples $\langle rc, c_1, c_2 \rangle$, where rc is a CAMEO root code and c_1 and c_2 are the country identifiers appearing as the event's Actor1CountryCode and Actor2CountryCode fields. As our aim is to learn generic norms that apply to all countries, we did not retain the country identifiers when training the SM. However, it was important to preserve the directionality of the events between the two countries: there is an important difference in the relative directions of the events in the first sequence below compared to those in the second and third sequences.

$$\langle rc_1, c_1, c_2 \rangle, \langle rc_2, c_1, c_2 \rangle \quad \langle rc_1, c_1, c_2 \rangle, \langle rc_2, c_2, c_1 \rangle \quad \langle rc_1, c_2, c_1 \rangle, \langle rc_2, c_1, c_2 \rangle$$

We therefore view each event as a combination of an event root code and a *direction*, where by convention the first event in a sequence is taken to be in the "forwards" direction. We denote a directed event by a pair $\langle dir, code \rangle$, giving the following representation for the first sequence above: $\langle F, rc_1 \rangle, \langle F, rc_2 \rangle$, where F denotes "forwards" and B denotes "backwards". The second and third sequences have the same representation: $\langle F, rc_1 \rangle, \langle B, rc_2 \rangle$. For simplicity, we denote a directed event by single variable, e.g. e, where we do not need to make the direction explicit.

Before training the SM, we replaced each event in a sequence with an integer code representing the combination of its event root code and a direction. While training the SM, we generated a second instance of each sequence in which the event directions are reversed. This is because the trained SM would be used to

[3] https://github.com/jgasthaus/libPLUMP.

look up likelihoods for previously unseen event sequences (encoded in the same way as the training data). The SM would first attempt to find a stored 'context' that completely matched the observed sequence. In the absence of an exact match, it would use the longest suffix of the observation that it could find in its internal storage. If we had not trained the SM with additional direction-reversed sequences, all stored contexts (from training inputs) would begin with events in the forwards direction (our convention during the original sequence generation), and this suffix matching would not work for observation suffixes that have an odd number of initial events omitted: the suffix would begin with a backwards event and thus match no stored SM context.

Finally, we appended a special end symbol to each sequence.

6 Normative Model

Given a set of candidate norms, for every observed event sequence σ in our dataset and each candidate norm we calculate the likelihood of the observation given the hypothesis h that the norm holds: $p(\sigma|h)$. We also calculate the observation's likelihood under the hypothesis that no norm holds (h_0). Bayes' Rule (the odds form of Bayes' Theorem) is then used to update the odds of the two hypotheses given the observation:

$$O(h\colon h_0|\sigma) = O(h\colon h_0)\frac{p(\sigma|h)}{p(\sigma|h_0)} \tag{1}$$

Here, we multiply the prior odds $O(h\colon h_0)$ by the ratio of the likelihoods of the observed sequence under the two hypotheses, to give the posterior odds.[4]

We reason with odds because, in general, candidate norms do not form a set of mutually exclusive and collectively exhaustive hypotheses, which is necessary to normalise probabilities when using Bayes' Theorem [9]. We work in log space. After initialising the prior log odds for all norm hypotheses to a uniform value, for each sequence s we calculate the log likelihood of s under all hypotheses. We then update the log odds for each hypothesis h by adding the difference between $log\, p(s|h)$ and $log\, p(s|h_0)$.[5]

6.1 Candidate Norms

We use the following language to define our set of candidate norms:

- $O(ec)$: an unconditional obligation to perform an event with event code ec.

[4] The priors were are initialised to 1 for all of the norms we consider. However, this choice has no significant effect as we are interested in the *relative* posterior odds.

[5] Note that this approach only reasons about single-norm hypotheses. Based on the log odds of individual norms, it would be possible to select combinations of most likely norms to form multi-norm hypotheses, but this requires a more complex model of observation likelihood than we have at present.

- $O(cec, ec, rel\_dir)$: a conditional obligation to perform an event with event code ec if a prior condition event with event code cec has occurred, and the two events have the relative direction specified by rel_dir (either 'same' or 'different', denoted + and −, respectively).
- $P(ec)$: an unconditional prohibition of events with event code ec.
- $P(cec, ec, rel\_dir)$: a conditional prohibition of events with event code ec if a prior condition event with event code cec has occurred, and the two events have the relative direction specified by rel_dir.

For conditional norms, the relative direction constraints are necessary to specify which country is subject to the norm once the condition occurs: the country that performed the event triggering the norm, or the other one.

The semantics of these norm types are defined using linear temporal logic interpreted over event sequences. For example:

$$\begin{aligned} O(cec, ec, +) \stackrel{\text{def}}{=} \; & \Box(\text{code}(cec) \wedge \text{dir}(\text{F}) \rightarrow \bigcirc\Diamond(\text{code}(ec) \wedge \text{dir}(\text{F}))) \wedge \\ & \Box(\text{code}(cec) \wedge \text{dir}(\text{B}) \rightarrow \bigcirc\Diamond(\text{code}(ec) \wedge \text{dir}(\text{B}))) \end{aligned}$$

where code and dir are predicates recording the event code and direction of the current event, and F and B denote the forwards and backwards event directions. $O(cec, ec, -)$ and the other norm types are defined in a similar fashion.

For our experiments, our set of candidate norms was formed by instantiating the $O(ec)$, $O(cec, ec, rel\_dir)$, $P(ec)$ and $P(cec, ec, rel\_dir)$ norm types with cec and ec ranging over the 20 CAMEO root codes and $rel\_dir \in \{+, -\}$. We therefore had 1640 candidate norms.

6.2 Computing Observation Likelihood Ratios

Let $\sigma = (\sigma_1, \sigma_2, \ldots, \sigma_N)$ be our dataset with $N = 513,906$ event sequences. Then, as each sequence is independently observed, we can express the conditional probability of the data given a norm hypothesis h as follows:

$$p(\sigma|h) = \prod_{i=1}^{N} p(\sigma_i|h)$$

Applying Eq. (1), taking logarithms, and considering the odds of a norm hypothesis holding versus the no-norm null hypothesis h_0, we calculate the log odds of the complete dataset as the sum of the prior log odds and the *log likelihood ratios* of each sequence under the two hypotheses.

$$log(O(h\colon h_0|\sigma)) = log(O(h\colon h_0)) + \sum_{i=1}^{N} (log(p(\sigma_i|h)) - log(p(\sigma_i|h_0)))$$

6.3 A State Machine for Our Norm Language

To calculate the log likelihood of an observed sequence given a norm, we need a model of how the countries act in the presence of norms. This has two parts. In this subsection we present a state machine that models the changes of state of a norm as each directed event in a sequence is observed. In the next subsection we define the likelihood of an event sequence given a norm hypothesis, which is defined recursively while using our model to track the norm state.

Various abstract state models for commitments and norms have been proposed in the literature, e.g. [11,31], often with the transition conditions defined as part of separate semantic rules. Our model differs from these as it is specifically intended to support our definition of the likelihood function and our language of unconditional and conditional obligations and prohibitions. We include a state indicating that a norm violation has been sanctioned, and define the complete transition semantics within the state machine (thus it is directly executable).

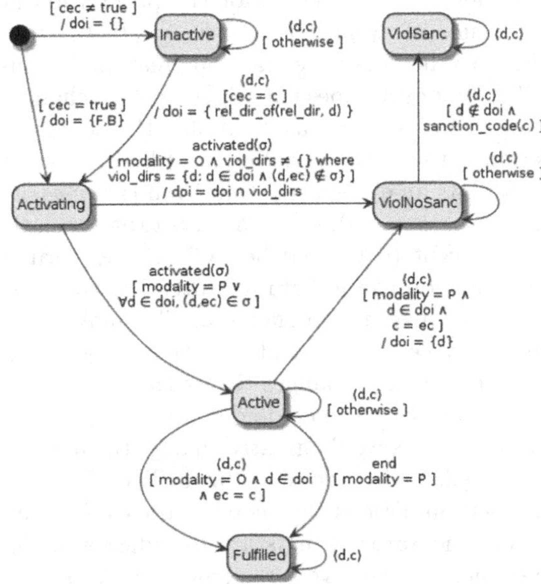

Fig. 2. The norm state machine

The norm state machine is shown in UML notation in Figure 2.[6] A separate state machine is created for each observed sequence and norm hypothesis. The variable `modality` is instantiated with the value `O` or `P`, representing an obligation or prohibition, respectively. The variables `cec`, `ec` and `rel_dir` record the corresponding norm parameters from Sect. 6.1. For unconditional norms, `cec` is

[6] The transition annotations have the format *trigger*[*guard*]/*action*. Transitions from the initial state have no trigger, and guards and actions are optional.

set to `true`. The observed events are passed sequentially to the state machine as $\langle direction, event\_code\rangle$ pairs, followed by an `end` event. The state machine uses the variable `doi` to track the "directions of interest" for checking events for norm fulfilment, violation and sanctioning.[7] For unconditional norms, `doi` is initially the set {F, B} (i.e., both forward and backwards), while for conditional norms, a singleton direction set is assigned to `doi` based on the direction of the triggering event and the norm's *rel_dir*.

From the initial state (represented by a filled circle), a prohibition norm or an eventually fulfilled obligation norm becomes `Active` (via an intermediate state `Activating`, explained below) if a triggering event occurs, or immediately for an unconditional norm. The norm can subsequently become `Fulfilled` if the norm's *ec* event code occurs (for an obligation) or doesn't occur (for a prohibition) in the correct direction. Norm violations cause a transition to the state `ViolNoSanc` (a currently non-sanctioned violation), and a subsequent sanction event (in the opposite direction to the violating event) causes a transition to `ViolSanc` (a sanctioned violation).

For example, consider a state machine for the prohibition norm $P(5, 13, -)$ and an observed sequence of events $\langle F, \mathit{4}\rangle, \langle F, \mathit{5}\rangle, \langle B, \mathit{13}\rangle, \langle F, \mathit{11}\rangle$. The state machine will transition to the `Inactive` state on creation, because the condition is not yet satisfied. The first event does not trigger a state change, but the second event causes a change to `Activating`, as it satisfies the norm's condition. A side effect of this transition is to set the variable `doi` (direction of interest) to $\{B\}$, because the norm prohibits an event with code 13 in the *opposite* direction from the triggering event (i.e. backwards). In the `Activating` state, the state machine receives an `activated` event (explained below). As the norm is a prohibition norm, this causes a transition to the `Active` state. The third event violates the prohibition, so the state changes to `ViolNoSanc`. The final event has a code that is classified as a sanction (see Sect. 4) and is in the opposite direction from the norm-violating event, so the state changes to `ViolSanc`.

We considered it impractical to include deadlines as parameters of our obligation norm hypotheses, as this would greatly enlarge the norm hypothesis space and require us to include dates in event encodings. Therefore, we have no way to filter out potential violation actions that come "too soon" after obligation violations. Instead, we use the `Activating` state to indicate to the learning agent that the remaining elements in the event sequence should be passed to the state machine as parameters of an `activated` event. This allows a look-ahead for obligation violations. If any are found, an early transition is made from `Activating` to `ViolNoSanc`, which allows sanction events to be handled immediately following activation. Otherwise, the norm state changes to `Active`. Thus, a transition from `Activating` to `ViolNoSanc` is made immediately if an obligation is violated by the remaining events in the sequence. In this case, sanctions will be recognised however soon they appear after norm activation.

[7] To simplify the model, only the first instantiation, fulfilment, violation and sanction of a norm within a sequence are tracked by the state machine.

6.4 Observation Likelihood

In this section, we define the likelihood of an observed sequence of events, given a candidate norm. This encodes our model of how norms influence the behaviour of interacting countries by varying the background probability of events (as modelled by the sequence memoizer).

Given a sequence of events σ (including the end symbol added before SM training), and the null hypothesis (h_0) that there is no norm, we define:

$$p(\sigma|h_0) = \prod_{i=1,\ldots,|\sigma|} p_{SM}(\sigma_i|\sigma^{\leq i}) \tag{2}$$

where $p_{SM}(e|h)$ denotes the probability of the event e given context history h returned from a sequence memoizer trained on the entire dataset, σ_i denotes the ith element of σ, $\sigma^{\leq i}$ is the prefix of σ of length i, and $|\sigma|$ is the length of σ.

For other (non-null) norm hypotheses, n, we define:

$$p(\sigma|n) = p(\sigma|s = nsm(n), h = \epsilon) \tag{3}$$

where $nsm(n)$ is a new instance of the norm state machine for norm n, and ϵ is the empty sequence, representing the sequence history prior to σ. In the following, we define the conditional probability $p(\sigma|s, h)$ appearing on the right hand side of Eq. 3 as a recursive function, with separate cases for the various states of the norm state machine.[8]

We use the following notation. Given a norm state machine s, we write $s.modality$, $s.ec$, $s.state$, and $s.doi$ to refer to the state machine's norm modality, norm event code, the current state and the value of the `doi` variable. We write $hd(\sigma)$ and $tl(\sigma)$ to denote the head and tail of the sequence σ, and $\sigma{:}e$ for σ with event e appended. Given a sequence σ and state machine s, we write s' as an abbreviation for $s.receive(hd(\sigma))$, i.e. the state machine resulting from sending $hd(\sigma)$ to s. In other words, wherever s' appears on the right hand side of an equation, the norm state machine has been invoked to update the state of the norm based on $hd(\sigma)$. For case $s.state = \texttt{Activating}$, we define $s^a = s.receive(hd(\text{activated}(\sigma)))$.

Case $\sigma = \langle\text{end}\rangle$**:**

$$p(\langle\text{end}\rangle|s, h) = p_{SM}(\text{end}|h)$$

Case $s.state \in \{\texttt{Inactive}, \texttt{Fulfilled}, \texttt{ViolSanc}\}$**:**

$$p(\sigma|s, h) = p_{SM}(hd(\sigma)|h)\; p(tl(\sigma)|s', h{:}\, hd(\sigma))$$

Case $s.state = \texttt{Activating}$**:** In this case we evaluate the conditional probability under three mutually exclusive additional assumptions: that the agent will be compliant with the norm, non-compliant but unsanctioned, and non-compliant and sanctioned. Two of these three assumptions will turn out be

[8] We perform the calculations in log space, resulting in a log likelihood, but for simplicity of presentation we do not show this.

inconsistent with σ and the norm embodied by the state machine s, and the corresponding conditional probabilities will therefore return 0. We write "comp" and "sanc" to denote the events of compliance and sanctioning occurring.

$$\begin{aligned} p(\sigma|s,h) = {} & p\_comp(n)^{|s.doi|}\, p(\sigma|s^a,h,\text{comp}) \\ & + (1 - p\_comp(n)^{|s.doi|})\, p\_sanc(n)\, p(\sigma|s^a,h,\neg\text{comp},\text{sanc}) \\ & + (1 - p\_comp(n)^{|s.doi|})\,(1 - p\_sanc(n))\, p(\sigma|s^a,h,\neg\text{comp},\neg\text{sanc}) \end{aligned}$$

Here, we assume that there are two key decisions that a country must make within a bilateral interaction in the presence of a norm: whether to *comply* with the norm, and whether to *sanction* a violation of the norm by the other party. Note that the negation of the decision-to-comply event is *not* the decision to be non-compliant. Rather, it is the lack of a decision to comply, which we take to mean that the country chooses not to care about the norm during the interaction. Once that choice is made, it may end up complying based on the background probability of events embodied in the sequence memoizer, but this is not due to normative reasoning. The *comply* and *sanction* decisions are governed by probabilities $p\_comp(n)$ and $p\_sanc(n)$, which we learn from the data on a per-norm basis. We count how many times each norm hypothesis is triggered,[9] violated, fulfilled and sanctioned across all the sequences in the dataset, and use add-one smoothing to address any zero counts.[10]

$$p\_comp(n) = \frac{\#t(n) - \#v(n) + 1}{t(n) + 2} \qquad p\_sanc(n) = \frac{\#s(n) + 1}{\#v(n) + 2}$$

where n is a norm hypothesis, t, v, s denote triggerings, violations and sanctions, and # abbreviates "number of".

In the case of unconditional norms, a sequence in which compliance is observed means that both agents have decided to be compliant. Thus, in the equation for $p(\sigma|s,h)$ above, we raise p_comp to the power of $|s.doi|$ (the number of "directions of interest", which is 2 in the case of unconditional norms).

Case $s.state = \texttt{Active}$:

$$p(\sigma|s,h,\text{comp}) = \begin{cases} p_1\, p_3 & \text{if } s.modality = \text{O and } \exists d \in s.doi,\ \langle s, s.ec\rangle \in \sigma \\ p_2\, p_3 & \text{if } s.modality = \text{P and } \forall d \in s.doi,\ \langle s, s.ec\rangle \notin \sigma \\ 0 & \text{otherwise} \end{cases}$$

and

$$p(\sigma|s,h,\neg\text{comp},v) = \begin{cases} p_1\, p_4 & \text{if } s.modality = \text{P and } \exists d \in s.doi,\ \langle s, s.ec\rangle \in \sigma \\ p_2\, p_4 & \text{if } s.modality = \text{O and } \forall d \in s.doi,\ \langle s, s.ec\rangle \notin \sigma \\ 0 & \text{otherwise} \end{cases}$$

9 In the case of unconditional norms, this is once for every observation.

10 Add-one smoothing involves adding one to both positive and negative counts, hence the "+2" in the denominator (the total count).

where v can be either sanc or $\neg$sanc and:

$$p_1 \equiv p_{incl(s.doi,\{s.ec\})}(hd(\sigma)|h),\ p_2 \equiv p_{excl(s.doi,\{s.ec\})}(hd(\sigma)|h)$$
$$p_3 \equiv p(tl(\sigma)|s', h\colon hd(\sigma), \text{comp}),\ p_4 \equiv p(tl(\sigma)|s', h\colon hd(\sigma), \neg\text{comp}, v)$$

p_1 and p_2 are defined in terms of some specialised conditional probability distributions:

$$p_{incl(doi,codes)}(e|h) \equiv p(e\,|\,h,\ h{:}e \sim \{\sigma \in D : \exists\langle d,c\rangle \in doi \times codes, \langle d,c\rangle \in \sigma\})$$

$$p_{excl(doi,codes)}(e|h) \equiv p(e\,|\,h,\ h{:}e \sim \{\sigma \in D : \nexists\langle d,c\rangle \in doi \times codes, \langle d,c\rangle \in \sigma\})$$

$p_{incl(doi,codes)}(e|h)$ is the probability of the directed event e occurring after event history h according to a language model trained on sequences from our dataset (D) that *include* an event with direction in *doi* and an event code in *codes*. This probability is used to determine the probability of an event under the assumption that there is an obligation norm and the norm is known to be active, or that a norm has been violated and will be sanctioned. In these cases, we know that the obligated event or a sanction should be one of the remaining events in the sequence, i.e. sequences that do not include such an event have a probability of zero. Therefore, to ensure we are using a correctly normalised probability distribution we must use a sequence memoizer trained only on data that excludes these sequences.

We are interested in $p_{incl(doi,codes)}(e|h)$ for cases where *codes* is a singleton set or the set of all sanction event codes. To implement $p_{incl(\cdots)}$, we train sequence memoizers for each case, using only sequences containing a forward-directed event with an event code in the *codes* set for that case. Given these, we can compute this probability for backwards-directed events *de* by reversing the event directions in both *de* and h[11].

Note that in cases of conditional norms, this probability is used as an approximation. To compute the correct probability, we would need to train the sequence memoizer on sequences that exclude such events only *after* the norm is activated by a norm's specific triggering event. This would involve using many more sequence memoizers, one for each pair of event codes (a triggering event and an obligated event). Thus, our specially trained sequence memoizer *underestimates* the probability, since it is trained on a superset of sequences compared to using a more specialised SM. This lower probability dampens the log odds of the norm, and thus our estimates of the log odds of conditional obligations are conservative. $p_{excl(doi,codes)}(e|h)$ is the probability of the directed event e occurring after event history h, according to a language model trained only on sequences from our dataset (D) that *exclude* events with direction in *doi* and an event code in *codes*. This probability is used to determine the probability of an event under the assumption that there is a prohibition norm and the norm is known to be

[11] Recall from Sect. 5 that we train sequence memoizers with two copies of each event sequences: one with its default directions (where the first event is taken to be "forwards" and a direction-reversed copy of the sequence).

active, or that a norm has been violated but will not be sanctioned. This probability distribution is implemented by modifying the probabilities returned by the default sequence memoizer p_{SM} (which is trained on the full set of sequences):

$$p_{excl(doi,codes)}(\langle d, c\rangle|h) = \begin{cases} 0 & \text{if } d \in doi \wedge \\ & \quad c \in codes \\ \frac{p_{SM}(\langle d,c\rangle|h)}{1-\sum_{d' \in doi, c' \in codes} p_{SM}(\langle d',c'\rangle|h)} & \text{otherwise} \end{cases}$$

Case $s.state$ = `ViolNoSanc`**:**

$$p(\sigma|s, h, \text{comp}) = 0 \quad (\texttt{ViolNoSanc} \text{ inconsistent with `comp' assumption})$$

$$p(\sigma|s, h, \neg\text{comp}, \text{sanc}) = \begin{cases} 0 & \text{if } hd(\sigma) \text{ is not a sanction in a direction in } s.doi \\ p_1\, p_3 & \text{otherwise} \end{cases}$$

and

$$p(\sigma|s, h, \neg\text{comp}, \neg\text{sanc}) = \begin{cases} 0 & \text{if } hd(\sigma) \text{ is a sanction in a direction in } s.doi \\ p_2\, p_4 & \text{otherwise} \end{cases}$$

where

$$p_1 \equiv p_{incl(s.doi,sanction\_codes)}(hd(\sigma)|h), \;\; p_2 \equiv p_{excl(s.doi,sanction\_codes)}(hd(\sigma)|h)$$
$$p_3 \equiv p(tl(\sigma)|s', h{:}\, hd(\sigma), \neg\text{comp}, \text{sanc}), \;\; p_4 \equiv p(tl(\sigma)|s', h{:}\, hd(\sigma), \neg\text{comp}, \neg\text{sanc})$$

Table 2. Top six norms

	log odds	triggers	fulfilled	viols	non sanc. viols	sanc. viols	pcomp	psanc
$O(4)$	75355.1	513906	115633	398273	349043	4230.0	0.225	0.011
$O(4, 4, -)$	65428.0	232767	115633	117134	114921	2213.0	0.497	0.019
$O(3)$	21550.6	513906	16384	497522	495551	1971.0	0.032	0.004
$O(3, 3, -)$	14569.4	56951	16384	40567	39548	1019.0	0.288	0.025
$O(5, 5, -)$	13814.1	66766	12618	54148	52404	1744.0	0.189	0.032
$O(4, 3, +)$	12092.1	232767	4750	228017	226077	1940.0	0.020	0.009

7 Results

To learn norms from the data, we estimated the probability of compliance and sanctioning for each norm, as discussed in Sect. 6.4, and ran the Bayesian inference procedure on our event sequence dataset and hypothesis set. This resulted in 173 norms with posterior log odds greater than 0 (i.e. odds greater than 1), and which were therefore found to be more likely hypotheses than the null hypothesis (that there are no norms). Among these 173 norms, there were 154 conditional obligation norms, 16 conditional prohibition norms and 3 unconditional obligation norms. The top six norms are shown in Table 2, along with their posterior log odds, counts of triggerings, fulfilments, violations and sanctions, and the inferred probability of compliance and sanctioning. These top norms can be understood as follows:

- $O(4)$: The CAMEO root code 4 (as seen in Table 1) stands for "Consult". This norm is an unconditional obligation to consult the other country. This norm is complied with 22.5% of the time which accounts for its high log odds. The violations in this norm were rarely sanctioned.
- $O(4, 4, -)$: This is triggered by a consultation, and the other party is then obliged to consult. More than half the time it is violated, but some of the violations (1.8%) are sanctioned. The 49.7% fulfilment rate and the sanctions account for this norm's very high log odds.
- $O(3), O(3, 3, -), O(5, 5, -)$: Much like the above two norms, these norms have high log odds. The first is the unconditional obligation to 'Express Intent to Cooperate'. The second is triggered by an expression of intent to cooperate, obligates the other party to express intent to cooperate in return. The third norm is the obligation to engage in diplomatic cooperation once the other part engages in diplomatic cooperation.
- $O(4, 3, +)$: This norm suggests that when a party consults the other party, it is also likely to express intent to cooperate.

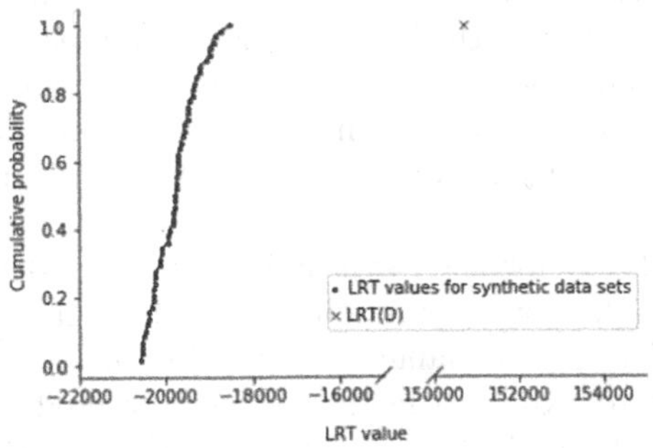

Fig. 3. $LRT(D)$ and the empirical distribution of $LRT(d)$

8 Evaluation

To address our research question *"Can the GDELT event dataset be better explained by a model combining event probabilities and explicit norms than by a probabilistic model?"*, we compare the total likelihood of the event sequence dataset under two models:

M_0: the probabilistic model embodied by the SM trained on all sequences, and
M_1: a model that uses normative reasoning about the top norm to modify the SM's probabilities (as presented in Sect. 6.4).

We denote the log likelihood of an event dataset d under these two models as $L_0(d)$ and $L_1(d)$, respectively. We write D to denote our GDELT-derived sequence dataset.

The total log likelihoods of all sequences in our GDELT-derived dataset under the two models were $L_1(D) - L_0(D) = 75355.051837$. Thus, M_1 is a better fit to the data than M_0. In order to determine whether the difference in log likelihood is statistically significant, we performed a likelihood ratio test. This test compared two hypotheses:

H_0: Model M_0 is the true model underlying the data. This is the null hypothesis.
H_1: Model M_1 is the true model underlying the data.

Under certain conditions related to model nesting and smoothness of the likelihood function, the null hypothesis implies that the likelihood ratio test statistic $LRT(d) = -2(L_0(d) - L_1(d)) = 2(L_1(d) - L_0(d))$ approximates a χ^2 distribution for large sample sizes, with degrees of freedom equal to the difference in the number of free parameters between the two models [33]. A standard one-tailed significance test can then be used to reject H_0 if $LRT(D)$ is less than or equal to the χ^2 value at the desired significance level. However, the conditions allowing the use of the χ^2 test do not apply in our case, so we compute an empirical distribution of the LRT statistic.

We used the posterior distribution of sequences, i.e. the trained SM, to generate 58 synthetic datasets[12] with the same size as the real dataset (i.e. 513,906 sequences) under the null hypothesis.[13] Sequences were sampled until the end symbol was reached from the sequence memoizer's conditional predictive distributions: $p(e|\sigma)$, where e ranged over all event root codes and σ is a known prior sequence of events.

We calculated $LRT(d)$ for each synthetic dataset and the p-value for the observed value $LRT(D)$. It was found that in each of these datasets, $LRT(d)$ was negative, indicating that the language model learned by the sequence memoizer is not sufficient to explain the top norm extracted from the real data. These negative values also indicate that the synthetic datasets are more likely to be probabilistically generated, which is true since they are generated from the SM. The p-value is the probability that $LRT(d) \geq LRT(D)$, $d \neq D$. Figure 3 shows the empirical distribution of $LRT(d)$. As $LRT(D)$ exceeds $LRT(d)$ for all synthetic datasets d, the p-value is less than $\frac{1}{58} \approx 0.017$, meaning that we can reject the null hypothesis at the 0.1 significance level. Thus, we can answer our

[12] The number was constrained by the highly time-intensive process of looking up the SM's conditional probabilities to generate and to evaluate the likelihood of these large datasets.

[13] Murphy discusses the relationship between sampling from the posterior and the well known *bootstrap* method for approximating the sampling distribution of a test statistic [22, p.192].

research question in the affirmative: our model including the top norm explains the GDELT dataset better than when using the sequence memoizer alone.

9 Conclusions and Future Work

We have presented a methodology for mining norms from a global political event database using a Bayesian norm-learning approach, and an algorithm for computing the log likelihood of observed sequences of actions given a norm hypothesis and a background probabilistic model of event sequences. A statistical evaluation showed that a model of event sequence likelihood that enhances the probabilistic model with normative reasoning fits the data significantly better than the baseline probabilistic model.

The primary contribution of this research is to propose a methodology for mining norms in international relations. With the growing presence of automated event datasets such as GDELT, research in this direction will provide tools for researchers and international organisations like the United Nations and the Inter-Parliamentary Union to gain a better understanding of the tacit norms that govern international relations. This work also provides a demonstration of how norm-learning techniques from multi-agent systems can apply to real-world human societies.

There are a number of limitations to our current approach that should be addressed in future work. We have focused on country actors with a government role, which could easily be extended to include other international organisations such as the United Nations, and police, military and intelligence agency roles.

We mined for norms using the full set of bilateral event sequences, so our inferred norms are those that apply globally, to all countries. It would be interesting to look for norms that are specific to particular groups of countries.

Our dataset was limited to a one-year period. A year is a short time in politics, and more interesting norms could be found from a dataset spanning a longer period, although this will require significantly greater computation time.

The detection of mutually relevant events relies on the ability of GDELT's automated event extraction techniques to assign the same identifier to an event across all mentions of it. The ability of GDELT's automated systems to uniquely identify events in this way has been questioned [32], and this warrants further investigation.

Our norm language is rather simple, and richer languages should be investigated in consultation with political science and peace and conflict studies experts. Our likelihood function can be easily adapted to other norm languages—this simply involves changing the logic for detecting norm violations and sanctions. However, a significantly richer norm language will lead to a much larger norm hypothesis set and increased computation time, even if an upper bound is placed on the complexity of hypotheses. This can be addressed by partitioning the set of hypotheses and distributing log likelihood computation for the partitions across different processors. The log odds updates for different norm hypotheses given an observed event sequence can then be computed in parallel and amalgamated in a final stage of computation.

A distinction has been made in the literature between "normal" and "normative" behaviour [18, Chap. 1]. It is argued that for observed "normal" behaviour to be considered normative, it must have an explicit internal representation as a norm (rather than simply being copied behaviour), and be the subject of social processes that account for its emergence. The external view of international events provided by event databases such as GDELT does not allow assessment of how explicitly the actors may be aware of the norms, and the only visible social mechanism is sanctioning. As sanctions were present for all of our inferred norms, there is reason to consider that these 'norms' are truly normative rather than simply normal behaviour. However, we see our research as only a first step in an investigation that will require input from social scientists to validate and refine our findings.

Acknowledgement. We thank Matt Schofield for statistical advice.

References

1. Andrighetto, G., Governatori, G., Noriega, P., van der Torre, L.W.N. (eds.) Normative Multi-Agent Systems, Dagstuhl Follow-Ups, vol. 4. Schloss Dagstuhl - Leibniz-Zentrum fuer Informatik (2013)
2. Avery, D., Dam, H.K., Savarimuthu, B.T.R., Ghose, A.: Externalization of software behavior by the mining of norms. In: 13th International Conference on Mining Software Repositories, pp. 223–234. ACM (2016)
3. Balke, T., Novais, P., Andrade, F.C.P., Eymann, T.: From real-world regulations to concrete norms for software agents: a case-based reasoning approach. In: International Workshop on Legal and Negotiation Decision Support Systems (LDSS), pp. 14–27. CEUR Workshop Proceedings (2009)
4. Blei, D.M.: Build, compute, critique, repeat: data analysis with latent variable models. Ann. Revi. Stat. Appl. **1**, 203–232 (2014)
5. de Cadenas-Santiago, G., Herrero, A.G., Vidal-Abarca, Á.O., López, T.R.: An empirical assessment of social unrest dynamics and state response in eurasian countries. Eurasian J. Soc. Sci. **3**(3), 1–29 (2015)
6. Campos, J., López-Sánchez, M., Esteva, M.: A case-based reasoning approach for norm adaptation. In: Corchado, E., Graña Romay, M., Manhaes Savio, A. (eds.) HAIS 2010. LNCS (LNAI), vol. 6077, pp. 168–176. Springer, Heidelberg (2010). https://doi.org/10.1007/978-3-642-13803-4_21
7. Conte, R., Dellarocas, C. (eds.). Social Order in Multiagent Systems. Springer, Boston (2001). https://doi.org/10.1007/978-1-4615-1555-5
8. Corapi, D., Russo, A., De Vos, M., Padget, J., Satoh, K.: Normative design using inductive learning. Theor. Pract. Log. Prog. **11**(4–5), 783–799 (2011)
9. Cranefield, S., Meneguzzi, F., Oren, N., Savarimuthu, B.T.R.: A Bayesian approach to norm identification. In: 22nd European Conference on Artificial Intelligence. Frontiers in Artificial Intelligence and Applications, vol. 285, pp. 622–629. IOS Press (2016)
10. Dam, H.K., Savarimuthu, B.T.R., Avery, D., Ghose, A.: Mining software repositories for social norms. In: 37th International Conference on Software Engineering, vol. 2, pp. 627–630. IEEE (2015)

11. Fornara, N., Colombetti, M.: A commitment-based approach to agent communication. Appl. Artif. Intell. **18**(9–10), 853–866 (2004)
12. Gao, J., Leetaru, K.H., Hu, J., Cioffi-Revilla, C., Schrodt, P.: Massive media event data analysis to assess world-wide political conflict and instability. In: Social Computing, Behavioral-Cultural Modeling and Prediction, pp. 284–292. Springer, Cham (2013). https://doi.org/10.1007/978-3-642-37210-0_31
13. Gao, X., Singh, M.P.: Extracting normative relationships from business contracts. In: International Conference on Autonomous Agents and Multi-Agent Systems, pp. 101–108. IFAAMAS (2014)
14. Gasthaus, J., Teh, Y.W.: Improvements to the sequence memoizer. In: Advances in Neural Information Processing Systems, **23**, pp. 685–693. Curran Associates, Inc. (2010)
15. The GDELT Event Database – Data format Codebook v2.0. http://data.gdeltproject.org/documentation/GDELT-Event_Codebook-V2.0.pdf (2015)
16. Jiang, L., Mai, F.: Discovering Bilateral and Multilateral Causal Events in GDELT. Paper presented at the International Conference on Social Computing, Behavioral-Cultural Modeling, and Prediction. Washington D.C. (2014)
17. Keertipati, S., Savarimuthu, B.T.R., Purvis, M., Purvis, M.: Multi-level analysis of peace and conflict data in GDELT. In: Proceedings of the 2nd Workshop on Machine Learning for Sensory Data Analysis, pp. 33–40. ACM (2014). https://doi.org/10.1145/2689746.2689750
18. Kelsen, H.: General Theory of Norms. Clarendon Press (1990)
19. Keneshloo, Y., Cadena, J., Korkmaz, G., Ramakrishnan, N.: Detecting and forecasting domestic political crises: a graph-based approach. In: Proceedings of the 2014 ACM Conference on Web Science, pp. 192–196. WebSci 2014, ACM (2014). https://doi.org/10.1145/2615569.2615698
20. Leetaru, K., Schrodt, P.A.: GDELT: global data on events, location, and tone, 1979–2012. In: Proceedings of the International Studies Association Annual Convention (2013). http://data.gdeltproject.org/documentation/ISA.2013.GDELT.pdf
21. Murali, R., Patnaik, S., Cranefield, S.: Bilateral government event sequences extracted from the GDELT database for the period 19 June 2018 to 20 June 2019. Dataset (2021). https://doi.org/10.6084/m9.figshare.13557809
22. Murphy, K.P.: Machine Learning: A Probabilistic Perspective. The MIT Press, Cambridge (2012)
23. Qiao, F., Li, P., Deng, J., Ding, Z., Wang, H.: Graph-based method for detecting occupy protest events using GDELT dataset. In: International Conference on Cyber-Enabled Distributed Computing and Knowledge Discovery, pp. 164–168. IEEE (2015)
24. Racette, M.P., Smith, C.T., Cunningham, M.P., Heekin, T.A., Lemley, J.P., Mathieu, R.S.: Improving situational awareness for humanitarian logistics through predictive modeling. In: Systems and Information Engineering Design Symposium (SIEDS), 2014, pp. 334–339. IEEE (2014)
25. Savarimuthu, B.T.R., Cranefield, S., Purvis, M.A., Purvis, M.K.: Obligation norm identification in agent societies. J. Artif. Soc. Soc. Simulat. **13**(4) (2010). https://doi.org/10.18564/jasss.1659
26. Savarimuthu, B.T.R., Cranefield, S., Purvis, M.A., Purvis, M.K.: Identifying prohibition norms in agent societies. Artif. Intell. Law **21**(1), 1–46 (2013)
27. Schrodt, P.A.: CAMEO: Conflict and Mediation Event Observations Event and Actor Codebook (2012). http://data.gdeltproject.org/documentation/CAMEO.Manual.1.1b3.pdf

28. Sen, S., Airiau, S.: Emergence of norms through social learning. In: Proceedings of the 20th International Joint Conference on Artificial Intelligence, pp. 1507–1512 (2007)
29. Shoham, Y., Tennenholtz, M.: On the emergence of social conventions: modeling, analysis, and simulations. Artif. Intell. **94**(1), 139–166 (1997)
30. Tan, Z.X., Brawer, J., Scassellati, B.: That's mine! learning ownership relations and norms for robots. In: Thirty-Third AAAI Conference on Artificial Intelligence, pp. 8058–8065. AAAI Press (2019)
31. Telang, P.R., Singh, M.P., Yorke-Smith, N.: A coupled operational semantics for goals and commitments. J. Artif. Intell. Res. **65**, 31–85 (2019)
32. Ulfelder, J.: Another note on the limitations of event data (2014). https://dartthrowingchimp.wordpress.com/2014/06/06/another-note-on-the-limitations-of-event-data
33. Wilks, S.S.: The large-sample distribution of the likelihood ratio for testing composite hypotheses. Ann. Math. Stat. **9**(1), 60–62 (1938)
34. Wood, F., Gasthaus, J., Archambeau, C., James, L., Teh, Y.: The sequence memoizer. Commun. ACM **54**(2), 91–98 (2011)
35. Yonamine, J.E.: A nuanced study of political conflict using the Global Datasets of Events Location and Tone (GDELT) dataset. Ph.D. thesis, Pennsylvania State University (2013)

Developers' Responses to App Review Feedback – A Study of Communication Norms in App Development

Bastin Tony Roy Savarimuthu[1(✉)], Sherlock A. Licorish[1], Manjula Devananda[1], Georgia Greenheld[1], Virginia Dignum[2], and Frank Dignum[2]

[1] Department of Information Science, University of Otago, Dunedin, New Zealand
{tony.savarimuthu,sherlock.licorish,manjula.devananda, georgia.greenheld}@otago.ac.nz

[2] Department of Computing Science, Umeå University, Umeå, Sweden
{virginia.dignum,frank.dignum}@umu.se

Abstract. Norms are general expectations of behavior in societies. Huge amount of computer-mediated interaction data available in the social media domain provides an opportunity to extract and study communication norms, both to understand their prevalence and to make informed decisions about adopting them. While interactions in social media platforms such as Twitter and Facebook have been widely studied, only recently researchers have started examining app reviews provided by users and the responses provided by developers in the domain of app development. In this vein, a lot of attention has been devoted to study the nature of user reviews, however, little is known about developer responses to such reviews. Additionally, no other prior work has scrutinized the nature of communication norms in this domain. Towards addressing these gaps, this work pursues three objectives using a dataset comprising user reviews and developer responses from Google's top-20 apps used to track running with a total of 24,407 reviews and 2,668 responses. First, based on prior literature in computer-mediated interactions, the study identifies 12 norms in responses provided by developers in three categories (obligation norms, prohibition norms and domain-specific response norms). Second, it scrutinizes the awareness and adoption of these norms. Third, based on the results obtained, this study identifies the need for creating a response recommendation system that generates responses to user reviews either automatically, or with some help from the developers. The proposed response recommendation system is a normative system that will generate responses that abide by the norms identified in this work, and will also monitor potential norm violations (if the responses were to be modified by the developers). Development of such a system forms the focus of future work.

Keywords: App reviews · Norms · Mining · Developer responses · Communication norms

A. Aler Tubella et al. (Eds.): COIN 2017/COINE 2020, LNAI 12298, pp. 57–75, 2021.
https://doi.org/10.1007/978-3-030-72376-7_4

1 Introduction

App reviews contain valuable information that can inform developers and users about issues that need to be fixed and enhancements and new features required [1]. The availability of 'big-data' comprising users' reviews and developers' responses has provided an opportunity to study the type of communication norms (patterns of excepted social behavior in communication exchanges, also known as communication etiquettes [2, 3]) among involved parties (users and developers), to understand their prevalence and to make informed decisions about adopting them. While several studies have investigated the nature of app reviews submitted by users [1, 4, 7], only a few have investigated the nature of responses provided to these reviews by app development firms [5, 6]. Additionally, these works have not investigated response provision from a normative perspective. This work aims to bridge this gap by investigating the patterns of developers' responses to users' reviews.

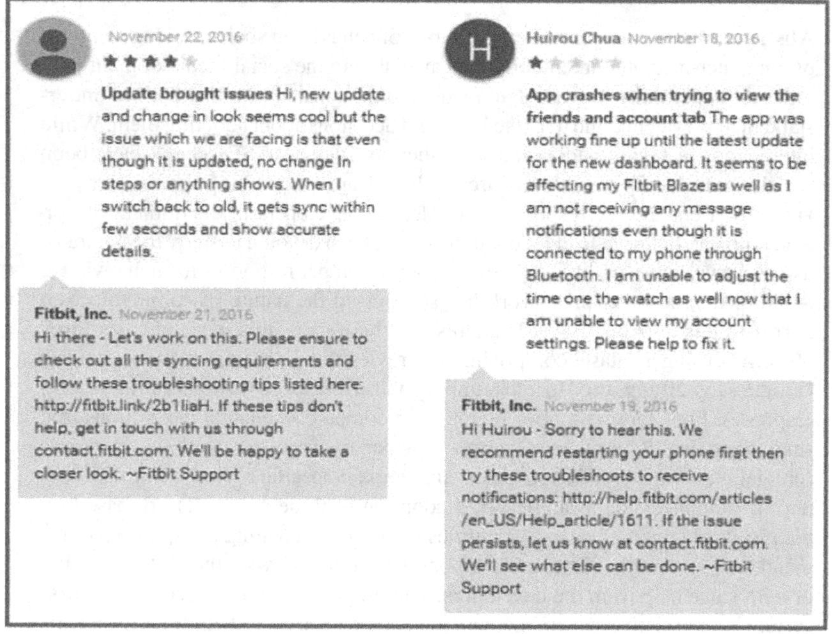

Fig. 1. Sample reviews from Fitbit app

Providing responses to reviews has only been a recent development, with Google Play enabling this service from 2013 [5, 6]. Examples of app reviews and responses are shown in Fig. 1. This new functionality to provide responses creates opportunities for researchers exploring the nature of responses provided, particularly from a norms perspective. It is important to study emergent norms in the new domain of app reviews for two reasons. First, insights on emergent communication norms between users and developers can be inferred. In this work, we evaluate these aspects using two metrics: norm *awareness* and norm *adoption* (discussed in the next section). Second, the study helps to identify requirements for response recommendation systems, proposing responses to reviews. Such systems would solve the problem of developers having to respond to voluminous reviews [7]. Some apps attract tens of thousands of reviews each day (e.g., Pokemon Go received 40,000 reviews per day between its release and January 2017), and it is cumbersome and expensive for humans to respond to each of these reviews. One solution is to develop a response recommendation system that can generate appropriate responses based on historical data (i.e., reviews and responses already available). The development of such a system needs the knowledge about prevailing communication norms. Once the system is aware of the prevailing communication norms it could respond appropriately considering such norms (i.e., a normative system).

This paper thus addresses three objectives: (1) it identifies a set of communication norms that can be identified in developer responses to user reviews, (2) it investigates norm awareness and adoption, and (3) it discusses the implications of the results for developing a normative response recommendation system. This paper is structured as follows. Section 2 provides background and related work considering communication norms. This section also introduces the domain of app development and how prior work has mined norms from large datasets including legal texts and business contracts. Section 3 presents the norms investigated in this study. Section 4 provides an overview of the adopted methodology, and Sect. 5 presents the results. Section 6 discusses the utility of the results in the development of a normative response recommendation system. Finally, Sect. 7 concludes the paper.

2 Background and Related Work

In communication studies, there has been a huge body of work focusing on the widely used email communication platforms [2, 3, 8–10]. From a norms perspective, researchers have focused on extracting patterns of common behaviors in email responses [3, 9, 10]. For example, the work of Kooti et al. [9] mined over 16 billion email interactions and noted that about 90% of emails are answered within a day. Research reported in [3, 10] focuses on different forms of greeting and closing norms in email messages. Beyond the email domain, researchers have focused on communication patterns in social-media platforms such as Twitter [11] and Facebook [12]. Kooti et al. [11] investigated the emergence and adoption of the retweet norm (i.e., the use of the 'RT' symbol for retweeting) when compared to the other proposals for retweeting. The work of Pérez-Sabater [12] investigated language conventions (greeting, closing, etc.) used by English and non-English speakers in Facebook posts.

In the context of software development, the domain of study of this work, there has been research investigating email discussions. For example, the work of Squire presents an overview of research work that uses email archives for various purposes including decision-making in software development [13]. Beyond emails, researchers have also investigated how users expressed their opinion on Twitter [14] about software they use (both desktop and mobile apps). Only recently, researchers have started investigating app reviews from a content-analysis viewpoint [1, 4]; we examine this body of work closely in the following sub-section.

2.1 User Reviews and Developer Responses in App Development

The app development domain has been popularized due to the rapid adoption of smart phones. After an app is released, users provide reviews that contain valuable information for other users and the developer(s) of the app. While prospective users read reviews to evaluate the suitability of apps for their needs, developers use these reviews for enhancing their app. The mechanism allowing users to provide reviews has been long implemented, however, the feature allowing developers to respond to reviews has only been enabled in app stores such as Google Play from 2013 (and this feature will be available for iOS only in the later part of 2017[1]). Since the provisioning of responses to reviews is relatively new, we believe norms in this domain might be in their formative stages, and hence, it is important to identify emergent norms so as to provide appropriate responses that conform to these norms.

Researchers have investigated the nature of reviews provided by users [1, 4, 7]. Maalej et al. [1] for instance have developed an approach that identifies whether reviews contain a bug report, a new feature request or a praise. The work of Chen et al. [4] proposes an approach for identifying informative reviews from noisy data and clustering reviews into relevant groups. Panichella et al. [7] have identified categories of users' requests (e.g., information giving, seeking) from reviews, thus, extending the work in [1]. However, developers' responses to users' reviews have not received a lot of attention. Developers' responses to users' reviews are important from a customer relationship management point of view since they: (a) indicate to the users that their feedback is listened to, appreciated, and appropriate action is taken to address their concerns, (b) provide solutions to problems, (c) help avoid losing customers [15] (reducing churn) which is wide-spread in the app community due to a large number of choices available, and (d) increase the reputation of brands and attract more customers (e.g., in the hotel industry, up to 60% increase in room sales as a result of providing responses (when compared to no responses) has been reported [16]).

A few studies have investigated responses to app reviews [5, 6]. The work of McIlroy [5] noted that providing responses had a positive impact on user rating (about 38% attracting improved rating). The work of Bailey [6] investigated how developers accommodated user reviews (i.e., what actions developers undertook). However, the actions of developers weren't explicitly communicated to the users as the work investigated apps in iOS store which did not have the response feature for direct communication. Nevertheless, this study showed the usefulness of reviews for informing developers about their product deficiencies. We note these works have not scrutinized communication norms in users-developers interactions, as we do in this paper.

2.2 Mining Norms in Normative Multi-agent Systems

The perspective of norms that we adopt in this work has been borrowed from the normative multi-agent systems' research work [17], where norms are treated as prohibitions, obligations and permissions. Researchers have identified applications of these types of

[1] https://techcrunch.com/2017/01/24/apple-will-finally-let-developers-respond-to-app-store-reviews/.

norms in many different domains [18]. For example, Gao and Singh have investigated a corpus of business contracts [19] that contain explicit specifications of prohibitions and obligations. Hashmi has proposed a methodology for extracting legal norms from regulatory documents [20]. Sadiq and Governatori [21] have discussed how various works have investigated norm compliance by investigating the extent to which business processes followed in organizations confirmed to norms (contractual obligations or legal requirements). Norms from textual documents in the abovementioned works (e.g., contracts [19]) are mined by the presence of explicit deontic modalities such as *must* and *must not* in sentences. For example, the phrase "One must pay his/her bills on time" would indicate the presence of an obligation. Researchers have also explored mining norms of software development from open source software repositories [22–24], applying and extending techniques previously developed for use in the multi-agent systems domain. For example, the work of Avery [22] scrutinizes the presence of different types of norms (prohibitions and obligations) in bug reports submitted by users and developers. Despite these developments, there is a gap in extracting and studying communication norms between users and developers in the software development context, a gap we address in this study. In the next section, we present the norms investigated in this work.

3 Norms Investigated

We investigate three types of norms in this work: (1) *domain-specific response norms* (norms 1–4 in Table 1), (2) *obligation norms* (norms 5–11 in Table 1), and (3) *prohibition norms* (norm 12 in Table 1). A brief description of all the 12 norms investigated in this work is provided in Table 1.

Domain-Specific Response Norms - The domain-specific response norms quantify the aggregate patterns in the domain of investigation (i.e., for all apps). These can be interpreted as conventions, i.e., quantifications of commonly observed behaviour in a domain reported in the form of descriptive statistics. These include *response rate* to reviews, *timeliness of responses*, *response length* and *review modification rate* (after the response is provided by the developer).

Obligation Norms - These norms describe communication patterns that are expected to be followed. For example, a response is expected to contain a greeting [3]. We divide obligation norms into three parts – (1) the *social etiquette norms*, (2) *direct help norms*, and (3) *extended help norms*. These have been divided into three parts based on prior work on social etiquette norms in communications [2, 3, 9, 10], and content-analysis based works that have scrutinized the nature of responses provided to customers (direct help and extended help in other domains such as hotel reviews [15, 25, 26] and film reviews [27]). We describe these three aspects below.

1) Social etiquette norms correspond to social aspects of communication, including the use of greeting words such as 'Hi' and 'Dear' [3, 10], the use of customer name in responses (personalization) [3, 10], appreciating feedback provided [28], apologizing for a complaint about the app [29], and sign-off (or closing) using developer's name or organization's name [3, 10]. These are norms 5–9 in Table 1. Figure 1 shows two sample responses. The response on the right conforms to the five norms mentioned above.

Table 1. Norms investigated in this work and their descriptions

ID	Norm	Description (in the question form)
Category 1 - Domain specific response norms		
1	Response rate	What proportion of reviews received a response?
2	Timeliness of responses	How long (in days) does it take developers to respond to reviews?
3	Response length	What is the length of the reviews (in characters)?
4	Response modification rate	What proportions of reviews are modified after receiving a response?
Category 2 - Obligation norms		
(5–9)	***Social Etiquette norms***	
5	Salutation (opening)	Do responses contain appropriate salutation (e.g., Hi and Dear)?
6	Personalization	Do responses include user's name?
7	Appreciation	Do responses exhibit appreciation for feedback provided?
8	Apology	Do responses contain apologies for the inconveniences experienced by the users?
9	Personalized sign-off	Do responses have a personalized sign-off (e.g., developer name or organization name)?
10	***Direct help norms***	
a)	Provides complete or partial solution	Do responses provide solutions to the users' problems with the app?

(*continued*)

Table 1. *(continued)*

ID	Norm	Description (in the question form)
b)	Indicates that solution will be available in the future or provides no solution	Do responses indicate that a solution will be available in the future or that a solution won't be available (for whatever reason)?
c)	Provides additional information/asks question/provides advise	Do responses contain additional information for the user, or offer advice or asks questions and provide answers?
11	***Extended help norms***	
a)	Details in a webpage (URL)	Does the review provide a URL of a web page for seeking additional help?
b)	Email	Does the review contain an email address for seeking additional help?
c)	Phone	Does the review contain a phone number for seeking additional help?
Category 3 - Prohibition norm		
12	Use of canned responses	Do developers use canned responses[a]?

[a]Canned responses are predetermined (or template) responses that are sent to many users.

2) Direct help norms correspond to the help offered towards solving an issue faced by the customer (norms 10a–c), or informing the customer that a solution will be available in the future. A direct help norm addresses a problem in full or part (norm 10a), or provide information about whether the solution will be available in the future (norm 10b) and/or offers helpful suggestions for the user (norm 10c). These norms are inspired by the findings of researchers in other domains (e.g., hotel reviews [15, 25, 26] and film reviews [27]) who have studied the nature of reviews. The responses in Fig. 1 provide direct help to the users.

3) Extended help norms (norms 11a-c) offer additional help to the customer. This help may be in conjunction with the direct help provided, or may be the only type of help offered. Literature on customer support channels notes there are numerous ways to listen to the customer such as phone, email, discussion boards and online chat. In fact, social-media platforms such as Twitter [30] also provide an opportunity to receive users' comments and facilitate service providers' responses. Content analysis of responses revealed the use of three channels for obtaining further help. These are: (1) a URL to a web page that can be used to communicate with the developers such as filling a web-based form (norm 11a), (2) an email address to write to the developers to obtain further help (norm 11b), and (3) a phone number to speak to a support person (norm 11c). The responses in Fig. 1 contain URLs to the support web pages.

Prohibition Norms – These proscribe certain actions or events. The prohibition norm that we investigate is the norm against using canned responses[2] that are perceived to be too impersonal (norm 12).

While some of the identified norms have been shown to hold in other relevant computer-mediated communication domains (e.g., social etiquette norms in email, and direct help norms in hotels' responses), we investigate whether these norms hold in the app review domain involving interactions between users and developers. We scrutinize this using two metrics – norm awareness and norm adoption. *Norm awareness* identifies whether the developers of an app are aware of a particular norm. If at least one of the responses from an app shows that the developer is aware of a norm, then the app is considered to be norm aware[3]. *Norm adoption* is the extent to which a norm is adopted in the responses provided, taking into account the number of times the norm is adhered to in a situation where it is expected to hold. For example, if there are 20 responses provided by an app, and if four of these contain greeting words, then the app developers are assumed to be aware of the greeting norm (norm 1), and the norm adoption is 20% (4 out of 20).

4 Methodology

This study investigated norms in one particular domain of apps – the top-20 apps on Google Play that tracked running (i.e., running apps). The apps considered in this study are shown in Table 2. A Java program was implemented to obtain the reviews and responses for these apps as ranked by Google on 20th November 2016. We obtained a total of 24,408 reviews of which 2,668 had responses. The number of reviews and responses for each app are shown in columns 3 and 4 of Table 2. We analyzed the 2,668 responses to study the nature of response norms across the 20-apps. To identify response norms, we initially automated the identification process for norms 1–9 and 12 using customized SQL queries, utilizing keywords. These were identified by the first author (who is a knowledgeable in the domains of normative systems and app reviews), based on previous research [2, 3, 8–10, 26], and also based on content analysis

[2] Examples of prohibitions of canned responses are listed in the guidelines for reviews by Amazon and TripAdvisor (refer to: https://www.amazon.com/gp/community-help/official-comment-guidelines and http://www.reviewtrackers.com/ultimate-guide-responding-tripadvisor-reviews/).

[3] We acknowledge that a developer may have followed a norm in question without consciously being aware of a norm. For example, a developer using salutation may have been exposed to that norm in a different domain (e.g. writing emails). However, in this work, we do not distinguish between the two situations. fo are multiple developers of an app, not all of them may be aware of the norm. This work assumes that if one of the developers is aware of the norm, there is norm awareness among the developers of an app. These aspects can be scrutinized further in a future work, for example by interviewing app developers.

pursued on the dataset (use of hi, hey, dear, hello etc. for the greeting norms). These keywords were reviewed and verified by the third author. While norms 1–9 and 12 could be fully automated using a keyword based approach, norms 10 and 11 required a manual interpretation due to the nature of the arguments presented in natural language.

In the process of manually interpreting the presence of norms 10 and 11, the presence of norms 5–9 were also validated. Note that the other norms (norms 1–4 and 12) do not require manual verification since the automation captures the metrics for these norms accurately (i.e., norms 1–4 report aggregated values and norm 12 checks for duplicate responses). To facilitate the verification process, we developed a tool which was used by two evaluators to indicate whether a response contains a particular norm (presence or absence of a norm). The first and the third author of this study divided the data into two parts to manually label the data for the presence of norms 5–11. For data analysis, we followed the interpretation guidelines for qualitative data [31]. The first author developed guidelines for coding the data, which was reviewed by the second author. After discussions between the two coders on how to interpret the presence of these norms, a sample of 20 developers' responses was coded and the results were discussed and adjustments were made to the interpretation guidelines. To formally evaluate the coding strength, a sample of 50 developers' responses was then coded by both investigators. The inter-rater reliability was computed using Cohen's kappa statistic measure which yielded a value of 0.94 for the two raters, which shows an almost perfect agreement (a value between 0.81 and 1 is considered to be almost perfect) [32]. The next section presents the results of our analysis of developers' responses.

5 Results

This section presents results for the three types of norms. The discussion of these results is presented in the subsequent section.

5.1 Domain Specific Response Norms

The results for the domain specific response norms are given in Table 2.

Response Rate (Norm 1) - The overall response rate across the apps is 11%. This figure in closer to the previous finding of 13.8% by other researchers [5]. It can be observed that the response rate varies across the top-20 apps (min = 0, max = 62, S.D = 22), as shown in column 5 of Table 2.

Timeliness (Norm 2) – We observed that 81% of responses across all apps were provided within 7 days (see column 6 of Table 2) and 75% responses were provided within 4 days. However, only 21% of the responses are provided within the first day. This is in contrast to email communication norms where 90% of the responses were provided within the first day [9].

Response Length (Norm 3) – The average response length across the apps is 159 characters (min = 55, max = 337, S.D = 105), which is less than half of the allowed response length of 350 characters. It can be observed from column 7 of Table 2 that some apps

Table 2. Results of the domain specific response norms for the top-20 running apps

App ID	App name	No. of reviews	No. of responses	Response rate	Timeliness (<7 days)	Response length	Review modification rate
1	Adidas train & run	805	252	31%	83%	293	12%
2	C25K® - 5K Running Trainer	1816	0	0%	0%	0	0%
3	Couch to 5K	732	4	1%	83%	118	0%
4	Endomondo - Running & Walking	1858	200	11%	84%	240	15.8%
5	FITAPP - Running Walking Fitness	196	121	62%	70%	151	0.6%
6	Fitbit	1161	339	29%	88%	278	12.4%
7	Fitso Running & Fitness App	389	83	21%	61%	240	11.4%
8	Garmin Connect Mobile	1263	150	12%	53%	217	39.8%
9	Google Fit - Fitness Tracking	1473	45	3%	82%	337	17.6%
10	Nike + Run Club	1402	0	0%	0%	0	0%
11	Run With Map My Run	2079	0	0%	0%	0	0%
12	Runkeeper - GPS Track Run Walk	2006	8	0%	44%	204	55.6%
13	Running Distance Tracker	1150	709	62%	95%	55	2.3%
14	Running For Weight Loss	709	58	8%	90%	215	3%

(*continued*)

Table 2. (*continued*)

App ID	App name	No. of reviews	No. of responses	Response rate	Timeliness (<7 days)	Response length	Review modification rate
15	Runtastic Running & Fitness	3146	28	1%	100%	132	0%
16	S Health	886	607	69%	89%	239	11.2%
17	Sportractive GPS Running App	94	10	11%	100%	122	10.5%
18	Sports Tracker Running Cycling	1274	13	1%	68%	143	0%
19	Strava Running and Cycling GPS	1727	0	0%	0%	0	0%
20	Zombies, Run! (Free)	241	41	17%	96%	185	4.4%
	Overall	**24407**	**2668**	**11%**	**81%**	**159**	**10%**

(app 1 and app 9) use the response length allowed more effectively (e.g., the reviews contained detailed information) than others (with average response lengths of 293 and 337 respectively).

Review modification (Norm 4) – After the responses are received users have modified 12% of the original reviews they had provided (min = 0, max = 56, S.D = 15). This modification included changes to the reviews and the review rating. We noticed that the average rating for reviews that were modified were higher (average = 3.12) than the ones that weren't modified (average = 2.98), pointing towards the utility of the responses in satisfying users and enhancing their feelings about apps, ultimately resulting in apps attracting higher ratings. Our results are in line with prior work that has reported that users upon receiving responses are likely to increase the review ratings upwards [5].

5.2 Obligation Norms

The results for the social etiquette norms, direct help norms and extended help norms (norms 5–11) are presented below.

Social Etiquette Norms (Norms 5–9) – We present the results based on two metrics – norm awareness and norm adoption. Results for norm awareness show that overall, developers of 70% of the apps are aware of the greeting norm (norm 5) and developers of 65% of the apps are aware of the personalization norm (norm 6). Eighty percent (80%) of the developers' responses towards reviews for the apps showed evidence for the awareness of the appreciation norm (norm 7). Awareness of apology norm was seen in 65% of the apps responses (norm 8). However, only 30% of the apps responses showed evidence for sign-off norm (norm 11). The results for norm adoption show that overall, 51% of responses had greetings (norm 5). The use of customers' name was present in 58% of responses (norm 6). In addition, 72% of responses contained appreciation (norm 7). However, only 35% of responses to reviews that had complaints contained apology (norm 8). Further, only 25% of the responses had a personalized sign-off (norm 11).

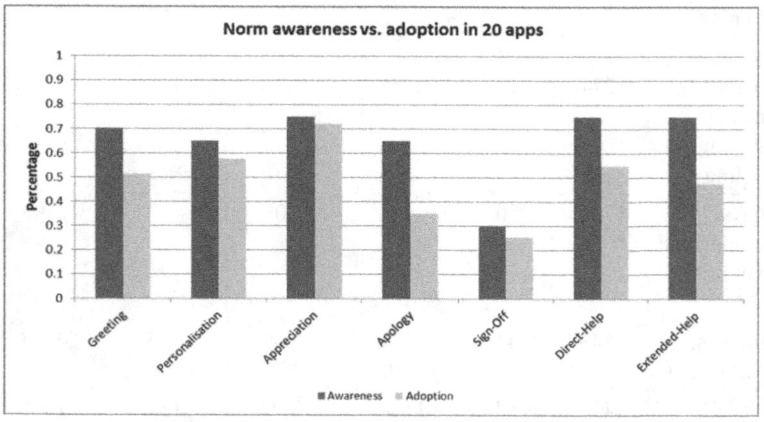

Fig. 2. Results for norm awareness vs. Adoption in 20 apps

The comparison for norm awareness versus adoption for the norms is shown in Fig. 2 (including results for direct and extended help norms). The results for norms 5–11 show that while the apps developers are aware of these norms (average of 65%), their adoption rate is low (average of 49%).

Direct Help Norms – Figure 3 shows the results for the nature of direct help messages (norm 9) across apps for three categories – (1) solution available, (2) solution unavailable or will be available in the future, and (3) other helpful information. It can be observed that out of 16 apps that provided responses (excluding apps 2, 10, 11 and 19 that had zero responses – see x-axis labels), 13 of them (81%) had a higher proportion of responses that contained solution (category 1) than the other two categories (categories 2 and 3). Only in two apps (apps 5 and 7) there were more 'other' help information than the other two categories. App 9's responses did not contain any direct help to the user. These results show that responses in general have pointed to the solutions for issues faced by the users. It is interesting to note apps used some form of canned responsesthat some apps have provided help messages to the fullest extent possible – i.e., 100% (apps 12 and 18), although, they had responded only to a small number of reviews (8 and 13 respectively). Overall, norm awareness for direct help messages was 75%, and norm adoption was 55% (results shown in Fig. 2).

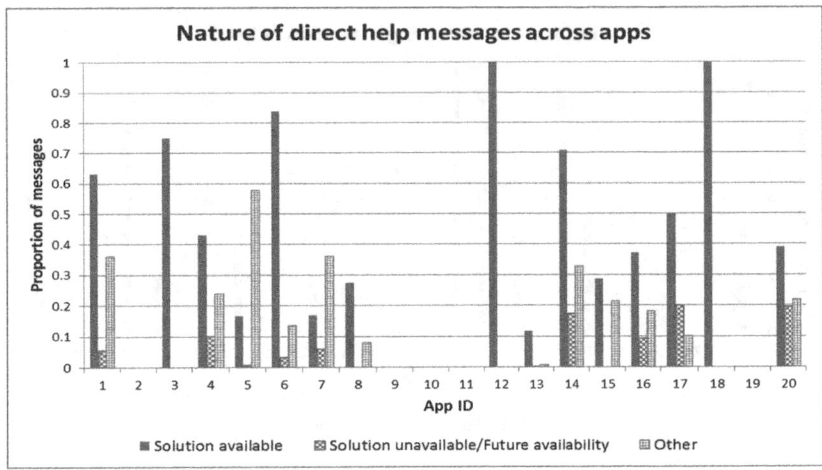

Fig. 3. Proportion of three types of direct help norms in responses across 20 apps.

Extended Help Norms – Figure 4 shows the results for the provision of extended help messagapps used some form of canned responseses by developers across the apps (norm 11). Messages contained extended help information to contact support staff through a web interface, an email or phone refer-ence. It can be observed that 15 out of 16 apps that provided responses (94%) used one of these three mechanisms for providing extended help, with 6 of them (38%) using two forms. Web interfaces and email addresses were used by 10 apps (63%), and the phone reference was least popular among the three options with only two apps using the option. However, the extent to which these extended help mechanisms were used varied. While apps 6 and 9 provided the URL for the users in more than 85% of the messages, apps 7 and 8 provided email addresses for a similar proportion of messages. These results show that the responses in general contained helpdesk details in an at-tempt to resolve the issues faced by users. Overall, norm awareness for providing ex-tended help messages was 75% and norm adoption was 47% (shown in Fig. 2).

We also examined the extent to which the three types of obligation norms influence review modifications. There were 255 reviews that were modified by the users subsequent to receiving responses from developers. We observed that in 93% of these cases where the users modified reviews, the developers' responses had followed social etiquette norms. Also, direct and indirect help norms were followed in 65% and 69% of the cases respectively. In 41% of the cases, all the three norms were followed. In the remaining 2413 reviews where there were no review modifications were observed, in 96% of the cases the social etiquette norms were followed. Direct and indirect help norms were followed in 54% and 45% of the cases respectively. In 34% of the cases all the three norms were followed. We also conducted correlation analysis between adhering to the three obligation norms and review modification by considering all the reviews in this study ($n = 2668$). Our results showed that there was a weakly negative correlation between social etiquette norms and review modification ($r = -0.06$, $p < 0.01$). The correlations for direct and indirect help norms with review modifications were weakly positive, with $r = 0.09$ for direct help norms and $r = 0.14$ for indirect help norms ($p <$

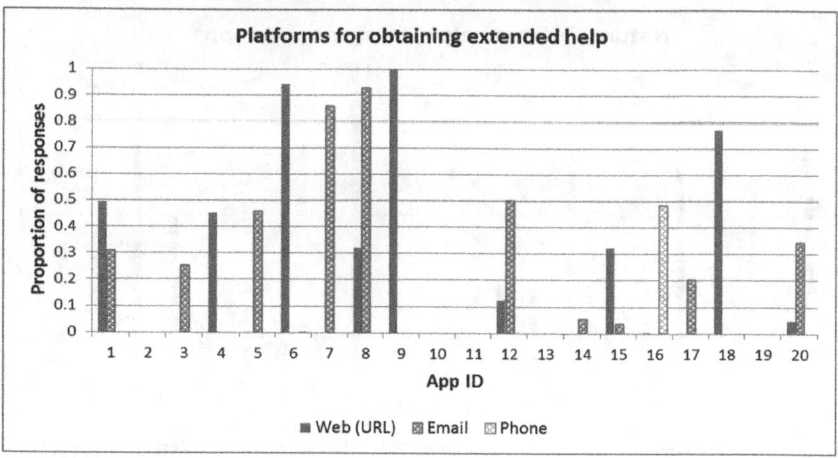

Fig. 4. Proportion of three types of extended help norms in responses across 20 apps.

0.01 in both cases). This result suggests that the direct and indirect help norms may be more important than the social etiquette norms to attract review modifications.

5.3 Prohibition Norms

Canned responses (norm 12) – there were about 30% (810 out of 2,668) of canned responses (reuse of the same responses). These messages did not have any personalization. Eight out of 16 apps used some form of canned responses (i.e., norm violated in 50% of the apps), with some apps using them \excessively. For example, 75% or more of posts from apps 8 and 13 contained canned responses and 100% of app 9 responses (45 responses) were the same canned response.

6 Discussion

In this section we provide a discussion of the results presented in Sect. 5, particularly discussing the implications of the results presented in the previous section for developing a recommendation system that provides responses to reviews which conforms to norms.

a) Domain specific response norms – The results for the response rate norm (norm 1) show that only 11% of the reviews are responded to by developers. Prior research suggests that one of the key advantages of social media platforms for businesses is their ability to facilitate dialogue with their customers (e.g., keeping them informed about actions taken based on their feedback). The low response rate presents an opportunity to develop a response recommendation system that generates responses to new reviews, thus improving response rates. The recommendation system can directly post responses to reviews in straightforward cases and also provide a template of a response for a human to complete in complex cases. While some app developers have indeed realized the importance of responding to reviews (apps 5, 13 and 16) and have responded to more than 60% of reviews, certain other apps have completely ignored responding to reviews (apps 2, 10, 11 and 19). Research has shown that there is tendency for apps receiving a lot of reviews [5] to ignore responding to issues raised due to the voluminous nature of reviews. This again points towards the opportunity to develop a response recommendation system. The result of the timeliness norm (norm 2) shows that 96% of reviews that receive responses attract responses within 7 days. However, only 21% are responded to within a day (unlike 90% of emails responded to within a day [9]). Research has shown that customer feedback needs to be responded to at the earliest since users' satisfaction and future repurchase intentions are directly related to the time taken to respond [33]. Additionally, in the app domain, users can easily try competitors' apps, hence, the timeliness of response needs improvement. A response recommendation system may be beneficial to provide responses in a timely fashion. The average response length for a message (norm 3) was 159 characters as opposed to 350 characters allowed. This also offers an opportunity to provide more detailed responses, which can be incorporated in generated responses (e.g., providing extended help as a part of every message and incorporating social etiquette norms). Our results for reviews' modification show that only 12% of reviews are modified after reading a response. Other researchers have noted that a significant proportion of users increased the ratings after reading a response, up to some 38% [5]. Hence, improving response provision rates through the proposed response generation system is likely to improve ratings.

b) Obligation norms – The results for the *social etiquette norms* (norms 5–9) indicate that norm adoption lags behind norm awareness. While app developers are (presumably) aware of these norms, they do not adopt these norms. Independent of the reasons for the failure to adopt norms, norm adoption can be improved using a response recommendation system that considers the social etiquettes (greeting, use of customer names, thanking, apologizing, and signing-off). A recommendation system (or a software agent), can be easily programmed to adhere to these norms. *Direct help norms* (norms 10a-c) had the highest proportion of adoption (55%), among all norms. This is understandable given that the main goal of providing a response is to help users to overcome the issues they face. However, the proportion of responses that contain helpful information can be increased further. Two approaches may be beneficial towards this end. The first is to use appropriate machine learning approaches for identifying responses provided by the developers in the past for issues that are similar to the ones reported in the new review (i.e., review for which a response needs to be generated) similar to the work in [34], that recommends auto completion phrases for creating new reviews. If issues reported in a review match a previous review for which a response is available (e.g., based on a pre-determined threshold for matching features), the response generated can be directly posted to the user. The second approach involves the creation of template messages by developers for new issues that the users face (e.g., a solution describing a fix for a new bug that has not been reported by users before). A response recommendation system needs to consider both of these approaches (as presented in the basic workflow of the normative response recommendation system in Fig. 5). *Extended help norms* (norms 10a-c) are easy to automate since they provide generic helpdesk information. However, these need to be customized based on the type of support (web, email or phone) the app development firm wishes to provide.

c) Prohibition norm – While the adoption of obligation norms can be ensured during the implementation of a response system, care should be taken to avoid violating prohibition norms. It is expected that developers will be presented with a template of a response which they can choose to modify. As a part of modifying the response, users may violate prohibitions. When these are violated, the system should warn the developer about potential issues. For example, if the developer replaces the response suggested by the system with an impersonalized canned response (norm 12), a warning can be generated. Note that 30% of the responses were canned responses. These responses do not use any personalization (i.e., without the use of greeting, customer name and developer sign-off). However, these elements can be easily incorporated in a response recommendation system (i.e., through the adherence of obligation norms 5–9). Additionally, warning messages can be generated if these norms are not adhered to when the developer posts the message. Thus, the response recommendation system should have a module that checks for violation of both types of norms (obligations and prohibitions) and provide appropriate warning messages to the developers.

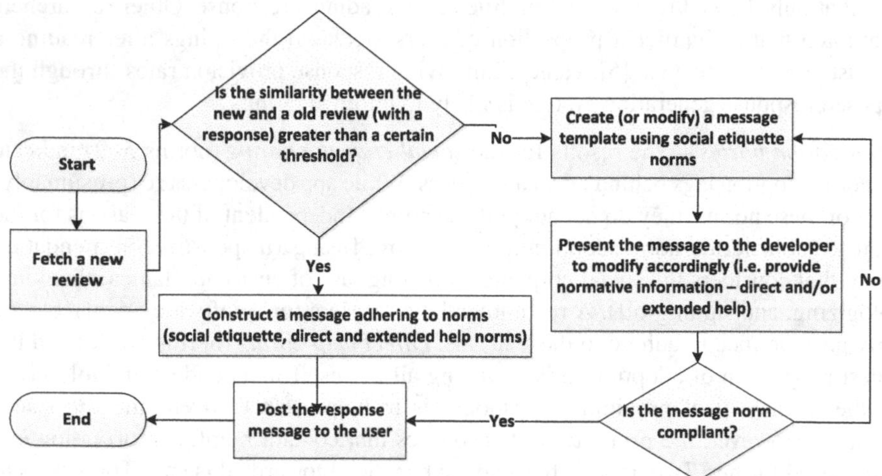

Fig. 5. Basic workflow of the normative response recommendation system

Further Considerations on the Normative Response Recommendation System – In addition to ensuring that the messages are norm compliant as shown in Fig. 5 the system will also need to *prioritize* which reviews should be responded to first by the developers (e.g., based on urgency inferred through rating, and also whether other users face the same problem). For example if 10 users had rated the app as being poor and 8 of them complained about a new bug and two about a known bug (for which the template solution exists) then the system should present the response addressing the new bug issue to the developer to make a decision due to its potential impact on multiple users. The recommendation system should also be provided with some *autonomy* to post responses to certain messages without the intervention of the developers (e.g., all reviews that have

5 star ratings that do not have any suggestions for improvement or questions can be thanked automatically), considering the volume of reviews posted for the most popular apps. Additionally, if the responses generated do not meet the threshold for automatic post, they can be presented to the developers in the form of a ranked-ordered (priority) list for their action and approval, taking into account considerations such as urgency. If a similar response has to be provided to multiple users, rephrasing responses can be considered using existing services[4] to avoid the issue of canned responses. Although, personalization of messages using appropriate usernames and sign-offs is likely to somewhat reduce the canned response problem. Implementing the outlined solution forms the focus of our subsequent work[5].

7 Conclusion

In the domain of app development, communication norms between users and developers have rarely been investigated. This work addresses this gap by first abstracting three categories of response norms for app reviews comprising 12 norms (4 domain specific response norms, 7 obligation norms and 1 prohibition norm). It scrutinizes awareness and adoption of these norms from a dataset of user reviews and developer responses in Google Play's top-20 running apps. The work demonstrated that there is a gap between norm awareness and adoption across apps. App developers, despite being presumably aware of these norms, do not adopt the norms effectively. To improve the provision of responses to users this work proposes a normative response recommendation system that also has the potential to improve user satisfaction [35], increase user ratings [5] and potentially reduce developers' workload [35] in responding to reviews.

References

1. Maalej, W., Nabil, H.: Bug report, feature request, or simply praise? On automatically classifying app reviews. In: RE, 2015 Conference, pp. 116–125 (2015)
2. Lewin-Jones, J., Mason, V.: Understanding style, language and etiquette in email communication in higher education: a survey. Res. PC Educ. **19**, 75–90 (2014)
3. Waldvogel, J.: Greetings and closings in workplace email. J. Comput.-Mediated Commun. **12**, 456–477 (2007)
4. Chen, N., Lin, J., Hoi, S.C., Xiao, X., Zhang, B.: AR-miner: mining informative reviews for developers from mobile app marketplace. In: ICSE Conference, pp. 767–778. ACM (2014)
5. McIlroy, S., Shang, W., Ali, N., Hassan, A.: Is it worth responding to reviews? A case study of the top free apps in the Google Play store. IEEE Software (2015)
6. Bailey, K.: Out of the mouths of users: examining user-developer feedback loops facilitated by app stores (2015)
7. Panichella, S., Di Sorbo, A., Guzman, E., Visaggio, C.A., Canfora, G., Gall, H.C.: How can I improve my app? Classifying user reviews for software maintenance and evolution. In: ICSME Conference pp. 281–290. IEEE (2015)

[4] https://www.gingersoftware.com/.

[5] A prototypical implementation of the system and the user evaluation are described in a subsequent work [35].

8. Markus, M.L.: Finding a happy medium: explaining the negative effects of electronic communication on social life at work. ACM TOIS **12**, 119–149 (1994)
9. Kooti, F., Aiello, L.M., Grbovic, M., Lerman, K., Mantrach, A.: Evolution of conversations in the age of email overload. In: WWW Conference, pp. 603–613. ACM (2015)
10. Bjørge, A.K.: Power distance in English lingua franca email communication1. Int. J. Appl. Ling. **17**, 60–80 (2007)
11. Kooti, F., Yang, H., Cha, M., Gummadi, P.K., Mason, W.A.: The emergence of conventions in online social networks. In: ICWSM Conference (2012)
12. Pérez-Sabater, C.: The linguistics of social networking: a study of writing conventions on Facebook. Linguistik Online **56** (2013)
13. Squire, M.: How the FLOSS research community uses email archives. Int. J. Open Source Softw. Processes (IJOSSP) **4**, 37–59 (2012)
14. Guzman, E., Alkadhi, R., Seyff, N.: A needle in a haystack: what do Twitter users say about software? In: RE Conference, pp. 96–105. IEEE (2016)
15. Chan, N.L., Guillet, B.D.: Investigation of social media marketing: how does the hotel industry in Hong Kong perform in marketing on social media websites? J. Travel Tour. Market. **28**, 345–368 (2011)
16. Ye, Q., Gu, B., Chen, W., Law, R.: Measuring the value of managerial responses to online reviews-a natural experiment of two online travel agencies. In: ICIS Conference (2008)
17. Andrighetto, G., Governatori, G., Noriega, P., van der Torre, L.W.: Normative multi-agent systems. Schloss Dagstuhl-Leibniz-Zentrum fuer Informatik (2013)
18. Singh, M.P., et al.: The uses of norms. Schloss Dagstuhl LZI (2013)
19. Gao, X., Singh, M.P.: Extracting normative relationships from business contracts. In: AAMAS Conference, pp. 101–108 (2014)
20. Hashmi, M.: A methodology for extracting legal norms from regulatory documents. In: EDOCW Workshop, pp. 41–50 (2015)
21. Sadiq, S., Governatori, G.: In: vom Brocke, J., Rosemann, M. (eds.) Handbook on Business Process Management 2. IHIS, pp. 265–288. Springer, Heidelberg (2015). https://doi.org/10.1007/978-3-642-45103-4_11
22. Avery, D., Dam, H.K., Savarimuthu, B.T.R., Ghose, A.: Externalization of software behavior by the mining of norms. In: MSR Conference, pp. 223–234 (2016)
23. Dam, H.K., Savarimuthu, B.T.R., Avery, D., Ghose, A.: Mining software repositories for social norms. In: ICSE Conference, pp. 627–630 (2016)
24. Savarimuthu, B.T.R., Dam, H.K.: Towards mining norms in open source software repositories. In: Cao, L., Zeng, Y., Symeonidis, A.L., Gorodetsky, V., Müller, J.P., Yu, P.S. (eds.) ADMI 2013. LNCS (LNAI), vol. 8316, pp. 26–39. Springer, Heidelberg (2014). https://doi.org/10.1007/978-3-642-55192-5_3
25. Ye, Q., Law, R., Gu, B.: The impact of online user reviews on hotel room sales. Int. J. Hosp. Manag. **28**, 180–182 (2009)
26. Sparks, B.A., So, K.K.F., Bradley, G.L.: Responding to negative online reviews: the effects of hotel responses on customer inferences of trust and concern. Tour. Manage. **53**, 74–85 (2016)
27. Basuroy, S., Chatterjee, S., Ravid, S.A.: How critical are critical reviews? The box office effects of film critics, star power, and budgets. J. Market. **67**, 103–117 (2003)
28. Khoo-Lattimore, C., Ekiz, E.H.: Power in praise: exploring online compliments on luxury hotels in Malaysia. Tour. Hospital. Res. **14**, 152–159 (2014)
29. Matzat, U., Snijders, C.: Rebuilding trust in online shops on consumer review sites: sellers' responses to user-generated complaints. J. CMC **18**, 62–79 (2012)
30. Malthouse, E.C., Haenlein, M., Skiera, B., Wege, E., Zhang, M.: Managing customer relationships in the social media era: introducing the social CRM house. J. Interact. Market. **27**, 270–280 (2013)

31. Merriam, S.B., Tisdell, E.J.: Qualitative Research: A Guide to Design and Implementation. Wiley, Hoboken (2015)
32. Landis, J.R., Koch, G.G.: The measurement of observer agreement for categorical data. Biometrics 159–174 (1977)
33. Miller, R.B.: Response time in man-computer conversational transactions. In: FJCC Conference, pp. 267–277 (1968)
34. Arnold, K.C., Gajos, K.Z., Kalai, A.T.: On suggesting phrases vs. predicting words for mobile text composition. In: UIST Symposium, pp. 603–608. ACM (2016)
35. Greenheld, G., Savarimuthu, B.T.R., Licorish, S.A.: Automating developers' responses to app reviews. In: 25th Australasian Software Engineering Conference (ASWEC), pp. 66–70 (2018)

Emergence and Social Metrics

Convention Emergence in Partially Observable Topologies

James Marchant and Nathan Griffiths(✉)

Department of Computer Science, University of Warwick, Coventry, UK
{james,nathan}@dcs.warwick.ac.uk

Abstract. In multi-agent systems it is often desirable for agents to adhere to standards of behaviour that minimise clashes and wasting of (limited) resources. In situations where it is not possible or desirable to dictate these standards globally or via centralised control, convention emergence offers a lightweight and rapid alternative. Placing fixed strategy agents within a population, whose interactions are constrained by an underlying network, has been shown to facilitate faster convention emergence with some degree of control. Placing these fixed strategy agents at topologically influential locations (such as high-degree nodes) increases their effectiveness. However, finding such influential locations often assumes that the whole network is visible or that it is feasible to inspect the whole network in a computationally practical time, a fact not guaranteed in many real-world scenarios. We present an algorithm, PO-Place, that finds influential nodes given a finite number of network observations. We show that PO-Place finds sets of nodes with similar reach and influence to the set of high-degree nodes and we then compare the performance of PO-Place to degree placement for convention emergence in several real-world topologies.

Keywords: Convention emergence · Partial observability · Local information

1 Introduction

Coordinating the actions of independent agents within a multi-agent system (MAS) increases efficiency within the system. Incompatible action choices made during interactions can cause clashes, which may incur resource costs and limit the overall effectiveness of the system. Establishing protocols of interaction, such as which action to choose in a given situation, minimises such clashes and helps to maximise the potential of the system.

However, it is not always possible to dictate such rules and protocols in a top-down manner. In multi-agent systems, with agents controlled by multiple parties or systems which lack a centralised control mechanism, it is often infeasible to establish this level of *a priori* coordination. Additionally, for systems where the range of choices available to agents is large or has no evident optimal selection, it may be undesirable to enforce rules of this nature.

A. Aler Tubella et al. (Eds.): COIN 2017/COINE 2020, LNAI 12298, pp. 79–97, 2021.
https://doi.org/10.1007/978-3-030-72376-7_5

Convention emergence allows a system to deal with these problems in a decentralised, online manner. A *convention* represents a socially-adopted expected behaviour amongst agents, for instance the correct course of action in a given scenario. Convention emergence has been shown to be possible in both static and dynamic networks with minimal requirements, needing only rational agents that are able to learn [7,16,26]. Convention emergence, and the related notion of norm emergence, is relevant to solving problems of coordination in application domains as diverse as logistics, healthcare, and manufacturing [12,19].

Fixed strategy (FS) agents are those that continue to choose the same action regardless of the behaviour of others around them or the results of their actions. Placing such agents within a system has been shown to affect the direction and speed of convention emergence, with small numbers of FS agents eliciting change in much larger populations [23]. In systems constrained by an underlying network topology, placing such agents by heuristics based on network features such as degree magnifies the impact of such FS agents, improving the speed of convergence [10,11]. While using FS agents clearly has a cost (e.g., a payment to a FS agent for acting in a particular way and to compensate for any mis-coordination costs), it has been shown that only a small number of FS agents are required relative to the population size [23] and so the cost can be outweighed by the benefits of coordination. For example, in a mobile ad-hoc network using convention emergence to learn how to allocate the frequency spectrum, the cost of each FS agent is mainly in terms of its failed communications while the benefits of successful population-wide communication after convergence outweigh this cost [8].

Previous work on convention emergence often assumes that the topology constraining agent interactions is fully observable, allowing highly influential locations to be found easily [14,21,23,25]. However, in many real-world applications such information is not always readily available [19]. This can be due to factors such as the problem size or external limitations such as restricted access to network information or a network's API as is the case with Twitter or Facebook.

In this paper we explore the effect of the restrictions placed on FS agent placement in partially observable topologies. We propose an algorithm, PO-PLACE, to find influential locations within such topologies given a highly limited number of network queries. We show the effectiveness of PO-PLACE at finding approximations of the highest degree locations for several real-world topologies under a number of restrictions on available information. We then apply PO-PLACE to select FS agents within these networks and examine the effect on convention emergence compared to placing with full topological knowledge. This approach allows an interested third party, with limited access to the system, to find the appropriate locations to target their influence efforts.

The remainder of this paper is arranged as follows. In Sect. 2 we explore related work on convention emergence and local information strategies for finding influential nodes. Section 3 describes the algorithm and its design, whilst Sect. 4

describes the network datasets and experimental setup. Section 5 contains the analysis and discussion of the results and Sect. 6 concludes the paper.

2 Related Work

Ensuring coordination in MAS allows increased system efficiency and conventions are a lightweight method of doing so. Conventions place 'soft constraints' on agent choices by encouraging mutually beneficial behaviour by adherence to the convention. Unlike *norms* there is no explicit punishment for going against the convention but doing so is likely to incur a cost to the agent due to increased clashes often represented as a negative interaction payoff [13,22]. Conventions can thus be described as "an equilibrium everyone expects in interactions that have more than one equilibrium" [28]. Agents adhering to the convention expect others to behave in a certain way and, because of this, can act efficiently when this expectation is met. Conventions have been shown to emerge unaided from local agent interactions in systems [7,14,24,26] and require no additional or assumed agent capabilities to enable punishment (as is the case for norms). The only assumptions necessary for conventions to emerge are that agents are rational and have the capability to learn from their interactions. Numerous works have shown that rapid and robust convention emergence occurs with these minimal assumptions [11,23,26]. It should be noted, that while conventions do not have the explicit punishments associated with norms, the payoff structure is typically such that non-compliance with a convention will incur a negative payoff [23], but is a direct consequence of the payoff structure rather than imposed by a third party or the system as in typically normative systems [12,19].

'Social learning' has been proposed as a way for agents to converge on a convention where agents monitor payoffs they receive from their choices when interacting with others and use a simplified Q-Learning algorithm to inform future decisions [23]. The payoffs directly quantify the notion of an action clash costing resources and convention emergence can occur without explicit memory of the interaction. However, the work does not consider a connecting topology that limits agent interactions. In many application domains such a topology is likely, whether it be a social network or a more explicit communication network and can have a large effect on the nature of convention emergence [6,25].

Despite lacking a connecting topology, Sen and Airiau's work introduces the concept of fixed strategy (FS) agents, those agents which always choose the same action regardless of the current situation or convention, as a way to influence convention emergence. They show that a small number of such agents is able to manipulate the convention emergence within a much larger population. Griffiths and Anand [11] expand on this by considering FS agents in a network topology. In their model, all agents are situated as nodes within the network and interactions are limited to neighbours. They showed that *where* FS agents are placed is a key factor in their effectiveness. Placing the FS agents at influential locations such as nodes of high degree or betweenness centrality offers substantially better performance than random placement. This was explored further by Franks et al. [9,10] who included more advanced placement metrics such as eigencentrality.

This previous work assumes full visibility of the network topology to inform FS placement. Indeed, little work on partial observability for convention emergence has been done. This paper expands the state of the art by considering the effect of restricted observations on the ability to robustly and efficiently place FS agents in static, real-world topologies. Convention destabilisation [17] and dynamic topologies [16] will be investigated in future work.

Related work exists in the fields of graph algorithms and influence spread, the latter sharing many qualities with convention emergence. For instance, Brautbar and Kearns present a novel model [2], *Jump and Crawl*, motivated by operations commonly available in networks such as Facebook. Their model consists of two aspects: *Jump* which moves to a randomly selected node in the network and *Crawl* which searches all neighbours of the selected node for high-degree nodes. They provide bounds for many different types of network but, for an arbitrary network, finding the highest degree node approaches $O(n \log n)$, a large factor for even medium-sized networks.

The influence maximisation problem [3,4] attempts to find a selection of nodes such that the spread of influence (often modelled as single chance 'cascades') from them is maximised. As in this paper, Mihara *et al.* [18] assume the network is initially unknown and show that influence maximisation effectiveness of 60–90% with 1–10% network observation is achievable. This work also uses a 'growing fringe' approach with priority based on degree estimation. As influence maximisation and convention emergence are similar in aim, this indicates that beneficial results are achievable for convention emergence under partial observability constraints.

Whilst many of these approaches are similar in application they differ in that our investigation focuses on the often encountered scenario of limited, finite observations. Making optimal use of these is paramount and so necessitates a different set of considerations.

3 Placement Strategy

In this paper, the partial observability problem for networks can be described as any scenario where a network's topology is initially unknown and is revealed incrementally within a local neighbourhood of nodes already explored [1]. As a solution to the partial observability problem for FS agent selection we propose a heuristic algorithm, PO-PLACE. This section describes the function of the algorithm as well as the justification for the design choices.

3.1 Partial Observability Algorithm

The placement strategy is presented in Algorithms 1 and 2 and has the following aim: Given a network, $G = (V, E)$, a desired number of locations, n, and a limited number of observations, o, find a selection of nodes $\{v_1, ..., v_n\} \subset V$ such that $\textit{deg-sum} = \textit{deg}(v_1) + ... + \textit{deg}(v_n)$ is maximised. We define an observation as a query that retrieves the list of neighbours, $N(u)$ for a given node, u. This

Algorithm 1. Partial Observability Placement

```
procedure PO-PLACE(G, n, o, s, p, f)
    Create empty node set, S
    Create empty mapping, N
    o_rem ← o

    while o_rem > 0 ∧ |S| < |V| do
        Select v u.a.r. from {V \ S}
        if o_rem mod s ≠ 0 then
            o_local ← min(⌈o/s⌉, o_rem)
        else
            o_local ← min(⌊o/s⌋, o_rem)
        end if
        o_rem ← o_rem − o_local
        o_unused ← Traverse(G, o_local, v, p, f, S, N)
        o_rem ← o_rem + o_unused
    end while

    return n highest-degree nodes in S
end procedure
```

functionality is frequently available in real-world network APIs (such as Twitter or Facebook) and so we assume that such information is available. This assumption is later relaxed to allow the algorithm to explore situations with only limited neighbour information. We assume that the set of nodes, V, is known but the set of edges, E, (and hence neighbours and degree of a node) is not. Finding the highest degree nodes is desirable since fixed strategy agent placement by degree consistently produces effective convention emergence [10,11,16,17] but without requiring computationally expensive metrics such as betweenness centrality. Previous work that uses FS agents to effect change in a population, e.g., by placing at high degree nodes, assumes full observability of both the set of nodes, V, and the edges, E. The degree of nodes can be entirely derived from local information and, as such, is an applicable heuristic within partially observable networks.

The algorithm begins by creating an empty set, S, to monitor which nodes have already been explored and an empty mapping, N, that maps a node v to $N(v)$, its set of neighbours. As we only consider static topologies in this paper, by storing this information we can avoid using observations redundantly.

Many of the other approaches [1,18] to finding high-degree nodes select a random starting node and then 'grow' outwards, selecting the highest degree nodes from the neighbourhood surrounding those already explored. However, this is not desirable in FS agent placement since, with limited observations, it is likely to produce a single cluster of well-explored nodes. Selecting from this cluster will then mean that all FS agents are close together, making some of their influence redundant. Instead, we build on the notion of *Jump and Crawl* [2]. We explore a local area up to a defined amount and then 'jump' to another location and explore around this new point. This helps to minimise the risk of overlap

Algorithm 2. Local area traversal algorithm

```
procedure TRAVERSE(G, o, v, p, f, S, N)
    Create max-priority queue, Q
    count ← 0
    if v not in N then
        N[v] ← N(v)
        Add v to S
        count ← count + 1
    end if
    Add (v, |N[v]|) to Q

    while |Q| > 0 ∧ count < o do
        Fringe ← top min(f, |Q|) elements of Q
        for all u in Fringe do
            Avail ← {N[u] \ S}
            num ← min(|Avail|, max(f, ⌊p × |Avail|⌋))
            Chosen ← u.a.r. select num members of Avail
            for all w in Chosen do
                N[w] ← N(w)
                Add w to S
                count ← count + 1
                if count = o then
                    return 0
                end if
                Add (w, |N[w]|) to Q
            end for
        end for
    end while

    return o − count
end procedure
```

between high-degree nodes, as well as ensuring that a bad initial random selection does not hinder the final selection.

To facilitate this, we introduce a parameter, s, which dictates the minimum number of separate local area explorations that will take place. The observations are split, as evenly as possible, between each of these explorations with the earlier ones receiving any spare observations (this is achieved between Lines 7 and 11 of Algorithm 1). This subset of observations is then passed to the local area traversal which is presented in Algorithm 2. If any observations are unused by the local area traversal (for instance if it finds a local maxima) they are returned to the pool of available observations and used in later, additional local traversals.

Algorithm 2, TRAVERSE, describes the local area traversals. It is passed both S and N, to avoid redundant exploration, as well as the initial start node of the local area, v. It is also passed its own local limit of observations and two additional parameters, p and f, which are explained below. It maintains a max-priority queue to determine which node(s) it should next explore by highest degree and begins by adding v to this queue. Throughout Algorithm 2, observation of a node's neighbour list is stored in N to avoid additional queries. The algorithm then performs the following, until either the queue is empty or all assigned observations have been used up:

1. Take the top f nodes from the queue (or all elements, if fewer).
2. For each of these nodes, find the set of unexplored nodes in its neighbours.
3. Choose a proportion, p, of these (or up to f if this proportion would be less than f).
4. Add these nodes to the queue after finding their neighbours.

Parameter f is the 'fringe size', the number of nodes that are expanded simultaneously before their neighbours are queued. This acts as a control over how 'breadth-first' or 'depth-first' the local traversal approach will be. Parameter p is the proportion of the node's neighbours that should be queried. This allows the algorithm to simulate situations where a node's full neighbour list is either not fully available (for instance, an API that only returns a subset) or where doing so incurs additional cost. In the latter case we seek to explore the effect that only querying p proportion of neighbours has on the performance of PO-Place. Whilst it will reduce the effectiveness, establishing the extent of this reduction, and whether the results are still close enough to degree placement, allows PO-Place to be effective over a wider range of scenarios.

4 Experimental Setup

This section defines the real-world topologies and the experimental setup used for analysis of PO-Place. We then describe the model of convention emergence used to study the efficacy of PO-Place for FS placement selection.

4.1 Networks

We make use of three real-world networks from the Stanford SNAP datasets [15]. These datasets represent a number of different methods of social interaction and, as such, each have different features allowing a wide-ranging look at the effectiveness of PO-Place. The three datasets chosen are: CA-CondMat, the collaboration network of the arXiv COND-MAT (Condensed Matter Physics) category; Email-Enron, the email communications between workers at Enron; and Ego-Twitter, a crawl of Twitter follow relationships from public sources (for our purposes we ignore the directed nature of the edges). These datasets are used frequently in both convention emergence and influence spread research [3, 9, 20, 27] as performance benchmarks.

For the purposes of monitoring convention emergence in these networks, we only want to examine a single, connected component. As such, all 3 networks were reduced to their largest weakly connected component (WCC). Additionally, any self-loops (edges from a node to itself) were removed as such edges artificially inflate a node's degree whilst not increasing its ability to influence others. Table 1 shows the number of nodes and edges in each network and the number of nodes and edges (without self-loops) in their largest WCC.

Table 1. Original and modified network sizes

	Network		Largest WCC	
	$\|V\|$	$\|E\|$	$\|V\|$	$\|E\|$
CA-CondMat	23,133	93,497	21,363	91,286
Enron-Email	36,692	183,831	33,696	180,811
Twitter	81,306	1,768,149	81,306	1,342,296

4.2 Experimental Setup

We performed simulations of PO-Place on the real-world networks described above. We varied both the number of nodes ($n = 5$ to $n = 30$) being requested as well as the number of observations provided ($o = 500$ to $o = 5000$ [$o =$ 3500 for CondMat]). To establish an upper bound and allow comparison a full-observability degree placement was also performed for each of the networks with the same range of values (equivalent to assuming that all edges of the network are observable [10,11,16,17]). Each set of parameters was averaged over 30 runs.

For convention emergence, a population of agents is situated in the topologies. Each timestep, each agent chooses one of its neighbours uniformly at random to play the 10-action coordination game [23] receiving positive or negative payoffs depending on whether their choices match. Agents use a simplified Q-Learning algorithm to learn the most beneficial choice. We utilise the 10-action game as used by Marchant et al. [17] to avoid the issues of small convention spaces raised in Sect. 2 and to allow comparison to previous work. Agents have a chance to randomly choose their action ($p_{explore} = 0.25$) or else choose the most beneficial one. FS agents replace the agents at the chosen locations and always choose their predetermined action.

5 Results and Discussion

In this section we present the analysis of PO-Place and compare it to the upper bound from degree placement. We explore the effects of the various parameters on PO-Place at different levels of observation. We then use these findings as insight to compare the performance of PO-Place to degree for convention emergence when used to place FS agents into the chosen networks.

5.1 PO-Place Output

We begin by looking at the isolated algorithm output, comparing it to the output generated by a degree placement scheme. As the aim of PO-Place is to maximise *deg-sum* this is our primary metric by which to evaluate PO-Place. The highest *deg-sum* possible in each network is that of the set of highest degree nodes. Establishing this as an upper bound allows evaluating the performance

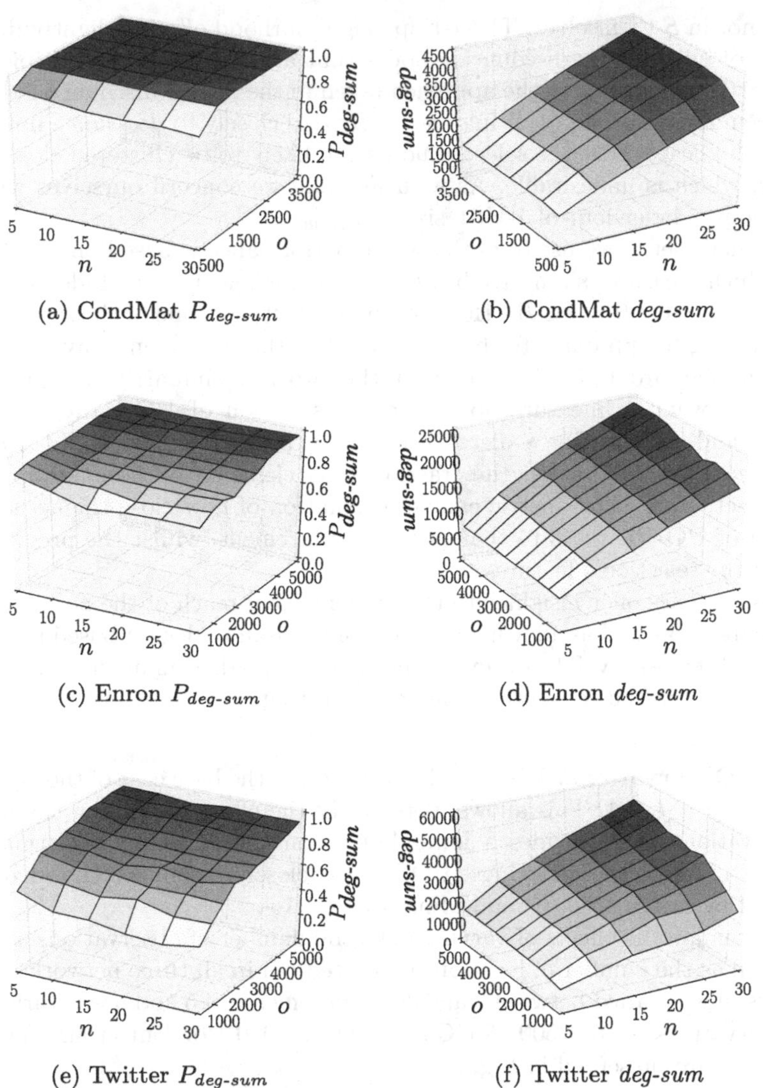

(a) CondMat $P_{deg\text{-}sum}$ (b) CondMat *deg-sum*

(c) Enron $P_{deg\text{-}sum}$ (d) Enron *deg-sum*

(e) Twitter $P_{deg\text{-}sum}$ (f) Twitter *deg-sum*

Fig. 1. $P_{deg\text{-}sum}$ and *deg-sum* performance of PO-PLACE for varying n (# of locations) and o (# of observations) in the real-world networks.

of PO-PLACE by comparing the *deg-sum* of its output as a proportion of that of the pure degree network. We denote this as $P_{deg\text{-}sum}$.

Whilst *deg-sum* describes the maximum reach of the nodes selected, another useful metric is the size of the 1-hop neighbourhood of those nodes. This can be defined as: $\text{1-HOP}(L, G) = \{v \in \{V \setminus L\} | \exists(u, v) \in E \wedge u \in L\}$ where L is the set of nodes selected for placement and $G = (V, E)$ is the network. That is, the 1-Hop neighbourhood is the set of nodes that are connected to a member of S

but are not in S themselves. The 1-Hop neighbourhood offers a slightly different measure of influence by discounting nodes that are connected to multiple members of S (this is similar to the approach taken in the degree discount method for influence maximisation [5]). Whilst normally tied closely to *deg-sum* a noticeable disparity indicates that the selected nodes are likely to be clustered close to one another, which is undesirable. As with *deg-sum* we concern ourselves with the proportionate behaviour of 1-HOP size, $P_{|\text{1-HOP}|}$.

The final metric we use to evaluate the performance is based on the Jaccard Index which measures similarity between two sets. The Jaccard Index is defined as $J(A, B) = |A \cap B|/|A \cup B|$. However, in our instance, one of the sets is static. We are trying to approximate that set with the other (i.e. a one-way similarity), whilst the Jaccard Index is looking at the two-way similarity between them. Instead we want to measure how close the selection of PO-PLACE is to the baseline, and so we define a distance measure, D_{Base}, thus: $D_{Base}(L, Base) = |L \cap Base|/|Base|$. That is, the fraction that elements of L make up of the baseline set, *Base*. This metric enables evaluation of how close the actual node selection of PO-PLACE is to that of degree placement, whilst the previous two measure the selection's features.

These metrics offer insight into the influence and reach of the nodes selected by PO-PLACE as well as allowing a direct comparison to degree-based placement with full observability. Thus they should be good predictors of the performance of PO-PLACE in the convention emergence setting.

Varying Observations. We begin by considering the base case of the algorithm where $s = p = f = 1$. This allows us to study the effect of varying the number of observations and provides a lower bound on the expected performance of PO-PLACE. With these settings, PO-PLACE closely resembles the algorithms presented by Borgs *et al.* [1] and Mihara *et al.* [18].

We examine the effects of varying both the number of observations available (o) as well as the number of locations requested (n) in all three networks. For all networks, n was varied between 5 and 30 in increments of 5 and o was varied from 500 observations up to 3500 (for CondMat) or 5000 (for Enron and Twitter). The results are presented in Fig. 1.

As can be seen in Fig. 1, all networks respond well, even with minimal numbers of observations. Even at $o = 500$, the degree sum of the nodes selected by PO-PLACE is often a substantial proportion of the optimal one. The performance varies across the three networks, with placement in CondMat doing best where it varies from 90% (±5%) at $n = 5$ to 83% (±5%) at $n = 30$. The algorithm similarly performs well in Enron, though to a lesser extent. The performance in Twitter is noticeably worse, varying from 61% to 48% with larger standard deviations for both. This is to be expected, as 500 observations represents a substantially smaller proportion of the population in Twitter than it does in CondMat or Enron (0.61%, 2.34% and 1.48% respectively) . Even with this, the percentage achieved in Twitter with such limitations substantially outperforms

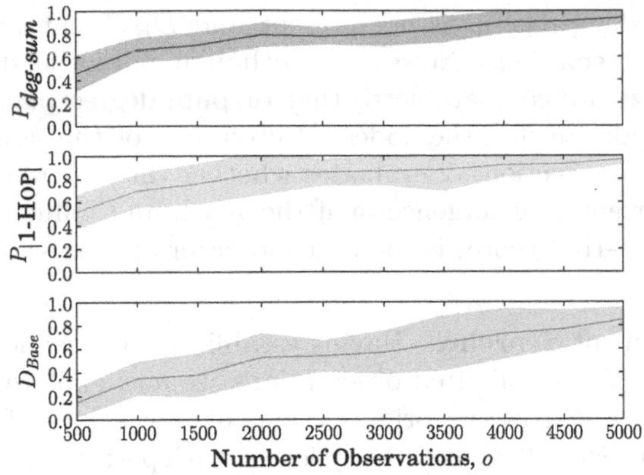

Fig. 2. Metric performances of PO-PLACE for the Twitter network, $n = 20$.

the naïve solution of using all observations at random locations (16% (±6%) for $n = 5$, $o = 500$, averaged over 100 runs).

Performance rapidly increases with the number of observations. For $n = 30$, the worst performing value of n, in both CondMat and Twitter $P_{deg\text{-}sum}$ exceeds 90% at round 5% network observation ($o = 1000$ for CondMat and $o = 5000$ for Twitter) and Enron exceeds 90% at around 10% observation ($o = 3500$). Figure 1 also shows that the relationship between $P_{deg\text{-}sum}$ and increasing o is one of diminishing returns, with improvements in $P_{deg\text{-}sum}$ most noticeable at lower values of o. This is to be expected, the relative increase in o is smaller at higher values, but dictates that increasing the effectiveness of PO-PLACE at low values of o will have the most benefit. Additionally, in each network, the difference in performance across the values of n becomes less noticeable at higher o. Thus, any increased performance from PO-PLACE will be most noticeable early on.

The other metrics we use to evaluate PO-PLACE show similar behaviour to $P_{deg\text{-}sum}$, increasing rapidly with the number of observations. Figure 2 shows a representative example of the three metrics' variation with o for the Twitter network when requesting 20 locations. The shaded regions represent the standard deviations. As can be seen, both the *deg-sum* and 1-HOP proportions increase rapidly up until $o = 2000$ and then any further gains occur over longer spans. The standard deviations for each of these decrease as well, from approximately 15% at $o = 500$ down to around 5% at $o = 5000$. This indicates that, not only is PO-PLACE finding sets of nodes with higher degree, it is doing so consistently at higher numbers of observations, a finding that is repeated across all networks and values of n. $P_{|1\text{-HOP}|}$ is consistently at the same level, if not better than, $P_{deg\text{-}sum}$. Whilst the two should be well-correlated, this shows that PO-PLACE is not simply choosing nodes close to one another and, indeed, is often choosing nodes that have a better neighbourhood size than the *deg-sum* would indicate.

The performance of PO-PLACE when evaluated by D_{Base} is noticeably different than the other two metrics and offers an interesting insight. The same pattern of diminishing returns is not present and D_{Base} continues to increase with additional observations. Note that, although both the degree sum and neighbourhood size are comparable to that of pure degree placement, the low values of D_{Base} indicate that the nodes selected are not the same as the actual highest degree nodes. Section 5.2 evaluates whether this difference has a noticeable effect on convention emergence or if the reach and influence indicated by high *deg-sum* and 1-HOP scores is the best indicator of success as hypothesised.

Varying Concurrent Searches. Having established a baseline for PO-PLACE and explored the effects of limited observations we now explore the variants of the algorithm. As noted in the prior section, at low values of o the *deg-sum* performance of PO-PLACE is consistently lower, with performance in the Twitter network as low as 48%. With very limited observations, making the best use of them is paramount. In Sect. 3 we hypothesised that splitting the available observations between multiple locations in the network and exploring them in parallel may offer improvements over crawling from a singular location.

To test this hypothesis, we varied s from 1 to 9 to determine the effect that these concurrent searches would have. Figure 3 shows a typical case in the Enron network for $n = 30$. Shaded areas represent the errors of each plot. The left-hand graph shows the effect on $P_{deg\text{-}sum}$ of varying the number of concurrent searches, splitting the observations between them. As can be seen, adding concurrent starting points has an immediate and noticeable effect, especially at low numbers of observations. At $o = 500$ the proportion achieved by *deg-sum* is 10% higher when additional starting locations are introduced and this difference becomes even more noticeable as o increases. Indeed, for most values of o, adding additional starting locations had significant benefits in both the Enron and Twitter networks, with the benefits become less marked at high o where $P_{deg\text{-}sum}$ approaches 1.0 unaided. Whilst there is a noticeable drop-off in effectiveness after initial parallelisation ($s = 5$ and $s = 7$, not included in the results to aid readability, offer little improvement over $s = 3$ for example) the effect at low values of s is substantial as can be seen. Concurrent starting points enable saturation of the algorithm's effectiveness at much lower values of o and not only increase $P_{deg\text{-}sum}$ and $P_{|1\text{-HOP}|}$ (not pictured) but, as shown in Fig. 3, cause marked improvement in D_{Base} as well, indicating that this change facilitates much better approximation of the degree placement.

However, it should be noted that this pattern is not consistent. In the CondMat network, increasing s had little effect and in a few settings was actually detrimental. This indicates that there is perhaps an underlying feature of the CondMat topology that benefits from localised crawling and will be an area of future study. The results of CondMat in Fig. 1a lend additional weight to this hypothesis, with behaviour that is substantially different than the other two topologies despite being of comparable size to Enron. Overall though, increasing s by even a small amount is likely to benefit the performance of PO-PLACE.

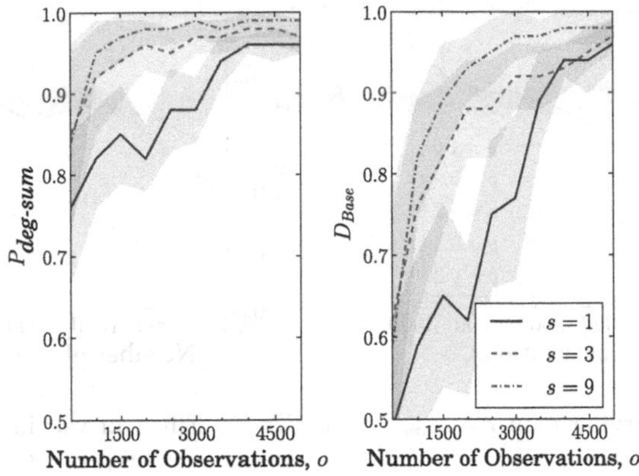

Fig. 3. Effect of varying s on $P_{deg\text{-}sum}$ and D_{Base}. Enron network, $n = 30$.

Partial Neighbour Lists. In many settings, retrieving the whole of an agent's neighbour list may also be impossible. Whether this is due to a technical limitation (only being able to retrieve a certain percentage of information) or because such information is not publicly available and is instead reserved for 'premium' or 'subscribed' users of such a network, ensuring that PO-PLACE is robust to such issues is a necessity to make it widely viable.

To simulate these restrictions, and measure their effect on the performance of PO-PLACE, the parameter, p, controls the proportion of an agent's neighbours that may be explored. Results until this point have assumed that the full neighbour list for any agent is available upon request (i.e. $p = 1.0$). We varied p between 0.3 and 0.9 to determine the impact of this limitation. Representative results are shown in Fig. 4 for the Twitter network and $n = 5$ but are applicable across all networks and values of o and n.

The results in Fig. 4 show that different values of p have minimal effect on the performance of PO-PLACE, indicating that PO-PLACE is effective at mitigating the impact of partial observability of neighbour lists. For all values of p, $P_{deg\text{-}sum}$ is comparable. Performing a 95% confidence interval Welch's t-test against the $p = 1.0$ results (i.e., full observability of a node's neighbours) at each point, only $p = 0.3$ ($o = 1500, 2000, 3500$) and $p = 0.5$ ($o = 1500, 3500$) are significantly worse. This pattern of minimal difference is repeated in all networks, with none seemingly more susceptible or affected by partial neighbour lists. This demonstrates that PO-PLACE is robust only having access to only partial information of a node's neighbour list and is largely unaffected by such limitations. Intuitively, values of p below 0.3 are likely to have more significant impact on performance as we asymptotically approach the case where there is no observation at all. Figure 4 shows that at $p = 0.3$ we are beginning to observe worse performance than other p values, although we only see statistically significant differences at $p \leq 0.5$.

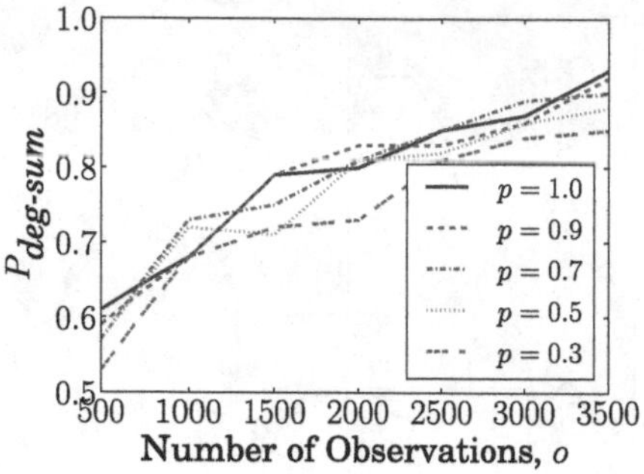

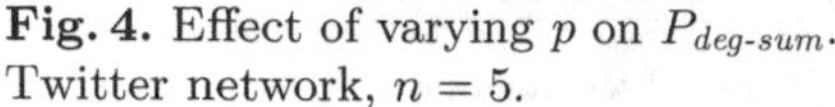
Fig. 4. Effect of varying p on $P_{deg\text{-}sum}$. Twitter network, $n = 5$.

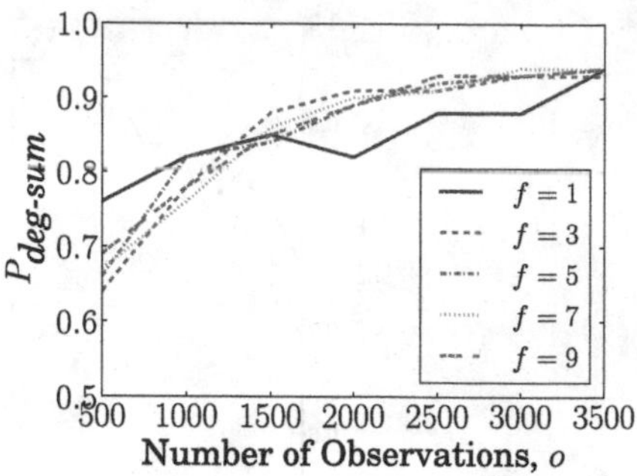

Fig. 5. Effect of varying f on $P_{deg\text{-}sum}$. Enron network, $n = 30$.

Breadth-First vs Depth-First Expansion. Finally, we turn our attention to the concept of breadth-first vs depth-first expansion in PO-PLACE. That is, when crawling the local area, should additional current area expansion be performed before considering new additions (breadth-first) or purely iteratively (depth-first). Where there is locally a clearly defined degree gradient we expect the latter to perform better. However, depth-first expansion also risks expending all the observations whilst exploring a suboptimal, locally maximal path.

Parameter f allows study of this by controlling how many of the current highest degree nodes that PO-PLACE is aware of are expanded concurrently. Experiments up until now have had $f = 1$ (depth-first). We now vary f from 1 to 9. Figure 5 presents these findings in the Enron network for $n = 30$. As with the previous results, it is our finding that the patterns here are replicated throughout the different topologies and values of n.

Similar to the findings when varying p, varying f has little absolute impact on the capabilities of PO-PLACE. However, using a 95% confidence interval Welch's t-test, all but $f = 9$ are statistically significantly worse at $o = 500$. This is likely due to the limited observations being focused too locally. All are significantly better between $o = 2000$ and $o = 3000$ but there is little gain in selecting values of f beyond 3 as the performance of PO-PLACE is almost identical. Overall, PO-PLACE seems to gain little from considering the local area more thoroughly before further expansion. Whether this is intrinsic in the design or a facet of the topologies being explored is ongoing work.

5.2 Convention Emergence Under Partial Observability

Having explored the performance of PO-PLACE under different topologies and types of partially observability, we now examine how PO-PLACE compares to degree placement [10,11,16,17] for FS agents in convention emergence in static networks, i.e., how close does it get given partial observability. Having established ranges of parameters that offer the best performance improvements for each topology, these will be utilised to compare the algorithm to degree placement. Additionally, basic settings (small numbers of observations, no concurrent placements) provide a baseline comparison of PO-Place.

A convention has emerged when the population has converged to have one action as the dominant choice of agents in the network. Most work considers this to be the case when the convention reaches 90% dominance [11,16,23]. However, much of this work utilises synthetic networks rather than real-world topologies and populations that are substantially smaller than those we consider. Preliminary experiments show that the topologies are relatively resistant to convention emergence, requiring both high numbers of FS agents as well as substantial time. As we are concerned with a comparison of the performance of PO-Place against pure degree placement we wish to find settings that are guaranteed to repeatably experience convention emergence. As such, we consider a convention to have emerged when the 80% Kittock criteria is met, $K_{80\%}$ [14]. That is, a convention has emerged when 80% of the population, when not exploring, would choose the same action. This indicates a high level of dominance of the desired action and allows more robust comparisons. We find that such a threshold is reliably reached, if it is likely to be reached at all, within 10000 iterations for the CondMat and Twitter networks and within 15000 iterations for the Enron network. As such, we measure the proportion of runs that have converged to the desired strategy within these time-frames across all networks.

The results are presented in Fig. 6. We utilise PO-Place and Degree Placement (with full observability of neighbours) to allocate FS agents across a range of FS group sizes found to exhibit noticeable changes in convention emergence rates with the parameters indicated. The values of o chosen within each topology are such that the number of observations is, at most, approximately 5% of the agent population. All runs are performed 50 times and the proportion of runs that produce the desired convention (defined as the strategy chosen universally at random at time $t = 0$ and assigned to all FS agents) is measured.

Figure 6a shows the results for the CondMat topology. As was expected, due to the behaviour of CondMat in the PO-Place experimentation, all of the chosen parameters produce comparable results to the pure degree placement (the latter with full observability). Even at the worst performing parameters ($o = 500, s = 1$) there is no discernible difference between the performance of degree placement and PO-Place, whilst at higher number of observations (where PO-Place was entirely approximating the highest-degree nodes as seen in Fig. 1a) the performance is as expected. Of note is the fact that, whilst it resulted in worse output of PO-Place in the prior section, increasing s does not noticeably affect the performance here.

Within the other networks the difference in performance is more noticeable but still indicates that PO-Place is generating close approximation of the degree placement, despite only having access to a small proportion of the edges. In both Enron and Twitter (Figures 6b and c) the minimal observation situation performs substantially worse than degree placement, particularly in the Twitter network. However, when given observations of 5% of the network, PO-Place performs noticeably better. Whilst it still falls behind the performance

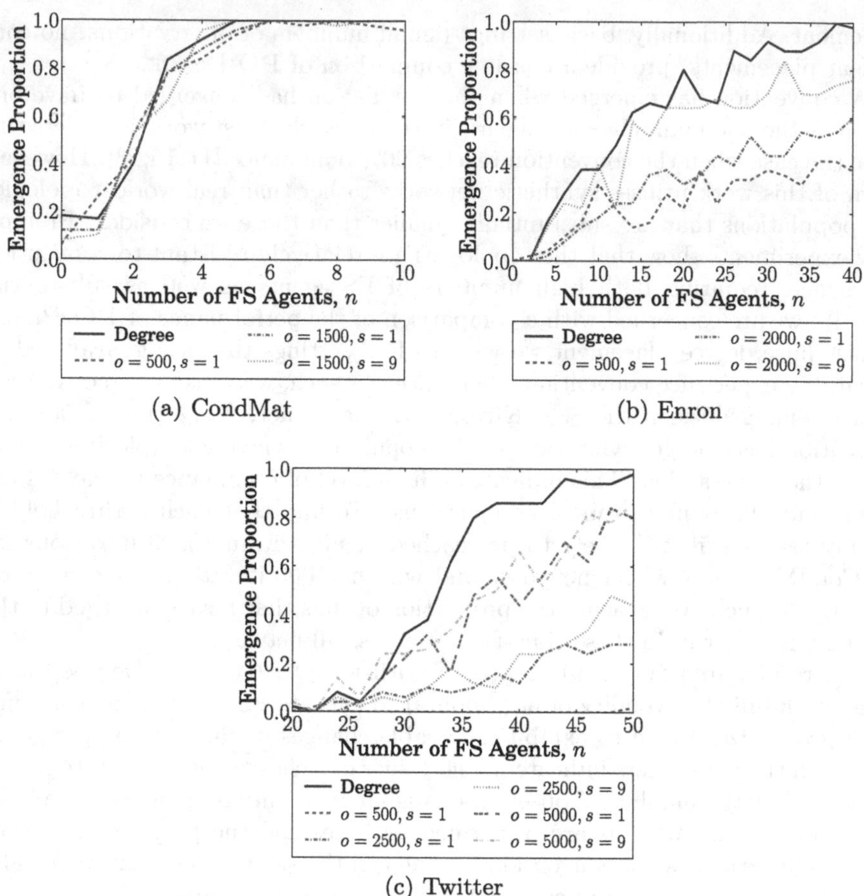

Fig. 6. Comparison of PO-PLACE and Degree FS agent placement for convention emergence in real-world topologies. The y-axis indicates the proportion of runs where the desired strategy emerged as the convention.

of degree placement in both networks the difference is substantially smaller with PO-PLACE performing around 50–70% as effectively on average as degree placement in both networks (0.52 ± 0.08 in Enron, 0.69 ± 0.18 in Twitter). However, when we increase s, as was found in Sect. 5.1, it improves this substantially to 0.82 ± 0.15 average effectiveness compared to degree placement in Enron and, less substantially, to 0.79 ± 0.3 in the Twitter network. We quantify these values by comparing the emergence proportions of PO-PLACE and degree at each value of n and calculating the ratio between them which we then average. We discount values where either placement is achieving less than a 0.1 emergence proportion to avoid noisy results influencing the measure. As 0.1 is the expected emergence proportion of our desired strategy in a convention emergence we do not influence, we believe discounting values below this allows a more accurate comparison between the two algorithms. In the Twitter network, we also consider $o = 2500$ as the effect of increased s was more pronounced for this value during Sect. 5.1. Whilst there is a noticeable improvement at higher n the average compared effectiveness differs only marginally: 0.24 ± 0.06 for $s = 1$ and 0.3 ± 0.11 for $s = 9$. In the Twitter network, o is the dominant factor. Intuitively, for larger graph sizes, the chosen real-world graphs enable us to see the difference across a range of sizes and so we would expect a similar pattern to be seen for even larger graphs. Specifically, we would see diminishing effectiveness as the number of observations becomes a smaller percentage of the graph size but still effective at very low percentages.

Overall, we have shown that even when only observing a small portion of the underlying topology, and strategically using these observations to maximise their effect, it is possible to achieve comparable performance to degree placement with full network visibility using PO-PLACE.

6 Conclusion

Finding influential positions within a network topology to maximise the effectiveness of fixed strategy agents is an ongoing area of research in convention emergence. The problem has many facets and variations that make it difficult to find an optimal yet general approach. In many cases, placing the fixed strategy agents at high degree nodes provides effective convention emergence with little computational overhead. Finding high-degree nodes in a network is trivial when the network is fully observable. In many domains, this may not always be possible. Technical limitations such as memory constraints or incomplete information and usage limitations such as finite API calls mean that often a network topology may only be *partially observable*. Finding effective placement for FS agents with these restrictions adds another level of complexity.

In this paper we presented a placement algorithm, PO-PLACE, that is designed for use in partially observable topologies. It uses finite observations to find sets of high-degree nodes and approximates the set of nodes that would be selected given full observability.

With small proportions of the network being observable, PO-PLACE can locate nodes with similar reach and influence as degree placement. We evaluate the performance in three real-world topologies and show that the addition of concurrent searches and splitting of observations improves the performance of the algorithm across all metrics. With 1–10% observation the algorithm is able to find sets of nodes with >90% of the reach and influence of degree placement.

Finally, we showed that PO-PLACE performs comparably to degree placement when used to facilitate convention emergence using fixed strategy agents whilst only observing 5% of a network topology. We found that the additional aspects of PO-PLACE benefit the placement mechanism and demonstrated that convention emergence is easily facilitated in partially observable networks. Future work will include investigation of dynamic network topologies, destabilisation of conventions, and the applicability of PO-PLACE to influence maximisation.

References

1. Borgs, C., Brautbar, M., Chayes, J., Khanna, S., Lucier, B.: The power of local information in social networks. In: Goldberg, P.W. (ed.) Proceedings of the 8th International Workshop on Internet and Network Economics, pp. 406–419 (2012)
2. Brautbar M., Kearns, M.J.: Local algorithms for finding interesting individuals in large networks. In: Proceedings of Innovation in Computer Science, pp. 188–199 (2010)
3. Chen, D.-B., Xiao, R., Zeng, A.: Predicting the evolution of spreading on complex networks. Sci. Rep. **4**, 6108 (2014)
4. Chen, W., Wang, Y., Yang, S.: Efficient influence maximization in social networks. In: Proceedings of the 15th ACM SIGKDD International Conference on Knowledge Discovery and Data Mining, pp. 199–208 (2009)
5. Chen, W., Wang, Y., Yang, S.: Efficient influence maximization in social networks. In: Proceedings of the 15th ACM SIGKDD International Conference on Knowledge Discovery and Data Mining (2009)
6. Delgado, J.: Emergence of social conventions in complex networks. Artif. Intell. **141**(1–2), 171–185 (2002)
7. Delgado, J., Pujol, J.M., Sangüesa, R.: Emergence of coordination in scale-free networks. Web Intell. Agent Syst. **1**(2), 131–138 (2003)
8. Di Felice, M., Chowdhury, K.R., Wu, C., Bononi, L., Meleis, W.: Learning-based spectrum selection in cognitive radio ad hoc networks. In: International Conference on Wired/Wireless Internet Communications, pp. 133–145-389 (2010)
9. Franks, H., Griffiths, N., Anand, S.S.: Learning agent influence in MAS with complex social networks. Auton. Agents Multi-Agent Syst. **28**(5), 836–866 (2013). https://doi.org/10.1007/s10458-013-9241-1
10. Franks, H., Griffiths, N., Jhumka, A.: Manipulating convention emergence using influencer agents. Auton. Agents Multi-Agent Syst. **26**(3), 315–353 (2013)
11. Griffiths, N., Anand, S.S.: The impact of social placement of non-learning agents on convention emergence. In: Proceedings of the 11th International Conference on Autonomous Agents and Multiagent Systems, pp. 1367–1368 (2012)
12. Haynes, C., Luck, M., McBurney, P., Mahmoud, S., Vitek, T., Miles, S.: Engineering the emergence of norms: a review. Knowl. Eng. Rev. **32** (2017)
13. Kandori, M.: Social norms and community enforcement. Rev. Econ. Stud. **59**(1), 63–80 (1992)
14. Kittock, J.: Emergent conventions and the structure of multi-agent systems. In: Lectures in Complex Systems: Proceedings of the 1993 Complex Systems Summer School, pp. 507–521 (1995)
15. Leskovec, J., Krevl, A.: SNAP Datasets: Stanford large network dataset collection, June 2014. http://snap.stanford.edu/data
16. Marchant, J., Griffiths, N., Leeke, M.: Convention emergence and influence in dynamic topologies. In: Proceedings of the 2015 International Conference on Autonomous Agents and Multiagent Systems, pp. 1785–1786 (2015)
17. Marchant, J., Griffiths, N., Leeke, M., Franks, H.: Destabilising conventions using temporary interventions. In: Ghose, A., Oren, N., Telang, P., Thangarajah, J. (eds.) COIN 2014. LNCS (LNAI), vol. 9372, pp. 148–163. Springer, Cham (2015). https://doi.org/10.1007/978-3-319-25420-3_10
18. Mihara, S., Tsugawa, S., Ohsaki, H.: Influence maximization problem for unknown social networks. In: Proceedings of the IEEE/ACM International Conference on Advances in Social Networks Analysis and Mining, pp. 1539–1546 (2015)

19. Morris-Martin, A., De Vos, M., Padget, J.: Norm emergence in multiagent systems: a viewpoint paper. Auton. Agent. Multi-Agent Syst. **33**(6), 706–749 (2019). https://doi.org/10.1007/s10458-019-09422-0
20. Pei, S., Tang, S., Zheng, Z.: Detecting the influence of spreading in social networks with excitable sensor networks. PLoS ONE **10**(5), e0124848 (2015)
21. Salazar, N., Rodriguez-Aguilar, J.A., Arcos, J.L.: Robust coordination in large convention spaces. AI Commun. **23**(4), 357–372 (2010)
22. Savarimuthu, B.T.R., Arulanandam, R., Purvis, M.: Aspects of active norm learning and the effect of lying on norm emergence in agent societies. In: Kinny, D., Hsu, J.Y., Governatori, G., Ghose, A.K. (eds.) PRIMA 2011. LNCS (LNAI), vol. 7047, pp. 36–50. Springer, Heidelberg (2011). https://doi.org/10.1007/978-3-642-25044-6_6
23. Sen, S., Airiau, S.: Emergence of norms through social learning. In: Proceedings of the 20th International Joint Conference on Artifical Intelligence, pp. 1507–1512 (2007)
24. Villatoro, D., Sabater-Mir, J., Sen., S.: Social instruments for robust convention emergence. In: Proceedings of the 22nd International Joint Conference on Artificial Intelligence, pp. 420–425 (2011)
25. Villatoro, D., Sen, S., Sabater-Mir, J.: Topology and memory effect on convention emergence. In: Proceedings of the 2009 IEEE/WIC/ACM International Joint Conference on Web Intelligence and Intelligent Agent Technology, pp. 233–240 (2009)
26. Walker, A., Wooldridge, M.: Understanding the emergence of conventions in multi-agent systems. In: International Conference on Multi-Agent Systems, pp. 384–389 (1995)
27. Wang, X., Su, Y., Zhao, C., Yi, D.: Effective identification of multiple influential spreaders by DegreePunishment. Physica A **461**, 238–247 (2016)
28. Young, H.P.: The economics of convention. J. Econ. Perspect. **10**(2), 105–122 (1996)

Improving Confidence in the Estimation of Values and Norms

Luciano Cavalcante Siebert[1,2(✉)], Rijk Mercuur[3], Virginia Dignum[3,4], Jeroen van den Hoven[2,3], and Catholijn Jonker[1,2,5]

[1] Faculty of Electrical Engineering, Mathematics, and Computer Science, Delft University of Technology, Delft, The Netherlands
l.cavalcantesiebert@tudelft.nl
[2] AiTech, Delft University of Technology, Delft, The Netherlands
[3] Faculty of Technology, Policy and Management, Delft University of Technology, Delft, The Netherlands
[4] Department of Computing Sciences, Umeå University, Umeå, Sweden
[5] Leiden Institute of Advance Computer Science, Leiden University, Leiden, The Netherlands

Abstract. Autonomous agents (AA) will increasingly be interacting with us in our daily lives. While we want the benefits attached to AAs, it is essential that their behavior is aligned with our values and norms. Hence, an AA will need to estimate the values and norms of the humans it interacts with, which is not a straightforward task when solely observing an agent's behavior. This paper analyses to what extent an AA is able to estimate the values and norms of a simulated human agent (SHA) based on its actions in the ultimatum game. We present two methods to reduce ambiguity in profiling the SHAs: one based on search space exploration and another based on counterfactual analysis. We found that both methods are able to increase the confidence in estimating human values and norms, but differ in their applicability, the latter being more efficient when the number of interactions with the agent is to be minimized. These insights are useful to improve the alignment of AAs with human values and norms.

Keywords: Autonomous agents · Values · Norms · Ultimatum game

1 Introduction

As autonomous agents (AAs) become more pervasive in our daily lives, there is a growing need to reduce the risk of undesired impacts on our society [2,12]. Hence, we need design and engineering approaches that consider the implications of ethically relevant decision-making by machines, understanding the AA as part of a socio-technical system [8, p.48]. For this, we need to ensure that the decisions and actions made by the AA are aligned with the stakeholders' values ("what one finds important in life" [23]) and norms (what is standard, acceptable or permissible behavior in a group or society [10]).

A. Aler Tubella et al. (Eds.): COIN 2017/COINE 2020, LNAI 12298, pp. 98–113, 2021.
https://doi.org/10.1007/978-3-030-72376-7_6

Values and norms can be seen as criteria for decision-making: values relating to more abstract and context-independent ideals, and norms as more concrete context-dependent rules. Furthermore, since humans use values and norms in their explanations, the use of these concepts allows for a better explanation of the AA [15–17]. People have a common base system of values and they are relatively stable over the life span of a person [4], however, values and norms vary significantly for each person and socio-cultural environment, making it difficult or even impossible to write down precise rules describing them. One approach to deal with this variance is to treat aligning the actions of the AA with human values as a learning problem [13,27]. However, estimating values and norms solely based on observed behavior may lead to ambiguous results. Different relative preferences towards values and norms can bring about the same behavior, i.e. there are many "reasons why" that might motivate a given observed behavior (ambiguity problem). In case that an agent's actions are driven by a "wrong" set of values and norms, strong ethical consequences may befall.

This paper studies the conditions under which AAs are able to make confident estimates of one's preference on values and norms from observed behavior. We studied the behavior of simulated agents driven by both values and social norms in the Ultimatum Game (UG), specifically in the proposer role. [20] has used the UG to study the relative importance of values across cultures. We focus on the relative importance of values and norms that guide individual decision making, aiming to provide useful insights to improve the alignment of AAs with human values and norms.

The main contribution of this paper is twofold. First, we propose an agent-based model to play the UG, expanded from [16], which uses both values and norms for determining the actions of the agents. Second, we present a method for estimating an agent's relative preferences to a given set of values and, if necessary, to improve the confidence in these estimations. This improvement is realized by interacting with the proposer agent in the UG, either by a free exploration of the search space or by the use of counterfactuals.

The remainder of the paper is structured as follows. The following section presents a brief context about the UG and how we model values and norms in this context. Section 3 presents both the method to estimate the relative preference attributed to an agent's values and norm, and the methods to reduce ambiguity on the estimation. Section 4 presents the main results of this research and Sect. 5 discusses these results. Finally, Sect. 6 presents the conclusions.

2 Values and Norms in the Ultimatum Game

2.1 Scenario: The Ultimatum Game

We simulate the behavior of the agents in the UG, first introduced by [11]. In the UG, two players negotiate over a fixed amount of money (the 'pie'). The proposer demands a portion of the pie, while the remainder is offered to the responder. The responder chooses to accept or reject this proposed split. If the responder chooses to 'accept', the proposed split is implemented. If the responder chooses to 'reject', both players get no money. The UG thus provides an environment where players have to make decisions about money based on their own judgment.

The remainder of the paper uses a version of the UG with the following specifics:

- An experiment has 32 players: 16 proposers and 16 responders.
- One experiment has 20 rounds. One round in the UG comprises one demand for each proposer and one reply for each matched responder.
- The players are paired to a different player each round but do not change roles.
- Players are anonymous to each other.
- The pie size P is 1000[1].

These specifics are chosen for pragmatic reasons: the paper uses an empirical dataset based on these specifics [3] and builds upon a model based on these specifics [16].

This paper models the decision-making of humans in the UG by using values and norms, but there have been many different approaches to it since its first appearance in [11]. One reason for its popularity is that the UG is a classical example of where the canonical game-theoretical agent (i.e., the *homo economics* that only cares about maximizing its direct own welfare) falls short. The *homo economicus* only cares about its direct welfare and thus will accept any positive offer in the UG. Humans, in contrast, reject offers as high as 40% of the pie [21]. Behavioral economics has aimed to explain humans by incorporating learning [25], reputation [9] or other-regarding preferences. Recently, [16] used values and norms to explain UG behavior. Using a series of agent-based simulation experiments, [16] showed that the model produces aggregate behavior that falls within the 95% confidence interval wherein human behavior lies more often than the other tested agent models (e.g., a learning *homo economicus* model). Moreover, the model uses concepts that humans use in their explanations. Thus because the model has been shown to reproduce human behavior and uses explainable concepts, the model of [16] provides a starting point to estimate preference towards human values and norms for value alignment.

2.2 Simulated Human Agent (SHA)

The simulated human agent (SHA) represents the human in the UG whose values and norms we aim to estimate. The model for the SHA is based on the value-based model and norm-based model presented in [16]. These models focus on the aggregate properties that emerge from pairing these agents in the UG. However, this paper focuses on estimating relative preference towards values and norms of individual agents. Therefore, we are interested in an agent model where one agent uses *both* values and norms. The remainder of this section presents the SHA model in three parts: the value-based agent (from [16]), the norm-based agent (extension of [16]) and an agent that uses both values and norms (new).

[1] For ease of presentation, we chose to present P with no monetary unit. Empirical work [21] shows that the effect of the pie size is relatively small.

Value-Based Agent. The value-based agent uses the importance an agent attributes to its values to determine what an agent (based on its values) should demand. [16] focuses on two values that are relevant in the UG: wealth and fairness and define di_a as the difference in importance an agent attributes to wealth versus fairness. Based on research by [26] and data on the UG [3], they then state a number of requirements for a function (see [16] for more details). First, they assume a (perfect) negative correlation between wealth and fairness. Second, valuing wealth is defined as wanting more money. Third, valuing fairness is defined as wanting an equal split of the pie. Fourth, agents should differ in how much money they demand, but not demand below 0.5P. The functions that map di_a to the demand $d \in \{0...P\} \subset \mathbb{Z}$ are given by

$$valueDemand(di_a) = \operatorname*{arg\,max}_{d \in \{0...P\} \subset \mathbb{Z}} u(d, di_a, P) \tag{1}$$

and

$$u(d, di_a, P) = -\frac{1.0 + 0.5di_a}{\frac{d}{P} + 0.5} - \frac{1.0 - 0.5di_a}{\frac{|0.5P - d|}{0.5P} + 0.5} \tag{2}$$

The agent thus calculates the utility for each demand d and returns the demand with the maximum utility. [16] shows these functions fulfill the stated requirements. By using (1) and (2), we enable our agent to choose a demand following theories on values [26] and [3] empirical results on the UG.

Norm-Based Agent. The norm-based agent uses the replies it observes from the other agent to determine what an agent (based on its norms) should demand. In [16], following theories by [5] and [10], it is stated that a norm exists for a particular person when that person perceives what most other people do or expect it. [16] provides a translation from this definition to a model for the UG. In the UG, the proposer cannot see what other proposers do, because the proposer is only paired with responders. Therefore, the proposer uses the responses of the responder to form an idea of what is expected (i.e., the norm). [16] provides the following function to map the observed responses (OR_{ak}) seen by agent a up to the current round k to a demand $d \in \{0...P\} \subset \mathbb{Z}$,

$$normDemand(OR_{ak}) = \frac{\min_{d \in RD_{ak}} d + \max_{d \in AD_{ak}} d}{2} \tag{3}$$

where $RD_{ak} \subset OR_{ak}$ is the set of demands that the proposer a has seen rejected and $AD_{ak} \subset OR_{ak}$ is the set of demands that the proposer a has seen accepted. The function thus uses two indicators to estimate the norm: the minimum of the rejected demands (RD_{ak}) and the maximum of the accepted demands (AD_{ak}). The rejection of a given demand indicates that the demand is higher than expected, thus the norm is lower than the minimum rejected demand. The acceptance of a given demand indicates that the demand is lower than expected (or perfect), thus the norm is higher (or equal) to the accepted demand. Equation (3) determines the norm as the average of these two indicators. By using

(3), we enable our agent to choose a demand following [5] and [10] theories on norms.

We extend the model provided by [16] to specify normDemand(OR_{ak}) for three edge cases: a case where there are no observed responses ($OR_{ak} = \emptyset$), a case with only observed rejections ($RD_{ak} = OR_{ak}$), and a case with only observed accepts ($AD_{ak} = OR_{ak}$):

- $OR_{ak} = \emptyset \rightarrow$ normDemand(OR_{ak}) is drawn from the normal distribution $N(561.8, 128.9)$, which is the normal distribution human demands follow in the empirical dataset we use of [3].[2]
- $RD_{ak} = OR_{ak} \rightarrow$ the agent averages between the minimum reject and halve the pie $((\min_{d \in RD_{ak}} d + 0.5P)/2)$.
- $AD_{ak} = OR_{ak} \rightarrow$ the agent averages between the maximum accept and the full pie $((\max_{d \in AD_{ak}} d + P)/2))$.

In [16], the agent determines a randomized demand as the norm in all these cases. By specifying these edge cases, we improve the SHA model aiming to better represent human behavior.

Agent with Values and Norms. This paper combines the value-based agent and the norm-based agent to model an agent that uses both values and norms. Values and norms are decision-making concepts the agent uses to decide what action is good and what action is bad [17]. [6] used values as more abstract ideals and norms as the more concrete context-dependent rules that follow from these ideals. Norms follow from values, but when agents copy the norms (but not values) from other agents the two can conflict. For example, one copies working over-hours although this is in conflict with its own values. This paper presents a model where an agent uses a weight (vw_a) to combine the best action based on values and the best action based on norms into the best action based on both values and norms.

For a proposer an action is defined as a demand $d \in \{0...P\} \subset \mathbb{Z}$. The demand d for an agent a in round k is determined by

$$\begin{aligned} d_{ak}(di_a, vw_a, OR_{ak}) = {} & vw_a \times valueDemand(di_a) \\ & +(1 - vw_a) \times normDemand(OR_{ak}), \end{aligned} \quad (4)$$

where di_a stands for the difference in importance an agent attributes to wealth versus the importance it attributes to fairness, $vw_a \in [0, 1]$ stands for the weight an agent attributes to its own values (versus the weight it attributes to norms) and OR_{ak} stands for the set of observed replies the agent has seen. Thus what an agent demands is the result of weighting the result of two functions described in [16]: the $valueDemand(di_a)$ (1) and the $normDemand(OR_{ak})$ (3).

[2] The norm that is drawn from the normal distribution is not used as input for the norm in subsequent rounds (i.e., the agent does not memorize it).

The above focuses on the demands of the SHA-proposer (SHA-P), but to simulate the UG we also need SHA-responders (SHA-R). The SHA-R is defined the same way as to the proposer model except that it determines a threshold $t \in [0, P]$ (instead of a demand d) and has to base its norms on a set of observed demands (instead of observed responses). The SHA-R uses the same function as the SHA-P (4) to determine the threshold. If the demand is higher than the threshold the responder rejects it, if the demand is lower than or equal to the threshold accepts it. The responder determines a threshold appropriate for its values analogue to the proposer, that is, by using (1) and (2). The responder determines the norm for the threshold by averaging over the observed demands (instead of the observed responses). The proposed demand is thus seen as a signal from the proposer that this is what the proposer considers 'normal'.[3] By using a threshold t based on its values and the norm (from observed demands), the responder uses values and norms to reject or accept the proposed demand.

Above we presented a model that uses both values and norms using two agent-specific variables: the difference in importance (di) and the value-norm weight (vw). The difference in importance specifies how much an agent values wealth over fairness and is normally distributed over agents $N(\mu_{di}, \sigma_{di})$, being μ_{di} the average value and σ_{di} the standard distribution of a normal distribution for di. The value-norm weight specifies how much an agent weighs values over norms and is normally distributed over agents $N(\mu_{vw}, \sigma_{vw})$. Both variables are constant over the different rounds. However, the $normDemand(OR_{ak})$ differs per round as the observed replies vary. To reproduce the demands and responses humans give, the parameters μ_{di}, σ_{di}, μ_{vw} and σ_{vw} need to be calibrated to the right settings.

2.3 Calibrating the SHA to Humans

We found that $\mu_{di} = 0.5$, $\sigma_{di} = 0.25$, $\mu_{vw} = -0.6$ and $\sigma_{vw} = 1.14$ produced simulated demands and responses that are closest to the empirical data on human demands and responses extracted from the dataset provided by [3]. This meta-study combines the data of 6 empirical studies to create a dataset of 5950 demands and replies made by humans in the same scenario as we describe in Sect. 2.1. We used five performance measures for which we compared the synthetic data on the SHA to the empirical data on real humans: average demand μ_d, standard deviation in demand σ_d, average acceptance rate μ_a, standard deviation in acceptance rate σ_a and the standard deviation in the demand solely based on values σ_{vd}.[4] The SHA is compared to humans on both round 1 and round 10. We used the following procedure to find the optimal parameter settings:

[3] To be exact, the proposed demand should be considered as what the proposer considers a 'normal' threshold. If it considered a higher threshold to be normal it would have demanded less, if it considered a lower threshold normal it would have demanded more.

[4] The standard deviation in the demand solely based on values σ_{vd} was added to ensure agents vary in what values they find important (di_a). The σ_{vd} for humans is postulated instead of extracted from empirical data.

1. Run simulations of the UG in Repast Simphony with different parameter settings ($\mu_{di} \in [-1, 1]$ and $\mu_{vw} \in [0, 1]$) and different random seeds ($r \in [1, 30]$) and obtain the resulting demands and acceptance rate (μ_d, σ_d, μ_a, σ_a);
2. For each run: average the performance measures with the same parameter settings, but different random seeds;
3. For each parameter setting: calculate the normalized root mean square error (NRMSE) between the simulated results and the human results;
4. Pick the parameter setting with a minimal NRMSE.

Table 1 compares the resulting demands and responses for the SHA (when NRMSE is minimized) and the empirical data on human results. We interpret these results as that our SHA can produce a distribution of demands and accepts that it is fairly close to that of humans (NRMSE = 11.0). The remainder of the paper uses these parameter settings to simulate human behavior based on values and norms.

Table 1. A comparison of the distribution of demands and responses between empirical data on humans and synthetic data on simulated human agents (SHAs) given the parameter settings with the best fit ($\mu_{di} = 0.5$, $\sigma_{di} = 0.25$, $\mu_{vw} = -0.6$ and $\sigma_{vw} = 1.14$).

Round	Source	Performance measures				
		μ_d	σ_d	μ_a	σ_a	σ_{vd}
1	Empirical (human)	561.8	128.9	0.806	0.40	128.9
	Synthetic (SHA)	557.9	91.1	0.876	0.29	109.2
10	Empirical (human)	584.2	98.66	0.868	0.34	122.5
	Synthetic (SHA)	646.8	90.89	0.923	0.23	109.2

3 Estimating Relative Preferences on Values and Norms

The conceptual model of the estimation process is presented in Fig. 1. The *Profiling Agent* (PA) is responsible to estimate the relative preference of a given SHA-P towards values and norms ($[\hat{di}_a, \hat{vw}_a]$), and whenever necessary, interact with the SHA-P to reduce ambiguity in the estimation.

The problem of estimating values and norms in the context of this work is translated to the estimation of di_a and vw_a, represented as $[\hat{di}_a, \hat{vw}_a]$. The estimation of relative preferences from behavior was assessed in different ways, such as via Inverse Reinforcement Learning (IRL) algorithms [1,12,14,18] and learning a utility function with influence diagrams [19]. In this work, we use the UG as a simple context (two values and one norm), aiming for clarity on understanding the conditions necessary to properly estimate the relative value

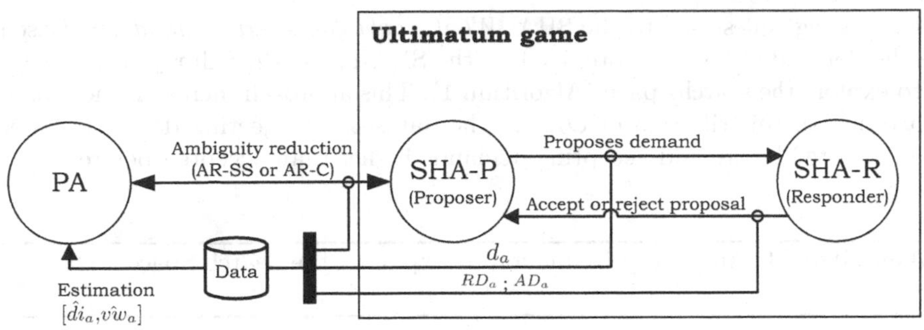

Fig. 1. Conceptual model.

and norm preference from behavior and, whenever necessary, how to reduce ambiguity.

In the context of the UG we can perform the estimation of the relative preferences by a exhaustive search process on the estimators, according to:

$$[\hat{di_a}, \hat{vw_a}] = \underset{di_a \in [-0.15;1.79]; vw_a \in [0;1]}{\arg\min} \frac{\sum_{k=1}^{m} \left| \hat{d}_{ak}(di_a, vw_a, OR_{ak}) - d_{ak} \right|}{k} \tag{5}$$

where $\hat{d_{ak}}$ is calculated by (4), and m represents the number of rounds from the UG analyzed in the estimation. In short, the estimators $\hat{di_a}$ and $v\hat{w}_a$ are defined as the preference set that minimizes the deviation between the observed demand (d_{ak}) and the demand that was calculated by an exhaustive search process ($\hat{d_{ak}}$). The range for di_a which has an effect on the demand by the SHA-P is $[-0.15; 1.79]$. With $vw_a \in [0; 1]$, and using a step of 0.01 to explore both variables, 19,392 evaluations of the fitness function are necessary for each estimation process.

3.1 Reducing Ambiguity

Ambiguity arises whenever the number of elements of $\hat{di_a}$ and $v\hat{w}_a$ is greater than 1. The PA will try to reduce this ambiguity by taking the role of the *responder* on the UG. This interaction might be interpreted as an elicitation process or, in simple, the PA will ask the SHA-P "questions". Different ways of "asking these questions" may produce higher or lower quality answers, and consequently a higher or lower change in the confidence on the estimation. We will explore two different approaches to how the PA interacts with the SHA-P. These interactions are a "side-game", i.e. changes in OR_a will not, by definition, influence future actions of the SHA-P.

Ambiguity Reduction by Exploring the Search Space (AR-SS). The approach to ambiguity reduction via exploring the search space ($AR-SS$) poses the following "question" to the SHA: *What would your next demand be?*. Based on the demand ("answer") provided by the SHA-P, the PA will reject or accept it to explore the search space (Algorithm 1). This approach increases the search space, i.e. the distribution of OR_a in the dataset, by rejecting demands lower than rejected before and accepting demands higher than accepted before.

Algorithm 1: Ambiguity Reduction by exploring the Search Space ($AR-SS$)

input : $\hat{di}_a$, $\hat{vw}_a$, max_{int},RD_a,AD_a,OR_a, d_a, k
output: $\hat{di}_a$, $\hat{vw}_a$,RD_a,AD_a,OR_a, $count$

$n_{solutions}$ ←number of solutions ($[\hat{di}_a, \hat{vw}_a]$)
$k \leftarrow k+1$
Calculate OR_{ak}
$count \leftarrow 0$
while $n_{solutions} > 1$ AND $count < max_{int}$ **do**
  Calculate $\hat{d}_{ak}(\hat{di}_a, \hat{vw}_a, OR_{ak})$ (4)
  Include OR_{ak} and $\hat{d}_{ak}$ to the data set
  Estimate $[\hat{di}_a, \hat{vw}_a]$ (5)
  $n_{solutions}$ ← number of solutions ($[\hat{di}_a, \hat{vw}_a]$)
  if $d_{ak} < min(RD_a)$ OR $\nexists$ RD_a **then**
    $RD_{ak} \leftarrow d_{ak}$
  else if $d_{ak} > max(AD_a)$ OR $\nexists$ AD_a **then**
    $AD_{ak} \leftarrow d_{ak}$
  $k \leftarrow k+1$
  Calculate $OR_{a,k}$
  $count \leftarrow count + 1$

Ambiguity Reduction via Counterfactuals (AR-C). Counterfactuals are mental representations of alternatives to events that have already occurred [24], frequently represented by conditional propositions related to questions in the "what if" form. Philosophical discussion on counterfactuals has been present for ages, including works from David Hume and John Stuart Mill [22], and it is considered an intrinsic element of causality. People use counterfactuals often in daily life to create alternatives to reality guided by rational principles.

Our approach to reduce ambiguity on the estimation of values and norms via counterfactual ($AR-C$) poses the following "question" to the SHA-P: *What would your next demand be if your opponent had accepted instead of rejected your proposal on round "x"?* or *What would your next demand be if your opponent had rejected instead of accepting your proposal on round "x"?*. As presented in Algorithm 2, the PA will 'ask' the 'question' related to the round that will lead to a broader search space in terms of the observed social norm (OR_a).

Algorithm 2: Ambiguity Reduction via Counterfactuals (AR-C)

```
input  : di^_a, vw^_a, RD_a, AD_a, OR_a, d_a, k
output: di^_a, vw^_a, RD_a, AD_a, OR_a, count
max_int ← k
count ← 0
n_solutions ←number of solutions ([di^_a, vw^_a])
while n_solutions > 1 AND count < max_int do
    for i = 1 : k do
        if ∃ AD_ai (Proposal was accepted in round i) then
            if d_ai < min(RD_a) OR ∄ RD_a then
                RD_ai ← d_ai
        else if ∃ RD_ai (Proposal was rejected in round i) then
            if d_ai > max(AD_a) OR ∄ AD_a then
                AD_ai ← d_ai
        Calculate OR_ai
        score_i ← min(|OR_ai − OR_a|)
    k ← k + 1
    OR_ak ← OR_az, where z is the iteration where score is maximum
    Calculate d^_ak(di^_a, vw^_a, OR_ak) (4)
    Include OR_ak and d_new to the data set
    Estimate [di^_a, vw^_a] (5)
    n_solutions ←number of solutions ([di^_a, vw^_a])
    count ← count + 1
```

4 Results

To test the methods presented in this paper we analyzed the behavior of agents acting as proponents (SHA-P) in 100 runs of the UG (each with 20 rounds), in terms of precision and confidence. The first will be evaluated by the root mean squared error (RMSE) between the observed demand (d) and the estimated demand ($\hat{d}$), while the latter by the number of elements in $[\hat{di}_a, \hat{vw}_a]$. A small number of elements represent high confidence (low ambiguity), while a large number of solutions represent low confidence (high ambiguity). It is guaranteed the number of elements of $[\hat{di}_a, \hat{vw}_a]$ is greater than zero, since we perform an exhaustive search in the complete range of di_a and vw_a. With these results, we aim to analyze the conditions under which the proposed methods can estimate preferences on values and norms in a precise and confident manner.

4.1 Estimation of Values and Norms

The precision in the estimation increased with the number of rounds used, given that an estimation is made by observing at least four rounds (Fig. 2(a)). Using less than four rounds the estimated values and norms ($[\hat{di}_a, \hat{vw}_a]$) predicted a demand ($\hat{d}$) that is very close to the real demand[5], but most of these estimations will not be able to generalize among other contexts (i.e. other observed response - OR_a).

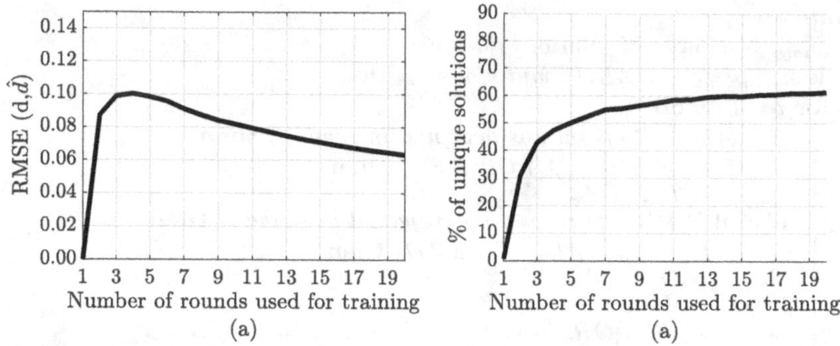

Fig. 2. (a) Precision of the estimation process. (b) Percentage of unique solutions for the estimation process.

When considering between one and four rounds the estimations were ambiguous: on average 69.2 different sets of estimations led to the same demand (Fig. 2(b)). Nevertheless, the confidence in the estimation increased with the number of rounds used. The steep curve reaching round four appears in both figures, showing a correlation between this initial precision in the estimation of the demand with the ambiguity on estimating preferences toward values and norms. Even with an increasing number of rounds observed, the percentual of unique solutions reached an average of only ca. 60%. These different estimations may lead to undesired properties of an agent that wants to act on behalf of the true values and norms of a given person.

4.2 Reducing Ambiguity

Both proposed methods were able to increase confidence in the estimation of preferences on values and norms ($[\hat{di}_a, \hat{vw}_a]$). Comparing Fig. 3(a) with Fig. 2(a), the RMSE between the calculated and observed demand are slightly higher, but still may be considered adequate in absolute values, given that $d \in \{0...1000\} \subset \mathbb{Z}$.

The methods $AR - SS$ and $AR - C$ did not increase confidence in the same manner, differing in their applicability. While $AR - SS$ was able to reach estimations with less ambiguity than $AR - C$ (Fig. 3(b)), it required in average of

[5] Given the deterministic model of the SHA, it might be expected that the RMSE should tend to zero. This is not the case because $[d, valueDemand, normDemand] \in \mathbb{Z}$, and therefore a rounding operator is used.

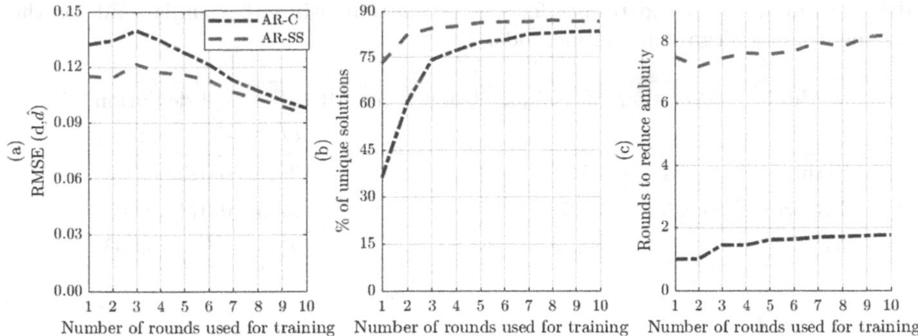

Fig. 3. Reducing ambiguity: (a) Precision; (b) Unique solutions; (c) Number of interactions made for reducing ambiguity.

4.9 more interactions with the user (Fig. 3(c))[6]. In 33.2% of the cases where the estimation was ambiguous, $AR - SS$ could provide a unique solution, while $AR - C$ provided it for 27.2% of the cases. Considering both the confidence and the number of interactions needed, $AR - C$ increased the number of unique solutions by 16.5% per interaction with the SHA-P, while $AR - SS$ increased it by 4.1% per interaction.

Table 2 summarizes the results when the estimation is performed using 10 rounds of observed data. We can see that precision varied only slightly, but the confidence in the estimation increased significantly when using any of the *ambiguity reduction* methods proposed. The columns related to the "Standard deviation" on Table 2 provide parameters to understand the dispersion of the search space[7] and of the estimations ($[\hat{di}_a, \hat{vw}_a]$). While the search space scatters with the ambiguity reduction methods, there is a reduction in the dispersion for the estimations. In other words, as the search space covered by OR_a increases, estimations become less ambiguous (and more gathered).

5 Discussion

AAs must be able to estimate human's relative preferences towards values and norms to align their behavior with them. This is not an easy task since a different set of preferences might lead to the same observed behavior (ambiguity problem). [18] demonstrated that 'normative assumptions' are needed to estimate an agent's reward function (in our case, values and norms). In this work,

[6] The x-axis in Fig. 3 relates to the number of rounds used during the initial estimation process, described in Sect. 4.1. The additional number of interactions performed by each method to improve the confidence in the estimations is not included in the x-axis but presented in Fig. 3(c).

[7] In our case OR_a: given that preference to values and norms are constant, demand is defined according to (4))

Table 2. Summary of the results for the estimation using 10 rounds, and for the subsequent ambiguity reduction methods.

Method	Precision	% Unique	Rounds on AR	Standard deviation		
				OR_a	$\hat{di}_a$	$\hat{vw}_a$
Estimation	0.082	57.4	–	36.1	0.021	0.008
AR-SS	0.095	86.7	8.2	42.6	0.011	0.003
AR-C	0.098	83.5	1.8	45.5	0.013	0.003

we proposed an ABM that uses both values and norms to account for these 'normative assumptions', and methods to estimate the SHA preferences and reduce the ambiguity in these estimations.

The first contribution, the proposed ABM, was built on previous works [15,17], and especially [16]. We extended the ABM works to use *both* values and norms for determining the actions of the agents. The model was calibrated to represent human behavior from empirical data. Future works can improve this model by specifying in more detail the use of norms and values, considering other values than wealth and fairness, constraining behavior by using deontic operators [16], and incorporating models that represent human bounded rationality. Furthermore, different application scenarios with a more complex view on value tensions e.g. non-zero sum game problems considering privacy and security can be modeled.

The second contribution of this work was focused on understanding to what extent the proposed methods were able to estimate the relative importance attributed to values and norms by a given agent. We show that even when considering 'normative' assumptions, represented by the PA's knowledge of the decision-making process of the SHA in a relatively simple context (the UG), ambiguity may still be present on estimating preferences for value alignment. To ignore this ambiguity might lead to great regret and unethical actions.

In the experiment performed we observed two general conditions under which an estimation of the preferences was possible, namely: heterogeneity on the observations and a sufficient number of observations. When observing at least four rounds of the UG, only 50 to 60% of the estimations were unambiguous. We proposed two methods for reducing ambiguity: one via exploring the search space ($AR-SS$) and one using counterfactuals ($AR-C$). The first approach, $AR-SS$, interacts with the SHA-P considering the last observed norm (OR_{ak}), which might be suitable for interacting with people in the real world due to the influence of short-term memory on decision making [7]. The latter approach, $AR-C$, uses counterfactuals, which are a part of causal reasoning. The results presented in the previous section show that targeting "imaginative" scenarios related to a specific round of the UG significantly increase the efficiency of the process. Nevertheless, it might be very demanding for a person to be able to go through this thought imaginary process and remind the precise social norm at a specific point in time. We can conclude that the $AR - SS$ method is more suitable where there are no restrictions regarding the number of interactions with the user, while $AR-C$ can improve confidence in situations where a limited number of interactions is desired.

Both methods act with the assumption that the only way the PA can interact with the SHA is by taking the role of the responder in the UG. Going beyond this assumption, we also evaluated a different approach: the PA can directly define a value for the social norm (OR_{ak}). If we consider $OR_a \in [0; 1000]$, the ambiguity was almost eliminated: 97% of unique solutions on average, considering up to 20 interactions. If we consider a more realistic assumption $OR_{ak} \in [500; 1000]$ the results were, in terms of the percentage of unique solutions, between the levels found by $AR - SS$ and $AR - C$ when using less than 6 rounds for training, and slightly better than $AR - SS$ when using 6 or more rounds. Future works can evaluate this hypothesis. We suggest that such experiments be done either considering improved models of human memory and cognition process or in laboratory settings.

The limitations of this works include the impossibility of directly generalizing the findings and methods to other contexts, the assumption that values are stable, and the lack of testing of the approach with humans in realistic settings as well as in more complex settings.

6 Conclusion

This paper aimed to investigate to what extent an AA might be able to estimate the relative preferences attribute to human values and norms, including methods to reduce ambiguity. Insight into the use of models to support the estimation of values and norms was obtained during the discussions, mainly the need for heterogeneity on the observations and also ways to reduce ambiguity. Especially the use of counterfactuals via the $AR - C$ approach showed it can be of great value in terms of a trade-off between increasing efficiency and avoiding excessive interactions/questions with humans. We showed that even in a simple context, considering models that represent values and norms ('normative assumptions'), and using a exhaustive search process, ambiguity cannot be easily be avoided in estimation of preference on values and norms. To ignore this ambiguity might lead to great regret and misalignment between machine behavior and human values and norms.

Acknowledgements. This work was supported by the AiTech initiative of the Delft University of Technology.

References

1. Abbeel, P., Ng, A.Y.: Apprenticeship learning via inverse reinforcement learning. In: Proceedings of the Twenty-First International Conference on Machine Learning (ICML). ACM (2004)
2. Amodei, D., Olah, C., Steinhardt, J., Christiano, P., Schulman, J., Mané, D.: Concrete problems in AI safety. arXiv preprint arXiv:1606.06565 (2016)

3. Cooper, D.J., Dutcher, E.G.: The dynamics of responder behavior in ultimatum games: a meta-study. Exp. Econ. **14**(4), 519–546 (2011)
4. Cranefield, S., Winikoff, M., Dignum, V., Dignum, F.: No pizza for you: value-based plan selection in BDI agents. In: Proceedings of the Twenty-Sixth International Joint Conference on Artificial Intelligence (IJCAI), pp. 178–184 (2017)
5. Crawford, S.E.S., Ostrom, E.: A grammar of institutions. Polit. Sci. **89**(3), 582–600 (2007)
6. Dechesne, F., Di Tosto, G., Dignum, V., Dignum, F.: No smoking here: values, norms and culture in multi-agent systems. Artif. Intell. Law **21**(1), 79–107 (2013)
7. Del Missier, F., Mäntylä, T., Hansson, P., Bruine de Bruin, W., Parker, A.M., Nilsson, L.G.: The multifold relationship between memory and decision making: an individual-differences study. J. Exp. Psychol.: Learn. Mem. Cogn. **39**(5), 1344 (2013)
8. Dignum, V.: Responsible Artificial Intelligence: How to Develop and Use AI in a Responsible Way. Springer, Cham (2019). https://doi.org/10.1007/978-3-030-30371-6
9. Fehr, E., Fischbacher, U.: The nature of human altruism. Nature **425**(6960), 785–791 (2003)
10. Fishbein, M., Ajzen, I.: Predicting and Changing Behavior: The Reasoned Action Approach. Taylor & Francis Ltd, Milton Park (2011)
11. Güth, W., Schmittberger, R., Schwarze, B.: An experimental analysis of ultimatum bargaining. J. Econ. Behav. Organ. **3**(4), 367–388 (1982)
12. Hadfield-Menell, D., Milli, S., Abbeel, P., Russell, S.J., Dragan, A.: Inverse reward design. In: Proceeding of the 31st Conference on Neural Information Processing Systems (NIPS), pp. 6765–6774 (2017)
13. Irving, G., Askell, A.: Ai safety needs social scientists. Distill **4**(2), e14 (2019)
14. Levine, S., Popovic, Z., Koltun, V.: Nonlinear inverse reinforcement learning with gaussian processes. In: Proceeding of the 31st Conference on Neural Information Processing Systèms (NIPS), pp. 19–27 (2011)
15. Malle, B.F.: How the Mind Explains Behavior: Folk Explanations, Meaning, and Social Interaction. MIT Press, Cambridge (2006)
16. Mercuur, R., Dignum, V., Jonker, C.M., et al.: The value of values and norms in social simulation. J. Artif. Soc. Soc. Simul. **22**(1), 1–9 (2019)
17. Miller, T.: Explanation in artificial intelligence: insights from the social sciences. Artif. Intell. **267**, 1–38 (2018)
18. Mindermann, S., Armstrong, S.: Occam's razor is insufficient to infer the preferences of irrational agents. In: Conference on Neural Information Processing Systems (NIPS), pp. 5598–5609 (2018)
19. Nielsen, T.D., Jensen, F.V.: Learning a decision maker's utility function from (possibly) inconsistent behavior. Artif. Intell. **160**(1–2), 53–78 (2004)
20. Nouri, E., Georgila, K., Traum, D.: Culture-specific models of negotiation for virtual characters: multi-attribute decision-making based on culture-specific values. AI Soc. **32**(1), 51–63 (2014). https://doi.org/10.1007/s00146-014-0570-7
21. Oosterbeek, H., Sloof, R., Van De Kuilen, G.: Cultural differences in ultimatum game experiments: evidence from a meta-analysis. SSRN Electron. J. **8**(1), 171–188 (2001)
22. Pearl, J.: The seven tools of causal inference, with reflections on machine learning. Commun. ACM **62**(3), 54–60 (2019)
23. Van de Poel, I., et al.: Ethics, Technology, and Engineering: An Introduction. Wiley, Hoboken (2011)

24. Roese, N.J.: Counterfactual thinking. Psychol. Bull. **121**(1), 133 (1997)
25. Roth, A.E., Erev, I.: Learning in extensive-form games: experimental data and simple dynamic models in the intermediate term. Games Econ. Behav. **8**(1), 164–212 (1995)
26. Schwartz, S.H.: An overview of the Schwartz theory of basic values. Online Read. Psychol. Culture **2**, 1–20 (2012)
27. Soares, N., Fallenstein, B.: Agent foundations for aligning machine intelligence with human interests: a technical research agenda. In: Callaghan, V., Miller, J., Yampolskiy, R., Armstrong, S. (eds.) The Technological Singularity. TFC, pp. 103–125. Springer, Heidelberg (2017). https://doi.org/10.1007/978-3-662-54033-6_5

Should I Tear down This Wall? Optimizing Social Metrics by Evaluating Novel Actions

János Kramár(✉), Neil Rabinowitz, Tom Eccles, and Andrea Tacchetti

Deepmind, London, UK
{janosk,ncr,eccles,atacchet}@google.com

Abstract. One of the fundamental challenges of governance is deciding when and how to intervene in multi-agent systems in order to impact group-wide metrics of success. This is particularly challenging when proposed interventions are novel and expensive. For example, one may wish to modify a building's layout to improve the efficiency of its escape route. Evaluating such interventions would generally require access to an elaborate simulator, which must be constructed ad-hoc for each environment, and can be prohibitively costly or inaccurate. Here we examine a simple alternative: Optimize By Observational Extrapolation (OBOE). The idea is to use observed behavioural trajectories, without any interventions, to learn predictive models mapping environment states to individual agent outcomes, and then use these to evaluate and select changes. We evaluate OBOE in socially complex gridworld environments and consider novel physical interventions that our models were not trained on. We show that neural network models trained to predict agent returns on baseline environments are effective at selecting among the interventions. Thus, OBOE can provide guidance for challenging questions like: "which wall should I tear down in order to minimize the Gini index of this group?"

Keywords: Deep learning · Governance · Interventions · Social modelling · Counterfactuals · Extrapolation

1 Introduction

A key interest in multi-agent research is to understand mechanisms that shift group behaviour towards some desirable goals or outcomes such as using institutions, or central agents, that can modify the environment in real time.

For example, suppose there's a traffic intersection that has inconvenienced many road users with its lengthy wait times and poor visibility, and we're advising a municipal government about whether to intervene, e.g. by installing a roundabout. There can be several desiderata, e.g. we may wish to reduce accidents and congestion.

One way to answer the question is to install the roundabout and measure the metrics of interest. This is scientifically simplest but practically prohibitive. Alternatively, one could simulate the change using a detailed traffic model. The

A. Aler Tubella et al. (Eds.): COIN 2017/COINE 2020, LNAI 12298, pp. 114–130, 2021.
https://doi.org/10.1007/978-3-030-72376-7_7

model may need to make substantial assumptions that might be broken by unanticipated circumstances, such as weather conditions, or unusual road users like electric scooters, etc. Further, designing and adjusting the simulator is a significant up-front research cost. Instead, the strategy we propose is to exploit the abundance of observational data (such as traffic patterns across a set of urban environments) and avoid relying on expensive experimental data (in which the intervention is tried, in either reality or simulation).

Our contribution is a method, which we call OBOE (Optimize By Observational Extrapolation), for building a central agent tasked with altering the physical environment where a group of agents interact, in pursuit of a group-level outcome. We construct this central agent by training a model to predict forward outcomes for each agent (e.g. forward returns) from environment states using purely observational data. Our central agent then uses these models to evaluate candidate interventions in real-time by modifying a snapshot of the environment, and selecting the intervention that produces the best result as estimated by the predictive model, and in terms of the desired outcome metric.

We evaluate our method on two socially complex grid-world environments, a variety of candidate interventions, and consider various model architectures. Our results show that predictive models trained on observational data can identify interventions that lead to desirable outcomes, and are thus well suited to build the central agent we set out to design. In some cases, we find that the resulting OBOE central agent is more effective than a simulation-based central agent that selects an intervention using multiple perfect (but stochastic) simulations of the environment.

2 Related Work

Multi-agent reinforcement learning has received considerable attention in recent years, both as a training paradigm to construct powerful individual agents [2,3, 35], and as a tool to study the role and emergence of human pro-social inductive biases and institutions in complex environments [20,25,26,32]. In this context, the idea of "opponent shaping", that is, constructing agents that actively influence the learning and behavior of others through conditional cooperation, or assuming the role of a central mechanism, has emerged as a key challenge to investigate [3,6,15, 22,27,30]. Unlike past work in this area, we investigate how to train such a central mechanism by generalizing entirely from observational data.

The recent advances of multi-agent reinforcement learning, and the challenges posed by agents that interact with other non/stationary, adaptive learners has sparked interest in "machine theory of mind" [33], as well as in the development of sophisticated behavioral models of multi-agent systems, often based on relational architectures [5,19,24,36]. We build on this work, adapting it for use as a central agent to achieve social goals.

The idea of changing elements of multi-agent environments so as to shepherd the behavior of groups towards outcomes that are desirable for the designer is a well-studied problem in economics. In particular, the sub-field of mechanism design has focused on analyzing the effects of changing payoff structures and reward signals, especially in the context of auction design [9,29,38]. Our work addresses these questions in the case where the mechanism is physical and where the agent behaviours are learned rather than perfectly rational – however it does not address how learning agents might change their policies in response to the central agent, which is a limitation.

In recent years there has been work on learning to simulate physical systems [34], make counterfactual physical predictions [4], and learn physical controllers [17]. Our work builds on this line of thought, targeting the challenges posed by a multiagent setting.

Finally, a number of researchers have investigated the effects of modifying the physical environment so as to promote or dissuade certain group behavior, especially in the context of pedestrian modeling and sheep herding [8,10,23,28]. We address this question in a broader context where the behavioural models must be learned rather than hand-coded.

3 Method and Experimental Set-Up

We introduce OBOE, a new method to construct a central agent that can optimize social metrics by intervening in the physical environment. Importantly, we assume that it is either hard or impossible to simulate the effects of these interventions, and therefore it is desirable to learn to estimate their efficacy based solely on an observational dataset, i.e. from trajectories of agents interacting in the environment, without any intervention whatsoever.

The OBOE method will proceed in 2 stages. In Sect. 3.1 we describe the dataset; then in Sect. 3.2 we describe the construction of the central agent. Following those subsections we'll describe the evaluation procedure. In Sect. 3.3 we describe how we generate a complete evaluation dataset of all possible interventions, and in Sect. 3.4 we describe how we use this dataset to identify which tasks are most suitable for evaluating the central agent.

Note that the training of the central agent in Sects. 3.1–3.2 and its evaluation in Sects. 3.3–3.4 are separate procedures. Evaluation requires counterfactual data for all possible interventions, which are not generally available in practice. For the purposes of this paper, we provide the ground truth counterfactual data (from additional simulations) for estimating the maximum achievable effect by a central agent. It's possible to validate our central agent itself much more economically, by only gathering data according to its prescribed interventions.

In our experiments we simplify the task for the central agent by only considering single interventions at a fixed timestep; this already pushes OBOE into new territory and gives a good indication of its promise, while still making it easy to generate a full evaluation dataset. The same central agents could also be used to intervene at multiple timesteps per episode.

3.1 Collect Observational Dataset

We first need to select environments and collect a dataset of many episodes, with no central agent nor interventions. Our environments and players are described in Sect. 4 and detailed further in Appendix B; in brief, we trained players with multi-agent reinforcement learning [25] on some Markov social dilemma games.

3.2 Construct a Central Agent

We consider a central agent whose objective is to optimise an episode social metric of interest M, which is computed per-episode as a function of individual agent' outcomes aggregated across the episode. In our environments these outcomes are the total returns across the episode: for agent i, we write this as $R_i = \sum_{t=1}^{T} r_i^t$, where r_i^t is reward. We can then write the metric as $M(R_1, \ldots, R_k)$. For example, the collective return is $M(R_1, \ldots, R_k) = \sum_i R_i$. We also need the representation of environment states s to let us construct intervention functions $s'_a(s)$ for each possible intervention a (e.g., build a wall) in the central agent's action space (Fig. 1).

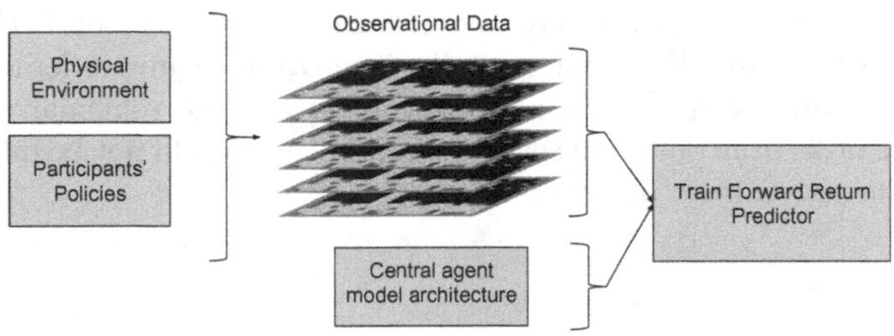

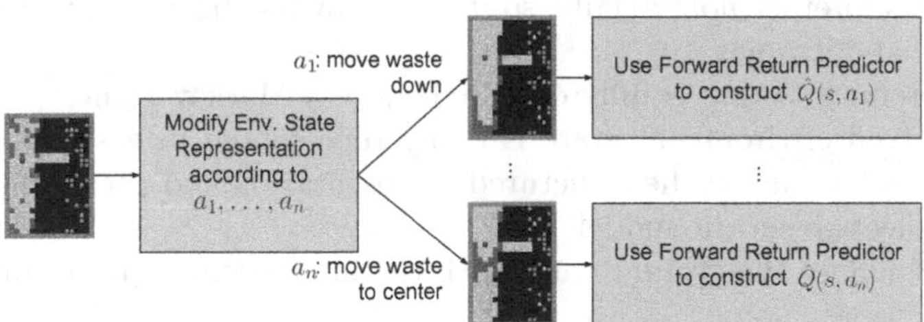

Fig. 1. An illustration of the OBOE method, with an example "move waste" intervention on the Cleanup game.

We use the observational dataset from Sect. 3.1 to train a forward return predictor[1] (or in general, forward aggregated outcome predictor) $\hat{R}^{>t}(s_t; i)$ (where

[1] This requires a model; we discuss model choices in Sect. 6.

the environment state s_t includes the timestep t, as well as the returns $R_i^{\leq t}(s_t)$ so far for agent i). Now, we can combine this with the intervention functions to estimate the central agent's action-value function $Q(s, a)$, i.e. the metric value that would result from the intervention a, as $\hat{Q}(s_t, a) = M(\hat{R}^{>t}(s'_a(s_t); 1) + R_1^{\leq t}(s_t), \ldots, \hat{R}^{>t}(s'_a(s_t); k) + R_k^{\leq t}(s_t))$. We propose a central agent policy that selects actions greedily according to this $\hat{Q}$.

3.3 Collect Evaluation Dataset

In order to evaluate the central agent, we collect an evaluation dataset. We record new trajectories of game play using, as before, our trained policies for participant agents. Importantly, however, here we do modify the environment state according to all possible interventions, and collect the various outcomes. With this data, we can compare the intervention selected via $\hat{Q}(s, a)$ to other possible actions, and evaluate the central agent.

3.4 Task Filtering

Finally, we use this second dataset to detect intervention families that result in no effect on social outcomes, or where the same intervention is always best. In applications it would be appropriate to detect such tasks and handle them more straightforwardly than OBOE; for example, it may not require a detailed model to predict that adding speed bumps will decrease average vehicular speed. We remove these tasks from our analysis as well, since they would not be informative. This procedure is outlined in detail in Sect. 5.

4 Tasks

In order to test the OBOE method, we need suitable tasks, where:

- The agents interact nontrivially, so it's not obvious how an intervention will affect social outcomes.
- The environment state is fully observed, as in a Markov game.
- The observed environment state is easily represented in a structured form, so we can intervene on the structured representation and get predicted intervention effects from the model.
- We can simulate the ground truth with the interventions (for evaluation).

We use two spatiotemporal social dilemma games which meet the above criteria: Cleanup, and Harvest. [12,20,22,31,40] In particular, the social outcomes are nontrivial to predict, both because the games pose social dilemmas to the players, and because the players are trained via deep RL. These games allowed us to construct several qualitatively different sorts of interventions, which was another desired criterion. The way the players were trained is detailed in Appendix B. While these games and players were adequate for our purposes, they're not special; OBOE is equally applicable in settings quite unlike them.

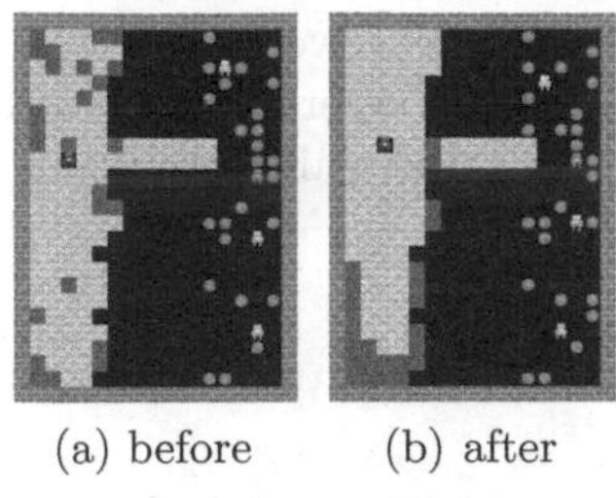

(a) before (b) after

Fig. 2. A "move waste" intervention for the Cleanup game.

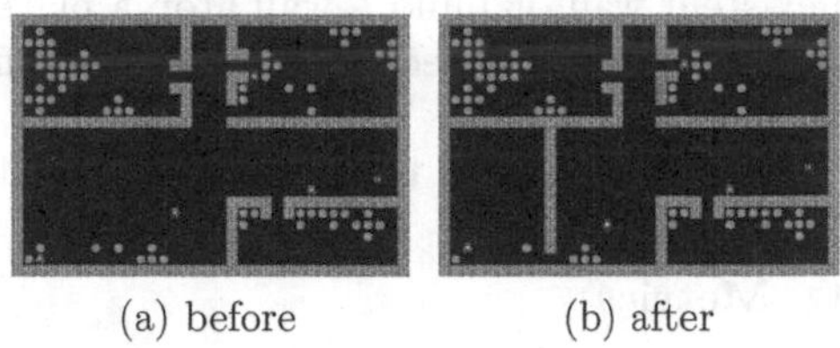

(a) before (b) after

Fig. 3. An "add wall" intervention for the Harvest game.

Cleanup: Cleanup (Fig. 2) is a public goods game in which 5 players collect apples from a field (right side), which grow only if the players collectively keep the waste accumulating in the aquifer (left side) at a low enough level, by cleaning it up. The simple primary objective of players in Cleanup is to collect as many apples as they can. However, the mechanics of the environment place players in a socially complex world: if the waste level is low, it's in each player's individual interest to remain in the field collecting apples. This neglect causes waste to accumulate, which negatively impacts the future apple spawn rate. This intricate dependency poses a dilemma between free-riding (collecting apples) and looking after the public good (cleaning the aquifer), which the players need to navigate.

Interventions: We consider three types of intervention for a central agent to make partway through a Cleanup game, at time 325 (out of 1000): 1) moving players (to one of 7 predefined locations[2], 2) moving waste (falling up, down, left, right, or towards the vertical center, among the aquifer map locations), and 3) moving apples (similarly to moving waste, but among the field locations). A "move waste" intervention is illustrated in Fig. 2.

Harvest: Harvest (Fig. 3) is a common pool resource game. As in Cleanup, the players collect apples from fields; but in Harvest, the apples only respawn if there are other intact apples nearby. The fields are located in corner rooms of the map, which is procedurally generated; and players can guard their rooms by firing a punishment beam at each other. In Harvest, players face a dilemma between their short- and long-term interests: if they don't distribute their harvesting across space or time, they deplete the apple stock, which may not recover; if they move around too much, other players will collect most apples.

Interventions: We considered two types of intervention in Harvest: adding walls, and removing walls, both at time 30[3] (out of 1000). Since the underlying map

[2] (1, 1), (1, 23), (16, 1), (16, 23), (9, 1), (9, 9), and (9, 23) on the 18×25 map.

[3] The timestep was chosen to be early so that apple areas would not yet be depleted (making the interventions more relevant), but not at the very start when player locations would be less typical.

is variable, we couldn't use a fixed set of interventions lest we tear down a nonexistent wall or build a wall atop a player, so we instead queried the central agent on 15 valid, procedurally generated candidates. An "add wall" intervention is illustrated in Fig. 3.

More details about the games are provided in Appendix B.

4.1 Metrics

To construct tasks for the central agent, we combine each of these 5 classes of intervention with 4 social outcomes, based on maximizing or minimizing. Two metrics are taken across each episode: the collective return, and the Gini index [16] (an inequality measure).[4] This gives a total of 20 intervention tasks for the central agent. Table 1 shows the mean metric values among the observational data; equivalently, these give the absolute performance of a "no-op" central agent.

Table 1. A summary of the interventions on the 2 games.

	Cleanup	Harvest
Maps	Standard	Procedural (rooms)
Baseline mean metrics	Collective return 1570.2 Gini index 0.1966	Collective return 584.6 Gini index 0.3139
Interventions	at $t = 325$ of 1000: – move players (each of the 5 players, to 7 fixed locations[a]) – move waste (up, down, left, right, center) – move apples (similarly)	at $t = 30$ of 1000: – add walls (15 random options provided) – remove walls (15 random options provided)

[a] (1, 1), (1, 23), (16, 1), (16, 23), (9, 1), (9, 9), and (9, 23) on the 18×25 map.

5 Task Analysis and Filtering

In this section we outline a brief analysis of the 20 intervention tasks just described. Our main goal here is to filter out tasks that do not probe the central agent's ability to consider and evaluate modifications to the physical environment in pursuit of an effect on some social outcome. In particular, we seek to select out tasks that fail to meet two intuitive standards:

1. It should be possible, by modifying the physical environment in the ways prescribed (e.g. by moving agents or adding walls), to affect the social outcome of interest (e.g. to maximize the welfare of our agents). In other words, we wish to prune out those tasks for which even an "ideal" central agent cannot help the situation better than by selecting a random action.

[4] Because the Gini index is nonlinear, strictly speaking the method of Sect. 3.2 will produce a biased result even if the forward return predictors are unbiased. We disregard this issue.

2. We are only interested in tasks where the optimal action depends on the environment state; for example, if we found that for a specific metric, no matter the state of the game, it's always best to move agents to the top left corner, we would filter out this task.

Here we describe the selection process, and the details of how we constructed three baseline central agents: an "ideal" one, a "random" one and a "constant action" one. These are constructed using an evaluation dataset with game episodes for both environments we consider (4×250 for Cleanup[5], 5000 for Harvest), in which every possible intervention was tried.

The "Random" Central Agent: We measured the average outcome of all possible interventions in each scenario.

The "Constant Action" Central Agent: We measured the performance of each intervention across all recorded episodes, and selected the intervention whose average was best[6]. We highlight that in Cleanup the interventions are defined across episodes (e.g. "move waste up"), whereas in Harvest the only consistent constant intervention is "do nothing", because the "add wall" and "remove wall" locations are procedurally generated.

The "Ideal", or "CV" Central Agent: As in OBOE, this central agent was constructed to select the candidate intervention based on its predicted effect on social outcomes. However, instead of extrapolating using a model, we used the *true environment simulator*: that is, we selected the best intervention according to the actual environment trajectories we recorded. Since both games and participants' policies are stochastic, doing this naïvely results in a selection bias; we eliminated this bias by using cross-validation. For every intervention we considered, we generated 5 different post-intervention completions of the episode by altering a random seed that's used for sampling from the players' stochastic policies. One of the 5 trajectories was used for evaluation, and the other 4 were used to produce an unbiased estimate of the social outcome (by averaging).

The CV central agent provides an interesting benchmark. It reflects the performance we'd expect if we had access to a perfect simulator of the interventions, and a reasonable (if naïve) budget to run such simulations. This allows us to select out tasks for which even an "ideal" agent cannot do better than random, or better than a "constant action" agent, and to put other central agents' performance into context. In Table 2 we present the achieved effect for each task[7] (relative to choosing no intervention) of selecting using the CV central agent, versus these other baselines. To conduct the task filtering, the table indicates for each task whether the CV central agent outperformed the baselines with statistical significance (at level $\alpha = 0.05$).

[5] Corresponding to the different player populations; see Appendix B.1.
[6] This creates a small selection bias.
[7] The "move apples" tasks in Cleanup were excluded because even the CV central agent could not produce any significant effect.

Table 2. Filtering intervention tasks. Each intervention task is determined by a game, a class of interventions (which always includes the null intervention), a social metric, and a direction to optimize the metric. For each task, we compare the mean effect of the CV central agent with two baselines. Where we have statistically significant evidence that CV outperforms both (at level $\alpha = 0.05$), we highlight the CV result; where we don't, we highlight the baseline(s) it didn't significantly outperform, with red for the random baseline (suggesting the intervention may have no effect at all) and yellow for the constant baseline (suggesting it may not be possible to do better than selecting the same intervention every time).

Cleanup[a]	move players (36 choices)				move waste (6 choices)			
	collective		Gini index		collective		Gini index	
	min	max	min	max	min	max	min	max
Random	−4.5	−4.5	0.0026	0.0026	6.8	6.8	0.0001	0.0001
Best constant	−54.6	11.3	−0.0023	0.0295	−5.2	29.1	−0.0004	0.0015
CV	−71.8	12.6	−0.0039	0.0481	−14.1	23.6	−0.0004	0.0005
Harvest	add walls (16 choices)				remove walls (16 choices)			
	collective		Gini index		collective		Gini index	
	min	max	min	max	min	max	min	max
Random	−1.5	−1.5	0.0152	0.0152	12.9	12.9	−0.0007	−0.0007
Null	0	0	0	0	0	0	0	0
CV	−99.1	71.2	−0.0219	0.0993	3.1	37.8	−0.0093	0.0092

[a] The "move apples" tasks in Cleanup were excluded because even the CV central agent could not produce any significant effect.

6 Models

As described in Sect. 3.2, we construct the central agent using models that predict the forward returns of each player, given a time step observation of the games. We use three architectures: two ubiquitous ones (a convolutional neural network (CNN) and a multi-layer perceptron (MLP)), and a Relational Forward Model (RFM) [36], chosen because it captures multi-agent interactions well and its structured input representation makes it easy to construct interventions. Details about model hyperparameters and training are provided in Appendix A. The three architectures call for slightly different input representations.

- For the RFM, we use a graph representation whose nodes are the individual agents as well as the potentially active map locations (all locations for Harvest, apple and waste locations for Cleanup). The node features are: x and y position, a one-hot for the non-agent content of the map location (for Cleanup: clean water, dirty water, empty field, apple; for Harvest: empty field, apple, wall, empty space), the player's identity (for Cleanup, i.e. prosocial or

antisocial; see Appendix B.1), the last action and reward, and the player orientation. The graph contains edges from every node to every agent node, and no input edge features are provided. Further, there is a single global feature: the timestep. All features are whitened to have mean zero and standard deviation 1.
- For the MLP, we use an input representation that contains all of the nodes' features, and the global feature, encoded as a concatenated vector.
- For the CNN, we provide separate channels for the agent node features, the non-agent node features, the global feature (timestep), and a channel that indicates which agent to predict forward return for.

7 Results

In Sect. 7.1 we describe the outcome of the task filtering we laid out in Sect. 5. In Sect. 7.2 we briefly compare the models in terms of their predictive performance on the validation subset of the observational data. In Sect. 7.3 we'll combine these tasks and models, establishing the resulting OBOE central agents' success on the filtered tasks.

It's useful to note that while the task filtering is useful here (because we don't know a priori what to expect from these interventions), we are only using the CV agent as a source of additional validation. The CV agent allows us to measure performance relative to an estimated optimum, but measuring the OBOE agents' performance in absolute terms would only require data for their selected interventions, rather than for all candidate interventions (as CV does).

7.1 Tasks

Before turning our attention to the trained models and resulting central agents, we review Table 2, in which we probe tasks by comparing the CV central agent with naïve baseline agents. On one of the tasks (5 including the "move apple" interventions[8]), the CV agent doesn't significantly beat a random baseline, so it may not be possible to achieve the desired social outcome using the available interventions. For an additional 4 tasks, there was a constant-intervention baseline that the CV agent couldn't significantly beat. This leaves 11 tasks (4 in Cleanup, and 7 of the 8 in Harvest) where we have evidence that the task meets the standards laid out in Sect. 5; we call these the *significant tasks*.

[8] The "move apples" tasks in Cleanup were excluded because even the CV central agent could not produce any significant effect.

7.2 Models

Following, we focus on the performance of the central agent design we propose. We trained models as described in Sect. 6, selecting the ones for each architecture that achieve lowest validation MSE on forward returns; the validation losses are displayed in Table 3.

Table 3. Best validation loss for each architecture in Sect. 6.

	MLP	RFM	CNN
Cleanup	775	757	748
Harvest	1485	1291	1205

All models achieved comparable validation loss on the no-intervention datasets. For each dataset, the convolutional model achieved lowest loss, followed by the relational model.

Table 4. Mean performance of the OBOE central agents on each task, with the random baseline and CV benchmark. The RFM OBOE agent always outperformed the random baseline – the other OBOE agents were worse than random on 2 tasks each.

Intervention class		Task		Mean intervention effect				
Game	Type			Random	CV	OBOE		
						MLP	RFM	CNN
Cleanup	Move players	Min	Collective return	−4.5	−71.8	−60.6	**−96.7**	−95.0
		Min	Gini index	0.0026	−0.0039	−0.0002	−0.0034	**−0.0050**
		Max	Gini index	0.0026	0.0481	0.0198	0.0464	**0.0485**
	Move waste	Min	Collective return	6.8	−14.1	−8.5	−7.8	**−19.8**
Harvest	Add wall	Min	Collective return	−1.5	−99.1	−12.1	−26.0	**−26.3**
		Max	Collective return	−1.5	71.2	6.5	**13.4**	0.0
		Min	Gini index	0.0152	−0.0219	0.0156	**0.0028**	0.0185
		Max	Gini index	0.0152	0.0993	0.0240	**0.0433**	0.0262
	Remove wall	Max	Collective return	12.9	37.8	31.2	**44.4**	42.3
		Min	Gini index	−0.0007	−0.0093	**−0.0138**	−0.0054	−0.0032
		Max	Gini index	−0.0007	0.0092	−0.0025	**0.0041**	−0.0036

7.3 Central Agents

Finally, we evaluate the OBOE central agents constructed using these models, on each of the significant tasks. In order to normalize the performance across the tasks, we compute a normalized score as:

$$\textit{effectiveness} = \frac{\bar{M}_{CA} - \bar{M}_{random}}{\bar{M}_{CV} - \bar{M}_{random}},$$

where $\bar{M}_{CA}$ is the sample mean of the metric M achieved by a central agent CA for a specific task. Figure 4 shows the mean cross-task effectiveness of each model; Table 4 shows a full breakdown of the mean effects.

Note that this is a very limited set of games and settings, so we can't generalise any conclusions from comparing the model architectures. Instead the main comparison of interest is between CV (which uses simulations to make an unbiased estimate of each intervention's effect) and the OBOE central agents (which use a learned model to extrapolate from observational data); the striking result is that the OBOE agents are able to do 56% as well on average as the CV central agent, even though the former are being applied outside their training distributions, and the latter has access to targeted ground-truth simulations.

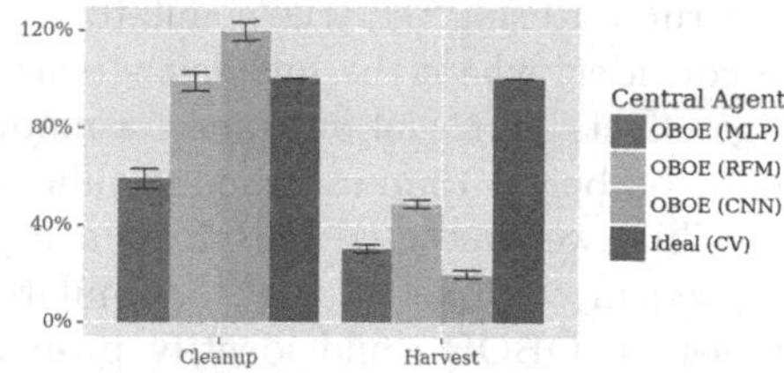

Fig. 4. Average percent effectiveness relative to CV, across significant tasks. The error bars indicate standard error.

8 Discussion and Future Work

We introduced OBOE, a novel, widely applicable method for constructing a central agent that selects modifications to a physical environment with multiple interacting agents, to maximize social metrics. In environments where it's prohibitively expensive to test out modifications, or run high-quality simulations of them, OBOE learns from observational data (i.e., recordings of the environment in which no intervention has been made), and constructs a state-action Q-function that predicts the effects of physical interventions on the social metric of interest.

We validated OBOE on a range of tasks consisting of different social metrics and games, using different candidate interventions and predictive architectures. Averaging across all of these, OBOE was 56% as effective as an estimated ideal central agent that was able to perfectly test each modification multiple times.

Notably, our constructed Q-function is a causal effect estimate based on correlations in the training set. It's worth discussing why this can work. The main principle is: if the environment (including players) is Markov then causal effects on future outcomes are equal to conditional expectations of those outcomes on the intervention timestep, and if the interventions are within the training distribution then a well-trained model will have low prediction error on them.

In our experiments we relied on two environments, using four families of candidate interventions which were effective in shifting the metrics. The environments were approximately Markov (with the only non-stationarity being the players' recurrent neural network states). However, the interventions were outside the training distribution to varying degrees (e.g. there are no free-floating walls in the training distribution), so the models needed to extrapolate using their inductive biases.

It is worth briefly discussing how actions picked using our model can sometimes lead to a better outcome than actions selected using cross-validation (i.e.

constructed using the true simulator as a model). In the high-variance settings we consider, where the inherent stochasticity of individual agents' policies has large effects on social outcomes, a model trained on large and diverse datasets might be better than unbiased simulators that only consider a few realizations.

While we presented OBOE as a replacement for a simulator, it could also be used in conjunction with a simulator that's accurate but expensive to run or design; OBOE could identify promising interventions quickly using a neural network forward pass, permitting better use of the simulation budget. The advantage would be increased if the environment had substantial stochasticity or if there was a larger action space to search through, requiring more simulations.

A requirement for OBOE is that the observational dataset contain the social outcomes of interest. This may be a limitation in settings where these outcomes are not measurable. This limitation could be addressed by learning agent reward functions or other designer preferences; however, this falls outside the scope of the current work.

Another limitation is that because OBOE extrapolates from existing agent behaviours, agents may strategically adapt their behaviours in response to the central agent in a way that violates OBOE's assumptions. This may be mitigated if similarly adapted behaviours can be incorporated in the observational dataset.

In the broader context of multi-agent research and simulation, OBOE constitutes an important tool to evaluate the effects planned modifications to the environment might have on complex social metrics.

Appendix A Model Details

Here we describe hyperparameters and training for the models in Sect. 3.

The RFM is constituted of an "edge block" ReLU MLP that computes a representation for each edge given the global and adjacent node features, feeding into a "node block" ReLU MLP that computes a representation for each node given the existing node features, global features, and incoming edge features. In the case of Cleanup, we used batch size 640; edge MLP layer sizes 64, 32, 32; and node MLP layer sizes 64, 32, 32, 1. In the case of Harvest, we used batch size 160; edge MLP layer sizes 5×128; and node MLP layer sizes 5×128, 1.[9]

For the MLP models, we again used batch size 640 for Cleanup and 160 for Harvest. The layer sizes for Cleanup were 64, 32, 32, 5, while for Harvest they were 128, 128, 128, 128, 5. (The final 5 corresponds to the 5 players.)

For the CNN models, we used batch size 160 and kernel sizes 3×3. For Cleanup, we used 8 layers, with channel counts 2×64, 3×128, 3×256, with strides 1, 1, $2 \times (2, 1, 1)$. For Harvest, we used 5 layers, with channel counts 2×64, 3×128, with strides 1, 1, 2, 1, 1. Each layer was followed by a batch normalizer and a ReLU activation, and the final layer was followed by an average pooling layer and a linear layer.

[9] The final 1 indicates that there is only one scalar prediction for each node; predictions for non-player nodes are ignored.

For learning the model parameters we used an RMSProp [37] optimizer with learning rate 10^{-4}, for $2.5 \cdot 10^6$ steps, or until convergence. Approximately $2 \cdot 10^5$ episodes of data were in the training set for each game; the validation set for each was 1000 episodes. The optimization criterion in every case was the mean squared error relative to the true forward returns of the players in the given episodes.

Appendix B Tasks

B.1 Cleanup: Game and Agents

Cleanup is a played on an 18×25 map, in which 5 players collect apples (each worth +1 reward) from a field. The field is sustained by a connected aquifer on which waste appears at a constant rate. The apple spawn rate falls linearly with the amount of waste in the aquifer, up to a saturation point where apples do not spawn. At the start of each game episode, no apples are present, and the waste level is just beyond saturation.

Each game episode runs for 1000 time steps. At each timestep, players observe a 15×15 RGB window centered at their position and orientation. Agents can move around or fire a "fining beam" or "cleanup beam", both of which have limited range. The fining beam gives -50 reward to a player that's within range if there is one, and -1 reward to the player using it. The cleanup beam removes waste within its range.

Standard RL algorithms for this task don't find a policy that responds effectively to the dilemma between collecting apples and tending to the public good [20]. Since this particular issue is outside the scope of this work, we side-stepped it by letting some agents be intrinsically motivated to clean the aquifer. Specifically, we trained 2 policies with additional reward per unit of waste cleaned: a "prosocial" policy that would receive +1, and an "antisocial" policy that would receive -1. These were co-trained using episodes in which players were randomly assigned them in a 1:4, 2:3, 3:2, or 4:1 proportion, using A2C [14]. After convergence, these populations behave in a sensible way in the environment and, as a group, collect close to the optimal number of apples in each episode.

B.2 Harvest: Game, Procedural Generation, and Agents

Harvest is a common pool resource game on a 35×23 map. In Harvest, the apple spawn rate in each field location depends on the number of nearby apples, and falls to zero once there are no apples within a certain radius. Each player's observations and actions are as in Cleanup, except there is no cleanup beam, the fining beam gives a reward of -30 to the target agent, and agents are not visually distinguishable (i.e. all agents appear red to other agents, and blue to themselves).

The maps were procedurally generated to have corner rooms of varying size enclosed by walls, sometimes perforated or absent. The exact procedure is as follows. Each corner of the map has a room, randomly assigned height 6 or 9 and width 12 or 15. For each room, we generate walls; 20% of the time, the wall will be "perforated" by letting each wall location remain as a hole with 10% probability. Next we add an entrance corridor to each room, as in Fig. 3; the location of the entrance must be a wall location that isn't in a corner or adjacent to a hole. (If no such locations exist, we don't add an entrance.) We then generate apple locations: we randomly choose 6% of eligible locations (rounded down), and add apples at those locations plus their immediate neighbours. All in-room locations are eligible apart from walls, holes, and entrance corridors. Finally, with 30% probability we randomly sample 1 or 2 (depending on whether height is 6 or 9) eligible locations as player spawn locations, and remove all of the walls. After this has been done for each room, we adjust the number of player spawn locations to 5, by either subsampling, or sampling from the non-room map locations.

In all other respects, the Cleanup and Harvest games are as published at [39].

In Harvest, we considered two types of intervention: adding walls, and removing walls, at time 30. As discussed in Sect. 4, these were procedurally generated to ensure they are valid. This was done by starting from a random suitable map location (wall for removing, non-wall non-player for adding), randomly choosing whether to extend horizontally or vertically, and then randomly choosing how far to extend in that direction. For removing, the length to extend in each direction was chosen uniformly between 0 and the maximum reachable amount of wall. For adding, the maximum length was broken into 3 partitions using a Dirichlet-multinomial distribution with parameters $(\frac{1}{2}, 2, \frac{1}{2})$, and the middle one was used as the wall segment.

As with Cleanup, standard RL algorithms can't find a sustainable policy for Harvest [20] so we modified the environment slightly: in our agent training, if a player moves to collect an apple with $k < 3$ apples within distance 2, collection would fail with probability 2^{-k}.

References

1. André, E., Koenig, S., Dastani, M., Sukthankar, G. (eds.): Proceedings of the 17th International Conference on Autonomous Agents and MultiAgent Systems (2018)
2. Baker, B., et al.: Emergent tool use from multi-agent autocurricula. CoRR abs/1909.07528 (2019)
3. Balduzzi, D., Tuyls, K., Pérolat, J., Graepel, T.: Re-evaluating evaluation. In: Bengio et al. [7], pp. 3272–3283
4. Baradel, F., Neverova, N., Mille, J., Mori, G., Wolf, C.: Cophy: counterfactual learning of physical dynamics. In: International Conference on Learning Representations (2020)
5. Battaglia, P.W., et al.: Relational inductive biases, deep learning, and graph networks. CoRR abs/1806.01261 (2018)
6. Baumann, T., Graepel, T., Shawe-Taylor, J.: Adaptive mechanism design: learning to promote cooperation. CoRR abs/1806.04067 (2018)
7. Bengio, S., Wallach, H.M., Larochelle, H., Grauman, K., Cesa-Bianchi, N., Garnett, R. (eds.): Advances in Neural Information Processing Systems 31 (2018)

8. Bennett, B., Trafankowski, M.: A comparative investigation of herding algorithms. In: Proceedings of Symposium on Understanding and Modelling Collective Phenomena (UMoCoP), pp. 33–38 (2012)
9. Conitzer, V., Sandholm, T.: Complexity of mechanism design. In: Darwiche, A., Friedman, N. (eds.) UAI 2002, Proceedings of the 18th Conference in Uncertainty in Artificial Intelligence, pp. 103–110 (2002)
10. Cowling, P.I., Gmeinwieser, C.: AI for herding sheep. In: Youngblood, G.M., Bulitko, V. (eds.) Proceedings of the Sixth AAAI Conference on Artificial Intelligence and Interactive Digital Entertainment. The AAAI Press (2010)
11. Dy, J.G., Krause, A. (eds.): Proceedings of the 35th International Conference on Machine Learning. PMLR (2018)
12. Eccles, T., Hughes, E., Kramár, J., Wheelwright, S., Leibo, J.Z.: The imitation game: Learned reciprocity in Markov games. In: Elkind et al. [13], pp. 1934–1936
13. Elkind, E., Veloso, M., Agmon, N., Taylor, M.E. (eds.): Proceedings of the 18th International Conference on Autonomous Agents and MultiAgent Systems (2019)
14. Espeholt, L., et al.: IMPALA: scalable distributed deep-RL with importance weighted actor-learner architectures. In: Dy and Krause [11], pp. 1406–1415
15. Foerster, J.N., Chen, R.Y., Al-Shedivat, M., Whiteson, S., Abbeel, P., Mordatch, I.: Learning with opponent-learning awareness. In: André et al. [1], pp. 122–130
16. Gini, C.: Variabilità e mutabilità. Reprinted in Memorie di metodologica statistica (Ed. Pizetti E, Salvemini, T). Libreria Eredi Virgilio Veschi, Rome (1912)
17. Grzeszczuk, R., Terzopoulos, D., Hinton, G.E.: Neuroanimator: fast neural network emulation and control of physics-based models. In: Cunningham, S., Bransford, W., Cohen, M.F. (eds.) Proceedings of the 25th Annual Conference on Computer Graphics and Interactive Techniques, pp. 9–20. ACM (1998)
18. Guyon, I., et al. (eds.): Advances in Neural Information Processing Systems 30 (2017)
19. Hoshen, Y.: VAIN: attentional multi-agent predictive modeling. In: Guyon et al. [18], pp. 2701–2711
20. Hughes, E., et al.: Inequity aversion improves cooperation in intertemporal social dilemmas. In: Bengio et al. [7], pp. 3330–3340
21. 7th International Conference on Learning Representations, ICLR 2019, New Orleans, LA, USA, 6–9 May 2019. OpenReview.net (2019)
22. Jaques, N., et al.: Social influence as intrinsic motivation for multi-agent deep reinforcement learning. In: Chaudhuri, K., Salakhutdinov, R. (eds.) Proceedings of the 36th International Conference on Machine Learning. Proceedings of Machine Learning Research, vol. 97, pp. 3040–3049. PMLR (2019)
23. Jiang, Z., Fan, W., Liu, W., Zhu, B., Gu, J.: Reinforcement learning approach for coordinated passenger inflow control of urban rail transit in peak hours. Transp. Res. Part C: Emerg. Technol. **88**, 1–16 (2018)
24. Kipf, T.N., Fetaya, E., Wang, K., Welling, M., Zemel, R.S.: Neural relational inference for interacting systems. In: Dy and Krause [11], pp. 2693–2702
25. Leibo, J.Z., Zambaldi, V.F., Lanctot, M., Marecki, J., Graepel, T.: Multi-agent reinforcement learning in sequential social dilemmas. In: Larson, K., Winikoff, M., Das, S., Durfee, E.H. (eds.) Proceedings of the 16th Conference on Autonomous Agents and MultiAgent Systems, pp. 464–473. ACM (2017)
26. Lerer, A., Peysakhovich, A.: Maintaining cooperation in complex social dilemmas using deep reinforcement learning. CoRR abs/1707.01068 (2017)
27. Letcher, A., Foerster, J.N., Balduzzi, D., Rocktäschel, T., Whiteson, S.: Stable opponent shaping in differentiable games. In: ICLR 2019 [21]

28. Martinez-Gil, F., Lozano, M., Fernández, F.: MARL-Ped: a multi-agent reinforcement learning based framework to simulate pedestrian groups. Simul. Model. Pract. Theory **47**, 259–275 (2014)
29. Mas-Colell, A., Whinston, M., Green, J.: Microeconomic Theory. Oxford University Press, Oxford (1995)
30. Mguni, D., Jennings, J., Sison, E., Macua, S.V., Ceppi, S., de Cote, E.M.: Coordinating the crowd: inducing desirable equilibria in non-cooperative systems. In: Elkind et al. [13], pp. 386–394
31. Pérolat, J., Leibo, J.Z., Zambaldi, V.F., Beattie, C., Tuyls, K., Graepel, T.: A multi-agent reinforcement learning model of common-pool resource appropriation. In: Guyon et al. [18], pp. 3643–3652
32. Peysakhovich, A., Lerer, A.: Prosocial learning agents solve generalized stag hunts better than selfish ones. In: André et al. [1], pp. 2043–2044
33. Rabinowitz, N.C., Perbet, F., Song, H.F., Zhang, C., Eslami, S.M.A., Botvinick, M.: Machine theory of mind. In: Dy and Krause [11], pp. 4215–4224
34. Sanchez-Gonzalez, A., Godwin, J., Pfaff, T., Ying, R., Leskovec, J., Battaglia, P.W.: Learning to simulate complex physics with graph networks. CoRR abs/2002.09405 (2020)
35. Silver, D., et al.: Mastering the game of go with deep neural networks and tree search. Nature **529**(7587), 484–489 (2016)
36. Tacchetti, A., et al.: Relational forward models for multi-agent learning. In: ICLR 2019 [21]
37. Tieleman, T., Hinton, G.: Lecture 6.5-rmsprop: divide the gradient by a running average of its recent magnitude. COURSERA: Neural Netw. Mach. Learn. **4**(2), 26–31 (2012)
38. Varian, H.R.: Economic mechanism design for computerized agents. In: First USENIX Workshop on Electronic Commerce (1995)
39. Vinitsky, E., Jaques, N., Leibo, J., Castaneda, A., Hughes, E.: Sequential social dilemma games (2019). https://github.com/eugenevinitsky/sequential_social_dilemma_games
40. Wang, J.X., Hughes, E., Fernando, C., Czarnecki, W.M., Duéñez-Guzmán, E.A., Leibo, J.Z.: Evolving intrinsic motivations for altruistic behavior. In: Elkind et al. [13], pp. 683–692

Conceptual Frameworks and Architectures

Impact of Different Belief Facets on Agents' Decision—A Refined Cognitive Architecture to Model the Interaction Between Organisations' Institutional Characteristics and Agents' Behaviour

Amir Hosein Afshar Sedigh[1](✉), Martin K. Purvis[1], Bastin Tony Roy Savarimuthu[1], Christopher K. Frantz[2], and Maryam A. Purvis[1]

[1] Department of Information Science, University of Otago, Dunedin, New Zealand
amir.afshar@postgrad.otago.ac.nz,
{martin.purvis,tony.savarimuthu,maryam.purvis}@otago.ac.nz
[2] Department of Computer Science, Norwegian University of Science and Technology, Ametyst-bygget, A205, Gjøvik, Norway
christopher.frantz@ntnu.no

Abstract. This paper presents a conceptual refinement of agent cognitive architecture inspired from the beliefs-desires-intentions (BDI) and the theory of planned behaviour (TPB) models, with an emphasis on different belief facets. This enables us to investigate the impact of personality and the way that an agent weights its internal beliefs and social sanctions on an agent's actions. The study also uses the concept of cognitive dissonance associated with the fairness of institutions to investigate the agents' behaviour. To showcase our model, we simulate two historical long-distance trading societies, namely Armenian merchants of New-Julfa and the English East India Company. The results demonstrate the importance of internal beliefs of agents as a pivotal aspect for following institutional rules.

Keywords: Institutions · BDI · Agent-based simulation · Facets of belief · Cognitive dissonance

1 Introduction

This paper extends a mental architecture to model dynamics in an agent's cognition. In other words, this paper presents a cognitive architecture inspired from the belief-desire-intention model (BDI) [10] and the theory of planned behaviour (TPB) [20] to investigate agents' interactions with institutions.

In this study, we use agents to divide a complex social system into smaller action components. Also, an agent impacts the system through its decisions. A challenge in agent-based simulation is modelling the agents' decision-making

A. Aler Tubella et al. (Eds.): COIN 2017/COINE 2020, LNAI 12298, pp. 133–155, 2021.
https://doi.org/10.1007/978-3-030-72376-7_8

process (i.e. action deliberation) [7]. A class of studies addresses this challenge by employing the beliefs-desires-intentions (BDI) cognitive architecture. Some well-known extensions of the BDI cognitive architecture include the BOID [11], EBDI [36] and the BRIDGE [18]. Also, a formalisation of BDI (n-BDI) was presented to take into consideration the norms and their internalisation [17]. Some researchers employed the BDI architecture to model agents' cooperation in institutionalised multi-agent systems [6,8]. In some studies, different components of information are considered in modelling agent architecture [13]. However, the stated study distinguishes the stored information based on their types and does not address the agents' interpretations given their enforcing meta-roles.

To our knowledge, none of the works in the area have taken into account a multi-faceted characterisation of beliefs as behavioural moderators, so as to produce nuanced behavioural outcomes that respond to the context and embedding of the agents therein. In this study, we are thus inspired from the BDI cognitive architecture and different belief facets of TPB. Also, we model the impact of different belief facets on agent decisions by drawing on extant social-psychological theories. More precisely, we model how institutional characteristics, including the fairness of institutions, impact agents' decisions. The impact of fairness on agents' decisions was studied by several researchers [28,29,35], in terms of fair behaviour of agents. In the stated studies the fairness concerned how individual agents punish each other, not the organisation (i.e. the focus of this paper).

Before providing the paper's organisation, we need to clarify that the nature of simulation and case studies contain some specification. Therefore, the simulation section cannot use the agent architecture as one may expect. The rest of this paper is organised as follows. Section 2 discusses our cognitive architecture. Section 3 discusses operationalisation of the central aspects of the model. Section 4 sketches a comparative overview of two historical cases, along with a simulation model for those societies that incorporates the proposed architecture. Section 5 presents the simulation results for the two societies. Section 6 discusses the findings and provides concluding remarks.

2 An Overview of the Cognitive Architecture

Our cognitive model inspired by the BDI and TPB models is depicted in Fig. 1. It includes a decision-making module that is expanded in the same figure in grey. What follows discusses different modules and their connections with one another. The architecture separates inputs, here referred to as "Events" that are external to the reasoning process from the actual cognitive architecture that operates on these inputs. The Cognitive architecture block represents an agent's cognitive decision-making components. Any action performed by an agent in a given iteration will be an input event for the agent itself and other agents in its social environment in the next iteration. For instance, an agent's cheating action in time t will be an action recognised by associated agents for the next period $(t+1)$. In the following, we will discuss the internal components and underlying assumptions of the architecture in more detail.

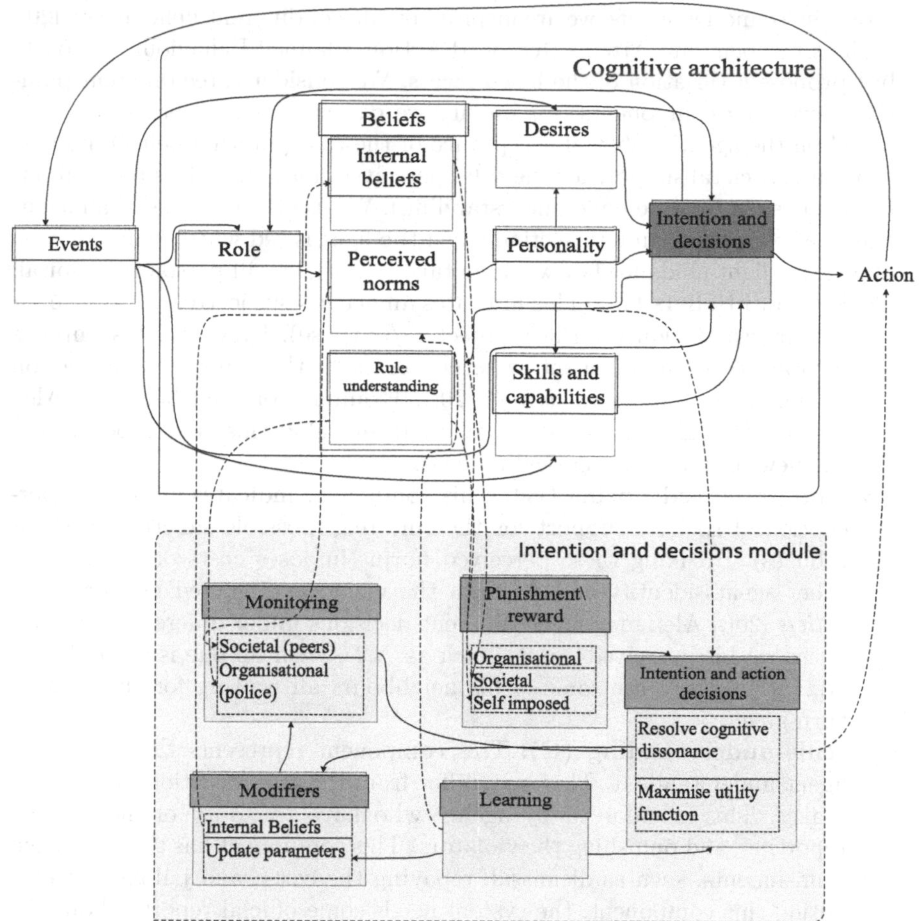

Fig. 1. A schematic diagram of the proposed cognitive architecture. The intention/decision module of the cognitive architecture is expanded in the dashed box (bottom block). The relationships between the modules of the cognitive architecture and the sub-modules of the "intention/decision module" is given by dashed-lines.

What follows discusses different modules and their connections with one another. As can be seen, there are two separate blocks, namely a left block called '*Events*' and a right block called 'Cognitive architecture'. The Events block represents the events from an outside environment. The *Cognitive architecture* block represents an agent's cognitive decision-making components. Note that when an action is performed by an agent, it will be an event for agents in the next iteration. What follows discusses the modules of cognitive architecture.

- **Roles:** An agent has a set of roles in society that indicate how a given rule impacts it [37].

- **Beliefs:** To model beliefs, we are inspired by idea of different belief facets [20], such as Fishbein and Ajzen's Reasoned Action/Planned Behaviour approach, but propose a variation of the belief facets. We consider three different punitive/rewarding components (for brevity we discuss them in terms of costs), based on the agent's internal acceptance of the rule (internal belief), its perception of societal support for the rule (perceived norms), and its belief about the purpose of the rule (rule-understanding). We use the example of an agent called Alex crossing an intersection when the light is red which is in violation of a traffic light abidance law when he takes a critically ill person to hospital:
  - **Internal beliefs (B):** This indicates an agent's subjective preference for rule interpretation (or rule's objective/purpose). Breaking this imposes mental costs on an agent, whether or not others observe the action (inspired by *behavioural beliefs* [20]). Examples of such beliefs of Alex include *B.1:* all rules must be followed and *B.2:* this rule is because of the new mayor's non-sensical policies.
  - **The perceived norms (N):** This component indicates an agent's perception of societal support for the rule (e.g. possible sanctions such as rebukes). Breaking these perceived norms imposes costs on an agent if other agents identify and sanction the violation (inspired by *normative beliefs* [20]). Alex may make different decisions under different situations based on his perceived norms, such as *N.1:* when no one is around, and *N.2:* when there are some of his neighbours all waiting for the light to turn green.
  - **Rule-understanding (C):** This component represents the rule as an agent understands it. This may differ from the real intention of the rule-maker. This is enforced by agents who have the duty of monitoring, reporting, and punishing the violators. This component has the most rigid punishments, such as dismissal, repaying the costs, and jailing. For executing this component, the system needs some official reports about the agents' behaviour (a formalised version of *control beliefs* [20]). Examples of theses include *C.1:* there is no police around, *C.2:* there is a working traffic control camera, and *C.3:* Alex may think he is allowed to cross the intersection the way that ambulances do (i.e. he thinks he would not be punished by the police).
- **Desires:** Agents have different desires with respect to the environment, their personalities, and the context, such as goals and ideal preferences.
- **Personality:** Personality of an agent impacts different aspects, such as its learning method and the way it weights its beliefs. We use MBTI (Myers-Briggs Type Indicator) [34] personality types. MBTI categorises personality types based on four dimensions: Introverted-Extraverted (I-E), Sensing-iNtuitive (S-N), Feeling-Thinking (F-T), and Judging-Perceiving (J-P). These dimensions are defined as follows:
  - Introverted versus Extraverted (I-E): This indicates where energy is oriented, or attitudes come from.
  - Sensing versus iNtuitive (S-N): This differentiates agents based on their *Perceiving* methods (i.e. collecting objective or abstract information).

- Feeling versus Thinking (F-T): This indicates how an agent makes decisions and *judges* (i.e. decisions are based on the demonstrable rationality or personal and social values).
- Judging versus Perceiving (J-P): This indicates how fast a person wants to reach a conclusion and 'achieve closure'. Also, "it describes the orientation to the extraverted world for every type" [34].

These dimensions indicate the extreme points (i.e. a person who is more Introverted is considered to be I).[1]

Another method used for the same purpose, i.e. to classify personalities, is called the *Big Five* personality factors [22]. The aspects (which are called traits by the designers) are measured by the model and its revised versions are: Agreeableness (the tendency to be cooperative or likeable), Conscientiousness (the extent to which an agent is achievement-oriented, dependable, and organised), Extraversion (how far an agent is socially-oriented, ambitious, and active), Openness (an agent's openness to experience and being unconventional), and Neuroticism (the inability of an agent to adjust to positive psychological states) [16].

- **Skills and capabilities:** Some determinants of an agent's behaviour and the impacts of such behaviours are its skills and capabilities.
- **Intention and decision:** An agent's intention to take an action and its decision about the final action is formed in this module (coloured in grey). The decision process includes normalising inputs based on aspects such as learnt parameters, personality, and roles, which results in an action. This action can be a modification of beliefs and roles or only performing a task. This module is at the core of the architecture and discussed in depth in the following section.

2.1 Intention and Decisions Module

This module is at the core of the architecture and indicated by grey and dashed box in Fig. 1. The dashed lines in Fig. 1 indicate all the relationships with the components now external to the decision module, including the visually conflated tripartite belief structure with its differentiated enforcement mechanisms explored previously. The components and moderators that integrate these in an agent's final decision are discussed below:

- **Monitoring:** This block indicates an agent's belief about the chances of being punished by each of the three belief facets for a given violation. Note that the internal belief component does not need external monitoring mechanisms to work.
- **Punishments/rewards:** As discussed earlier, the punishments/rewards associated with internal beliefs and perceived norms depend on the agent's

[1] In our model agents may have different values associated with different dimensions and this weight impacts their behaviour. Note that the weights are complementary (i.e. 10% Introverted means 90% Extraverted).

beliefs. However, the rules generally have explicit and less ambiguous consequences than social norms in terms of punishment and rewards.
- **Modifiers:** As discussed earlier, an agent may decide about modifying its internal beliefs, role, and beliefs about the system for reasons such as cognitive dissonance (incurred costs for inconsistent internal beliefs [4]) and new information. This block thus functions as a moderator across the different influence factors.
- **Learning:** This block indicates an agent's interpretation of its observations, suggestions, and past information. Furthermore, the agent can increase its skills (including general skills) by observation or by practising over time.
- **Intentions and action decisions:** This block coordinates the decisions with cognitive or organisational consequences in terms of performing modifications or turning an intention into an action.

To have a better understanding of the way these modules work, let us explore those from a process perspective. First, an agent accounts for the consequences of an action with respect to *monitoring* and *punishment/rewards*. It also learns and updates its *learning* of the system's characteristics with respect to its observations, and experience. Then given an agent's *intention, it assesses and revises its cognition to take an action.* If the agent decides to modify the beliefs and roles, it uses the *modifier* for doing so. The agent also improves its cognition about system characteristics by employing a *learning* procedure to improve and modify its understanding.

In the following, we attempt to draw general links between weighing of beliefs and empirical data, so as to replicate diverse compliance behaviour as found in real-world settings.

2.2 Impact of Personality

As depicted in Fig. 1, personality influences the decision module (i.e. an agent's personality impacts its decision). Furthermore, the decision module is a mediator for modifying different cognitive aspects (e.g. to resolve cognitive dissonance). In the following we discuss the impact of personality on an agent's utility function.

Weighting Perceived Norms and Internal Beliefs: To model the impacts of personality on norm conformance, we use the result of correlations between behavioural tendencies as measured by the *California Psychological Inventory* (CPI) [23,32]. The measured aspect of interest for us is the classification of agents into the norm following vs. -questioning groups. The correlations between the CPI scales and the MBTI scores indicated that Sensing and Judging (S-J) in the MBTI personality types are correlated to norm-favouring personalities [21]. Conversely, iNtuitive-Perceiving agents (N-P) appear to have the strongest tendency to question norms (i.e. weigh their internal beliefs higher than the perceived norms).

Dynamics in Internal Beliefs: Perceived fairness of the system has disparate impacts on the agents' behaviour in terms of rule-following. The Thinking-Feeling (agreeableness for Big Five [22]) aspect significantly influences agents' behaviour [12,40]. The impact of perceived fairness on "*organisational retaliatory behaviour*" that was measured by several studies [1,12,40] indicate that an agent *deliberately* changes its behaviour as a reaction to an unjust situation.

Mobility Versus Residency: Residency in a place gradually leads to formation of friendship among agents; also, friendships have certain impacts on the agent's behaviour [3]. The Feeling types, weight keeping harmony in the society more [34]. In our model, this effort can be modelled, based on the weights of the connections.

Having provided a high-level overview of the agent's cognition and decision-making modules, we describe an agent decision-making procedure using an example. For this purpose, we consider the condition under which an agent (A) observes that another agent (B) uses the company's properties for self-interest. First, we state how the *Cognitive architecture* impacts agent A's decisions. Given the architecture presented in Fig. 1, the agent A's role impacts its decision. For example, if agent A is a manager of agent B reporting the action might be considered as a part of its responsibilities, while if it is a peer of agent B the same behaviour (i.e. reporting agent B) might be considered as whistle-blowing. Such a change in role impacts agent A's beliefs about its actions—i.e. agent A may consider whistle-blowing the same as a betrayal to its friendship with agent B.

Also, agent A has different beliefs (i.e. facets of belief) regarding whistle-blowing. For example, it may consider the rules too strict and considers the action a mild violation (internal belief)—e.g. agent B used company's copy machine to make copies of its own documents and the rule dictates firing of employees for such an action. Furthermore, agent A may have learnt that most of his colleagues consider whistle-blowing as a taboo (perceived norm). Finally, agent A interpretation of the rule may differ from the real intention of the company—e.g. company does not consider using a copy machine for making copies of a document as a violation.

Agent A's desires, personality, and skills and capabilities impact its decision. In the example stated earlier, maybe the agent A has certain desires for whistle-blowing [9], such as hatred of agent B. Agent A's personality impacts its desires, skills [27], and weighting its different belief facets [21] (see Subsect. 2.2 for a clarification). Agent A's normalises its inputs in the intention and decisions resulting in the final action.

We use the stated example to describe an example to clarify how *intention and decisions module* impacts an agent's final action. As indicated in Fig. 1, agent A's decisions are impacted by some external factors, including monitoring and punishment means. For instance, if agent A decides to report agent B's behaviour, it may change its mind to avoid social sanctions when the rest of it colleagues are present in the manager's room (i.e. punishment and monitoring for perceived norm). Under the same circumstances, agent A may decide to report agent B, because its manager identified agent B's behaviour and there are strict punishments for collusion among agents (i.e. punishment and monitoring for rules).

To explain the learning and modifiers modules consider the earlier situation. Agent A learns the organisation's intentions of rules, its peers' expectations, and the punishments and rewards associated with a behaviour and modifies its earlier beliefs based on collected information and its observations. Also, there are situations such as agent A's loyalty to the organisation which bring it into the conflict between its peers' expectations. Therefore, agent A is afflicted with the cognitive dissonance that needs to be resolved by modifying its beliefs. This is exemplified by showing how smokers who were aware of the harms ranked their smoking habit milder than their counterparts [43] (i.e. changed their beliefs about their smoking behaviour). Note that this modification of beliefs impacts agents' future behaviours.

The stated example clarifies how different modules interact. However, there are instances such as the agency problem (known as the *principal-agent problem*) where the monitoring cannot be performed easily [38]. The principal-agent problem concerns the dilemma where the self-interested decisions of a party (agent) impact the benefits of the other person on whose behalf these decisions are made (principal) [33]. Note that we consider utilitarian decisions made by agents who play an incomplete information game.[2] In such games, agents learn the system's characteristics over time and use a utility function to make a decision. In the following section, we describe how we operationalise an agent's decision-making process by defining its utility function.

3 Operationalisation

In this section, we concisely explain how an agent makes its decisions. We briefly describe an agent's utility function and the way it forms and updates its perception of norms. Note that an agent learns system's characteristics based on its personality.

3.1 Agent's Decision Utility Function

Agent A takes an action (x) that maximises its utility function presented in Eq. 1 ($U_A(x)$). The utility function has four parts. The first part indicates the revenue that agent A earns for an action ($R(x)$). The second part shows how the agent is mentally punished for such an action ($IBP_A(x)$), given its personality ($(N_A + P_A)/2$).

$$\begin{aligned} U_A(x) =& R(x) - \left(IBP_A(x) \times \frac{N_A + P_A}{2} \right) - \\ & \left((PN_A(x) \times NM_A) \times (1 - \frac{N_A + P_A}{2}) \right) - (RP(x) \times RM(x)) \end{aligned} \tag{1}$$

The third term shows the agent's perception of the punishment by its connections (social sanctions). Agent A estimates this, based on its perception of

[2] This approach was used for modelling agency problems [39].

punishment for such an action ($PN_A(x)$), and it is moderated based on its estimation of its connections' monitoring strength (NM_A) and its personality $\left(1-(N_A+P_A)/2\right)$. Finally, it takes account of organisational punishment regarding violation ($RP(x)$) and moderates its impact, based on its estimation of organisational monitoring ($RM(x)$). The next subsection discusses how agent A estimates monitoring strength associated with norms.

3.2 Perception of Norms

The perception of norms differs from that of the rule by the vagueness of punishments associated with norms. To model an agent's perception of norms, we should note that a person expresses his/her beliefs, based on the weight he/she allocates to people's expectations. To consider this effect, we consider the impact of personality on an agent's norm conformance (i.e. expectations with undefined consequences).

$$PN_A^t = wi \times \left(\frac{\sum_{i \in C_{A,N}} EN_i^t}{K_A} + \frac{(K_A - K_{A,N}) \times PN_i^{t-1}}{K_A}\right) + (1-wi) \times PN_A^{t-1} \tag{2}$$

Equation 2 shows how agent A (agent of interest) collects its associated agents' opinions about the norm (they may express their opinions different than their real internal beliefs), and updates the society's expectations from itself at time t $\left(PN_A^t\right)$ (in former formula we skipped t for simplicity). The agent associates some weights with the recent information (i.e. wi). Furthermore, the agent averages the recommended scores by its connections with whom it has strong relationships (i.e. the associated $wi \geq 0.5$). From those connections, it takes account of the ones who have at least the same experience as itself; we call the subset of such members from C_A (i.e. the whole connections of A) as $C_{A,N}$. Also, K_A and $K_{A,N}$ indicate the number of members of C_A and $C_{A,N}$, respectively. This procedure states that an agent would not ask for less experienced agents' recommendations because of the feeling that it knows better. Furthermore, an agent does not criticise people's expectations unless it knows the audience well (i.e. the ones who have a higher w_{iA}). In addition, agent A assumes that the rest of the connections (i.e. $K_A - K_{A,N}$) realise the norm the same as himself $\left(PN_i^{t-1}\right)$. Then the agent associates the rest of the weights (i.e. $1-wi$) with its past perception about expectations (i.e. PN_A^{t-1}).

Now we discuss how other agents express their beliefs to agent A. Agent i does it through a weighting of its perception of social expectations (PN_i) and its beliefs (IB_i). Equation 3 shows how weighting the outer world impacts an agent's expression of beliefs. As discussed earlier, the personality of agent i (a friend of agent A) impacts its expression of its beliefs about the outer world's expectations. EN_i^t indicates agent i's expression of what people do and what they should do at time t. As discussed earlier, the iNtuitive and Perceiving aspect of an agent decreases weights given to other people's expectations; hence, agent i straightforwardly expresses its own beliefs and expectations at that time (i.e. IB_i^t, the first term on the right of Eq. 3). The second term on the right shows the opposite—i.e. how personality of agent i impacts its expression of ideas, based on the value it associates with other agent's expectations (i.e. PN_i^t).

$$EN_i^t = (IB_i^t \times \frac{N_i + P_i}{2}) + (PN_i^t \times (1 - \frac{N_i + P_i}{2})) \tag{3}$$

4 Simulation, Algorithms, and Parameters

In this section, first, we discuss the underlying assumptions of the simulation. Then we provide an overview of two historical societies studied for simulation, namely the English East India Company (EIC) and Armenian merchants of New-Julfa (Julfa). Then we briefly discuss their aspects of interest for us and the simulation procedures used to represent agents' behaviour in these societies.

4.1 Assumptions

This paper is inspired by empirical studies on the importance and effects of cognitive dissonance—tensions formed by conflicts between different cognitions [4]—on agents' behaviour. This leads to creating some justification for taking one of the conflicting actions. Empirical studies attributed workers' productivity to cognitive dissonance formed by fairness of institutions [2]. Studies showed that procedural justice (having fair dispute resolution mechanisms) [42], and payment schemes (e.g. underpaying or overpaying) [1] impact agents' behaviour. Also, as discussed earlier, the impact of fairness of institutions on agents' behaviour varies based on their personalities.

4.2 Societies

Armenian Merchants of New-Julfa (Julfa): Armenian merchants of New-Julfa were originally from old Julfa in Armenia. They re-established a trader society in New-Julfa (near Isfahan, Iran) after their forced displacement in the early 17th century [26]. They used commenda contracts (profit-sharing contracts) in the society and also used courts to resolve disputes. The mercantile agents were responsible for buying and selling items and moved among different nodes of the trading network expanded from Tibet (China) and Manila (Philippines) to Marseille (France) and Venice (Italy) [5].

The English East India Company (EIC): During the same time, the English contemporaneous counterpart of Julfa (i.e. the English *East India Company* (EIC, AD 1600s-1850s)) had a totally different perspective on managing the society. They built settlements for their mercantile agents to stay in India [24]. Also, they paid their employees fixed wages and fired agents based on their beliefs about their trading behaviour [25].

Note that the EIC's trading period covers two events, namely a) granting permission for private trade (1665–1669) and b) a significant budget deficit on part of employees (around 1700). The EIC reduced its employees wages when granted the permission for private trade (i.e. fairness of the system had decreased because agents' already performed private trade without such a permission). Furthermore, agents were desperate for their living costs because of the budget deficit[3]. In the simulation model, we regenerate those events in iterations 70 and 100.

Fairness: Another difference between the two historical long-distance trading societies is associated with their payment schemes and adjudication processes. The EIC rarely employed an adjudication process, and they paid low wages to their employees [25]. However, in Julfa a mercantile agent was paid based on his performance [5]. Julfans had adjudication processes to resolve disputes considering available evidence [5]. However, the Julfa society had certain characteristics that questioned its complete fairness—for instance, in the Julfa society, the capital of the family was managed by the elder brother[4] [26]. This rule deprived younger brothers of managing their own capital.

Agent's Mobility: Another difference in the policy of the two historical long-distance trading societies concerns whether or not the mercantile agents stayed in a certain place to perform trades. In the EIC, the company built its own factories and mercantile agents (but not sailors) resided there [24]. This introduces issues such as forming an informal community within the company that could have operated based on the norms of friendship [14].

Note that the events of years 70 and 100 are regenerated for unfair societies.[5] Note that once private trade is permitted, the fairness of the society decreases (because of a decrease in wages).

4.3 Algorithms

In this section, we discuss the procedures employed to use the above-described model to simulate the two aforementioned societies. The simulation model is split into four distinctive procedures and one sub-procedure. The first procedure is the meta-algorithm that executes other algorithms in an appropriate sequence and updates parameters required for them. The second procedure models the societal level activities of the simulation, including creating an initial population and staffing (hiring new recruits) to create a stable population. The fourth procedure models *mercantile agents*' decision-making and learning the system's parameters. The fourth procedure also includes a sub-procedure for defining new parameters associated with hired mercantile agents. The fourth procedure covers the decision-making and learning procedure associated with managers (i.e. monitoring agents).

---

[3] This deficit was because of lower wages and profits and higher living costs due to an increase in the number of private traders as a consequence of formation of the New East India Company (see p. 17 of [31]).

[4] This rule helped the families to work like a firm.

[5] Some discussions suggest that agents tend to break bureaucratic rules that seemed to be harmless for organisation [19].

Algorithm 1: Meta-algorithm

```
  /* Intialise the system starting with iteration ← 0.                  */
1 Create 500 new agents with status ← new, random personality aspects, and
  random parameters
2 Assign appropriate roles (i.e. mercantile, managers, and directors) to created
  agents
  /* Call algorithms in an appropriate sequence.                         */
3 repeat
4 |   Run Algorithm 2
5 |   Run Algorithm 4
6 |   Run Algorithm 5
7 |   if Private trade is legalised and iteration = 100 then Mercantile agents
  |   feel desperate for basic living costs
8 |   iteration ← iteration + 1
9 until iteration = 250
```

Algorithm 1 shows how the simulation is initialised, other procedures are executed, and the system's characteristics are modified. In iteration 0, the system is initialised by creating 500 new agents with random parameters (line 1). The roles are assigned to created agents (about 2% directors, 5% managers, and the rest mercantile agents)[6], and they have 0 years of experience (line 2). The rest of the algorithm is repeated until the termination condition is met (lines 4–9).

Algorithm 2: Societal level set-up

```
  /* n equals deceased and fired agents (mercantile agents and
     managers) in the former iteration.                                  */
1 The most experienced mercantile agents get promoted to a managerial role to
  keep the number of managers constant.
2 Create n new agents status ← new, Experiene ← 0, randomly initialise
  personality aspects and other parameters (discussed in Table 1)
```

In each iteration, the simulation begins with the societal algorithm (i.e. Algorithm 2, line 4). Then the algorithm associated with the mercantile agents is run (i.e. Algorithm 4). Note that the Algorithm 3 associated with the newly recruited mercantile agents is called inside Algorithm 4. After 100 years, in unfair system, private trades are legalised and the mercantile agents face financial issues and feel financially desperate. This phenomenon was observed in the EIC after a decrease in wages, coupled with fewer opportunities for private trade because of the establishment of the New East India Company. Note that for simplicity, when we modelled the phenomenon, we did not consider a gradual decrease (line

[6] These numbers are inspired from the numbers in the EIC [24].

6). Finally, the simulation iteration increases by one, and the stop condition is checked (line 8).

Algorithm 2 shows how the societal level of the system is simulated. The organisation hires and promotes agents to sustain the number of agents per role—i.e. by replacing deceased agents (lines 1–2).

Algorithm 3: Initialising the mercantile agent's algorithm

```
1 Fair ← RandomUniform(0, 1)
  /* Rule-understanding and the internal belief about rules.       */
2 Agent has a random perception of norms and rules
3 Status ← Experienced
```

Algorithm 3 shows how the parameters of newly introduced mercantile agents (i.e. new agents) are initialised. This algorithm is executed only for inexperienced agents (i.e. new recruits). An agent has a completely random understanding of the system's characteristics (lines 1–2). After initialisation, the agent updates its status to *experienced* so that the system can identify it (line 3).

Algorithm 4: Mercantile agent's algorithm

```
/* Upadate parameters for new recruits.                                */
if Status = New then Set agent's parameter using Algorithm 3
if Experience > 3 then
    /* Make a decision on cheating using Equation 1.                   */
    Cheat ← 0
    /* Viol is a set of random violations.                             */
    foreach viol ∈ Viol do
        util ← Utility(viol)
        if Util > Utility(Cheat) then Cheat ← viol
if Desperate then
    foreach Violation level do
        /* Punishment of internal beliefs decreases significantly      */
        Change the costs of internal belief violations
/* Agent (I) increases the weight of fellows.                          */
W_Ij ← W_Ij × (1 + #Rnd(FriendIncrease)) ∀ j∈frinds
if Moving to a new place then
    /* Most of the former fellows are replaced with new fellows        */
    Replace Mob% of fellows with new fellows.
Learn system parameters and modify your internal belief and perceived norm
/* Agent may die                                                       */
Experience ← Experience + 1
if Rand(1) ≤ MortalityProbability(Experience + 15) then Die
```

Algorithm 4 shows the procedures associated with mercantile agents' cognition and decision-making processes. Note that in this algorithm $\#Rnd(x)$ indicates a random number generated in the interval $(0, x)$. As stated earlier, if the status of the mercantile agent is new, he goes through an initialisation algorithm (i.e. Algorithm 3, line 1). Experienced mercantile agents decide whether to cheat based on a set of potential violations (lines 2–6). Lines 7–9 model the scenario when mercantile agents faced a decrease in wages and a drop in private trade's revenue such that they were desperate to pay for their living costs. As a consequence, costs associated with violating the internal beliefs decrease (lines 7–9). Also, the mercantile agent increases the weight of social bonds with his associated agents (line 10). And when moving to a new place, the majority of a mobile mercantile agent's work fellows (e.g. Julfans) are replaced (lines 11–12). Finally, the mercantile agent learns system parameters, modifies his beliefs, increases his experience, and dies with an estimated probability (lines 13–14).

Algorithm 5: Manager's algorithm

```
  /* Manager reports (and eventually punishes) a number of employees
     who violate the rules of the organisation beyond its tolerance
     level.                                                          */
1 PotPunish ← employees with violations more than TolPunish
2 if The number of members of PotPunish > MaxPunish then
     /* The manager has a limit for the number of agents he can punish
        called MaxPunish.                                            */
3    Punish MaxPunish out of PotPunish that have the most violation
4 else
5    Punish all PotPunish members.
6 Experience ← Experience + 1
7 if Rand(1) ≤ MortalityProbability(Experience + 15) then Die
```

Algorithm 5 shows the procedures associated with managers. A manager creates a set that consists of violators with unacceptable violations (i.e. it tolerates violations to some extent, see line 1). Note that the manager reports about the violators and punishes a certain number. If the number of violators exceeds a certain threshold, it punishes the worst violators (lines 2–3). Otherwise, all the violators are punished (lines 4–5). Finally, the agent's experience and age increase, and the agent may die (lines 6–7).

4.4 Simulation Parameters

In this subsection, we discuss the important parameters employed in the simulation (see Table 1), along with the justification for the parameterisation. Note that we used 250 iterations to reflect the longevity of the EIC (it was active with some interruptions and changes in power from 1600 to 1850). Each iteration thus models one year of activity in these systems. In Table 1, column 'Name' indicates the name of parameters, column 'Comment' shows additional information if required, column 'Distribution' indicates the probability distribution of these parameters, and column 'Values' indicates the values of parameters estimated for the two historical long-distance trading societies. Note that these parameters can be easily revised to reflect other societies.

Table 1. Parameters associated with the model

Name	Comment	Distribution	Values
Fairness	Unfair: Fair	Constant	$-0.4 : 0.6$
Perception of fairness of system		$Uniform$	$(-1, 1)$
Rule monitoring	The lower bound (lb) The learnt probabilities	$Uniform$	$(0, 1)$ $(lb, 1)$
Norm monitoring strength		$Uniform$	$(0, 1)$
Minor violation punishment	Probability	$Uniform$	$(0, 1)$
Weight of the connections	Fellows	$Uniform$	$(0, 1)$
Modifier for mental costs	Cognitive dissonance	$Uniform$	$(0, 0.3)$
Modifier for connections	Friendship	$Uniform$	$(0, 0.2)$

Fairness: Note that as stated earlier, Julfa had fairer institutions than the EIC due to profit sharing and using adjudication processes. We set system fairness for fair and unfair societies as 0.6 and −0.4, respectively. We believe that neither of these two societies was completely fair or unfair (e.g. EIC managers justified the firing of agents in their letters, which indicates some efforts towards interactional fairness [25]).

Perception of Fairness: An inexperienced agent has a completely random understanding of system characteristics.

Rule and Norm Monitoring: The agents believe the more serious violations are more likely to be punished. They use a Uniform probability distribution that is identified by its lower and upper bounds. For the upper bound, they use 1 (i.e. completely violating the rule such as stealing all the money). However, they are unsure about the lower bound for tolerance of peers and managers; hence, a continuous Uniform probability distribution in (0,1) is used. For the strength of the norm monitoring (i.e. how often agents punish each other), agents have a random understanding. However, these parameters are updated by continuous learning.

Minor Violation Punishment: In the model, we assume the agents have doubts about being fired for minor violations. This doubt is modelled by using uniform random numbers.

Weight of the Connections: To model all the possibilities for new links, such as knowing one another in advance, we used a random number (0,1) for new friendship links and links between mercantile agents and middle managers.

Modifier for Mental Costs: When an agent violates a rule, it randomly discounts the costs associated with such an action by a maximum of 10% of its initial point and on average the initial costs decreases by 5% of its initial point.

Modifier for Weights of Connections: For changes in weights of connections, we increase the connection's weight as a proportion of the current weight (i.e. $weight \times x$). Due to the ongoing interactions, the weight of friendships increases randomly between (0, 0.2).

Learning: Furthermore, we parametrise the agents' learning as follows. Agents discount past information using a weight of 30% (i.e. a weight of 70% for recent information). This reflects the importance of recent information for agents, because they are not sure about the stability of the system's behaviour in the long run. Also, we use entrepreneurs' personalities as a representative of personality of these trading agents [46] (see Table 2).

Table 2. Tendency of personalities to be entrepreneurs and the impact of them on an organisation's performance

Big five[a]	MBTI[b]	Intention[c]	Performance[d]
E	*E*	0.11	0.05
O	*N*	0.22	0.21
A	*F*	−0.09	−0.06
C	*J*	0.18	0.19

[a]**E:** extraversion, **O:** openness to experience, **A:** agreeableness, **C:** conscientiousness.

[b]**E-I:** Extravert-Introvert dimensions, **S-N:** Sensing-iNtuitive dimensions, **T-F:** Thinking-Feeling dimensions, **J-P:** Judging-Perceiving dimensions. Note that initials show the aspect used—for instance, E is the degree to which the person has the Extravert aspect. Note that as with their earlier study, we assume that results of different tests are interchangeable (see Appendix of [45]).

[c]It shows the correlation between personality and the *intention* of the person to be an entrepreneur.

[d]It shows the correlation between personality and the *performance* of the person as an entrepreneur.

5 Results

In this section, we discuss the simulation results considering four different combinations of two characteristics, namely a) mobility of agents and b) fairness of institutions.

We utilised *NetLogo* [44] to perform our simulation. We also used 30 different runs for each set-up and then averaged their results. Table 3 indicates the characteristics for the *four* simulated societies and societies they represent. The set-ups (i.e. societies) are identified by the first letter of the characteristics, namely M and F that are representatives of the **m**obility of agents across trading nodes (M) and **f**airness of the institutions (F), respectively. We used a Boolean index to indicate whether such an attribute is included (i.e. 1) or not (i.e. 0). Likewise, in the table, a tick indicates that the society possesses such an attribute, and a cross indicates the society does not possess such an attribute. In the absence of detailed knowledge, we assume an explorative approach that starts off with a prototypical EIC configuration, and incrementally approximates the Julfa configuration by hypothesised intermittent society configurations. This approach allows for a nuanced analysis of the individual influence factors, so as to isolate their respective influence on the simulation outcome. Table 3 reflects this by gradually modifying individual characteristics of the EIC (M_0F_0) society towards the Julfa (M_1F_1). In the following figures, we use two vertical dashed-lines that indicate the year that permissions for private trade was granted and the year that agents face issues with their living costs (i.e. year 70 and 100, respectively).

Table 3. System specification based on different characteristics

Characteristics	M_0F_0 (EIC)	M_0F_1	M_1F_0	M_1F_1 (Julfa)
Mobility	✗	✗	✓	✓
Fairness	✗	✓	✗	✓

Certain characteristics of societies impact agents' tendencies to violate rules. Figures 2a–2d present the percentage of mercantile agents who violated the rules (i.e. cheaters) in a year. In these plots, the y-axis represents the percentage of cheaters. As can be seen, the most influential characteristic is the fairness of institutions (Fig. 2c versus 2d) that reduces the number of cheaters significantly. Also, mobility of agents (Fig. 2a versus 2b) reduces the number of cheaters moderately. Note that as shown in Fig. 2d, even in fair societies some cheaters are available; however, this number is not noticeable because of high percentages of cheaters in other configurations. Also changes in fairness of institutions (first dashed-line) and financial issues that lead to an increase in the percentage of cheaters.

Another important issue regarding cheating is the seriousness of a violation. Figures 3a–3d present results for this phenomenon. In these plots the y-axis indicates the average of the seriousness of violations of cheaters. As can be seen, societies with fair institutions and the mobility of the agents had less serious violations in the long-run. In other words, Figs. 3a–3d indicate relatively the same patterns with respect to the percentage of cheaters shown in Figs. 2a–2d.

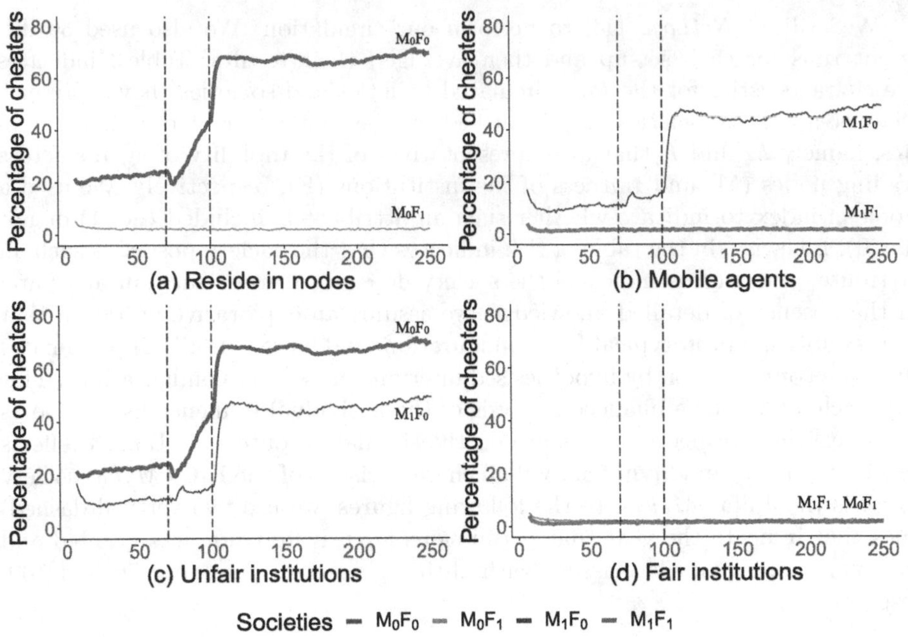

Fig. 2. Cheating frequency

Note that the combination of these results indicates that, in a society with unfair institutions where the agents reside in a node (e.g. the EIC), a higher percentage of agents cheat and the cheaters commit more severe frauds (i.e. frauds with more costs for the company). Our model mirrors the results what was observed in the EIC. For instance, the real EIC situation was much worse than that of our simulation results. The following case is an example that indicates another popular cheating mechanism (i.e. embezzlement) and its extent in the system:

> "The most common practice of partial defraudment in the Indies was to enter large sums of money in the name of fictitious Asian merchants as advance payment for goods and use the money to finance the private trade of the servants. " [15, p. 466]

As Aslanian points out, the "cases of cheating and dishonesty are rarely mentioned in Julfan correspondence" [5, p. 249]. Furthermore, based on the historical evidence, he notes that blacklisting in Julfa was extended to cases such as refusing to pay the share of taxes [5, p. 249, footnote 66]. This indicates the honesty of Julfan traders that made it possible to boycott society members for reasons other than violating trade rules.

Another instance concerns the historical evidence from the chartered companies (e.g. EIC) and Julfa to evaluate the patterns suggested by our simulation

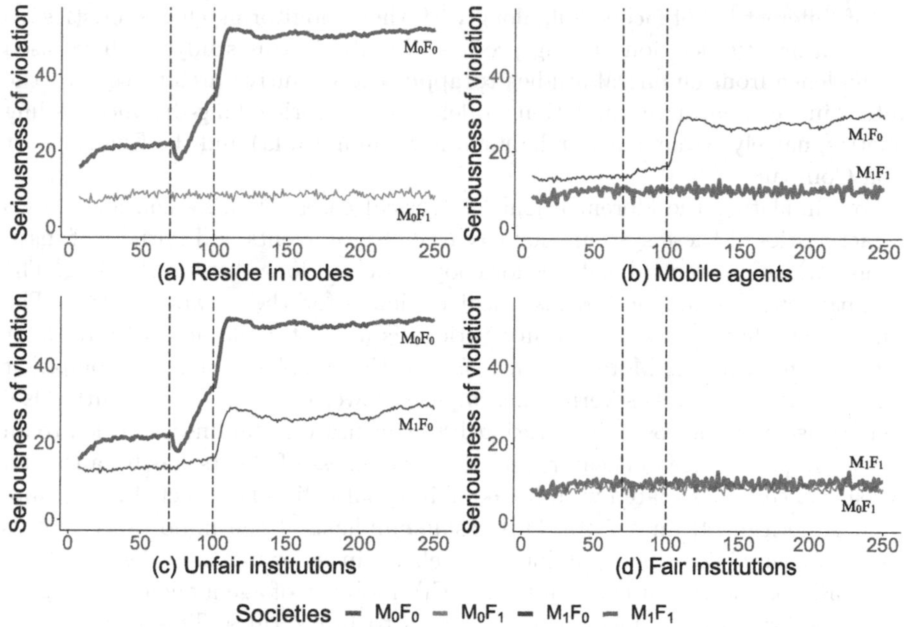

Fig. 3. The seriousness of violations

results. The evidence is presented in the form of quotations from historians. The passage below belongs to the EIC:

> "There were even fraudulent attempts to charge the Company [EIC] a higher price by buying it [pepper] during the cheap season and then entering in the books the later price which had been raised by the demand from private traders arriving late on the coast. In fact, the Court of Directors felt so strongly about the expenses incurred at Tellicherry [sic] under the management of Robert Adams that they were prepared to abandon the settlement altogether unless the charges were drastically reduced." [15, p. 325]

Chaudhuri notes that the reason for the court's decision was a downswing in the pepper market inside Europe [15]. However, this argument not only suggests the cheating behaviour and acceptance of it, but it also points to the beliefs about some coalitions.

6 Discussion, Concluding Remarks, and Future Directions

This study has presented a conceptual agent cognitive architecture inspired from the BDI [10] and TPB [20] models to investigate the interactions of different belief facets with institutions. More precisely, in this study we have used the idea of different belief facets [20], along with their monitoring characteristics, to model an agent's decision-making process. Finally, in this study, we have used the evidence from empirical studies to apply the cognitive architecture to the context in a comparative simulation model of two historical long-distance trading societies, namely Armenian merchants of new Julfa (Julfa) and the English East India Company (EIC).

For simulating the aforementioned historical cases, we have considered two characteristics of these systems, namely mobility of agents and fairness of institutions, which are central features for cooperation in long-distance trading. The simulation results mirror the historical evidence for these two societies. The results show that the fairness of institutions is a pivotal characteristic to deter agents from cheating. Moreover, in a fair institutional setting, non-compliant agents cheated with less severity (i.e. imposed lower costs on the system). Also, the increase in living costs (in iteration 100—second vertical line), that led to an increase in percentage of cheaters and the seriousness of cheats was because of a decrease in costs associated with breaking internal beliefs (see Sect. 4.2, footnote 3 and Algorithm 4, lines 7–9). This result emphasised the importance of this aspect of agents' cognition (i.e. internal beliefs) in following the rules.

Finally, as shown in Figs. 2 and 3 (M_1F_0), mobility of agents helps the organisation by lowering the inclination of agents to break rules. This is caused by higher mobility, and thus fewer opportunities for agents to form strong friendship bonds and express their real beliefs to each other; leading to overall higher levels of compliance. The impact of fairness of institutions on agents' behaviour translates well in modern settings; in organisational studies it is referred to as organisational citizenship (i.e. cooperative working environment) and counterproductive work behaviour (i.e. agents deliberately decrease their cooperation) [41]. The impact of internal beliefs (e.g. religions) on agents' behaviour has also been observed by political philosophers such as Machiavelli.[7]

As a future extension of the current study, detailed interactions between other modules of the cognitive architecture presented in Fig. 1 deserves more attention. The societal model can be extended to take account of a wider range of characteristics such as apprenticeship programmes, and considering the impact of those on organisational profitability so as to sketch a more realistic picture of these historical trading societies.

References

1. Adams, J.S.: Inequity in social exchange. In: Advances in Experimental Social Psychology, vol. 2, pp. 267–299 (1965)
2. Adams, J.S., Rosenbaum, W.B.: The relationship of worker productivity to cognitive dissonance about wage inequities. J. Appl. Psychol. **46**(3), 161–164 (1962)

[7] Machiavelli discussed internal beliefs could help a governor to bring order into society: "[T]hose citizens whom the love of fatherland and its laws did not keep in Italy were kept there by an oath that they were forced to take; [... t]his arose from nothing other than that religion Numa [sic] had introduced in that city" (p. 34 of [30]).

3. Argyle, M., Henderson, M.: The rules of friendship. J. Soc. Pers. Relatsh. **1**(2), 211–237 (1984)
4. Aronson, E., Aronson, J.: The Social Animal, 10th edn. Worth Publishers, New York (2007)
5. Aslanian, S.D.: From the indian ocean to the mediterranean. Ph.D. thesis, Columbia University, New York (2007)
6. Balke, T., De Vos, M., Padget, J., Traskas, D.: On-line reasoning for institutionally-situated BDI agents. In: The 10th International Conference on Autonomous Agents and Multiagent Systems, AAMAS 2011, vol. 3, pp. 1109–1110. International Foundation for Autonomous Agents and Multiagent Systems, Richland, SC (2011)
7. Balke, T., Gilbert, N.: How do agents make decisions? A survey. J. Artif. Soc. Soc. Simul **17**(4), 13 (2014)
8. Balke, T., De Vos, M., Padget, J.: Normative run-time reasoning for institutionally-situated BDI agents. In: Cranefield, S., van Riemsdijk, M.B., Vázquez-Salceda, J., Noriega, P. (eds.) COIN -2011. LNCS (LNAI), vol. 7254, pp. 129–148. Springer, Heidelberg (2012). https://doi.org/10.1007/978-3-642-35545-5_8
9. Baltaci, A., Balci, A.: Reasons for whistleblowing: a qualitative study. Eğitim Bilimleri Araştırmaları Dergisi **7**(1), 37–51 (2017)
10. Bratman, M.E., Israel, D.J., Pollack, M.E.: Plans and resource-bounded practical reasoning. Comput. Intell. **4**(3), 349–355 (1988)
11. Broersen, J., Dastani, M., Hulstijn, J., Huang, Z., van der Torre, L.: The BOID architecture: conflicts between beliefs, obligations, intentions and desires. In: AGENTS 2001, pp. 9–16. ACM, New York (2001)
12. Buboltz Jr., W.C., Williams, D.J., Thomas, A., Seemann, E.A., Soper, B., Woller, K.: Personality and psychological reactance: extending the nomological net. Pers. Individ. Differ. **34**(7), 1167–1177 (2003)
13. Castelfranchi, C., Dignum, F., Jonker, C.M., Treur, J.: Deliberative normative agents: principles and architecture. In: Jennings, N.R., Lespérance, Y. (eds.) ATAL 1999. LNCS (LNAI), vol. 1757, pp. 364–378. Springer, Heidelberg (2000). https://doi.org/10.1007/10719619_27
14. Chaudhuri, K.N.: The English East India Company: The study of an early joint-stock company 1600–1640, 1st edn. Frank Cass & Co., Ltd., London (1965)
15. Chaudhuri, K.N.: The Trading World of Asia and the English East India Company: 1660–1760, 1st edn. Cambridge University Press, Cambridge (1978). https://doi.org/10.1017/cbo9780511563263
16. Costa, P.T., McCrae, R.R.: The revised NEO personality inventory (NEO-PI-R). In: Boyle, G.J., Matthews, G., Saklofske, D.H. (eds.) The SAGE Handbook of Personality Theory and Assessment: Volume 2 — Personality Measurement and Testing, vol. 2, pp. 179–198. SAGE Publications Inc. (2008). https://doi.org/10.4135/9781849200479.n9
17. Criado, N., Argente, E., Botti, V.: Normative deliberation in graded BDI agents. In: Dix, J., Witteveen, C. (eds.) MATES 2010. LNCS (LNAI), vol. 6251, pp. 52–63. Springer, Heidelberg (2010). https://doi.org/10.1007/978-3-642-16178-0_7
18. Dignum, F., Dignum, V., Jonker, C.M.: Towards agents for policy making. In: David, N., Sichman, J.S. (eds.) MABS 2008. LNCS (LNAI), vol. 5269, pp. 141–153. Springer, Heidelberg (2009). https://doi.org/10.1007/978-3-642-01991-3_11
19. Erikson, E.: Between Monopoly and Free Trade: The English East India Company, 1600–1757, 1st edn. Princeton University Press, Princeton (2014)
20. Fishbein, M., Ajzen, I.: Predicting and Changing Behavior: The Reasoned Action Approach, 1st edn. Psychology Press Ltd., New York (2011)

21. Fleenor, J.W.: The relationship between the MBTI and measures of personality and performance in management groups. In: Fitzgerald, C., Kirby, L.K. (eds.) Developing Leaders, 1st edn, pp. 115–138. Davies-Black Publishing, Palo Alto (1997)
22. Goldberg, L.R.: An alternative "scription of personality" the big-five factor structure. J. Pers. Soc. Psychol. **59**(6), 1216–1229 (1990)
23. Gough, H.G.: The California psychological inventory. In: Watkins, C. Edward, J., Campbell, V.L. (eds.) Testing and Assessment in Counseling Practice, 2nd edn, pp. 37–62. Lawrence Erlbaum Associates Publishers, Mahwah (2000)
24. Hejeebu, S.: Microeconomic investigations of the English East India Company. Ph.D. thesis, University of Iowa, IA, January 1998
25. Hejeebu, S.: Contract enforcement in the English East India Company. J. Econ. Hist. **65**(2), 496–523 (2005)
26. Herzig, E.M.: The Armenian merchants of New Julfa, Isfahan. Ph.D. thesis, Oxford University, Oxford, UK (1991)
27. James, K., Asmus, C.: Personality, cognitive skills, and creativity in different life domains. Creativity Res. J. **13**(2), 149–159 (2001)
28. Knaak, N., Kruse, S., Page, B.: An agent-based simulation tool for modelling sustainable logistics systems. In: International Congress on Environmental Modelling and Software, Osnabrück, Germany (2006)
29. Levy, N., Klein, I., Ben-Elia, E.: Emergence of cooperation and a fair system optimum in road networks: a game-theoretic and agent-based modelling approach. Res. Transp. Econ. **68**, 46–55 (2018). https://doi.org/10.1016/j.retrec.2017.09.010
30. Machiavelli, N.: Discourses on Livy, 1st edn. University of Chicago Press, Chicago (1998). Originally published in 1531
31. Marshall, P.J.: East Indian Fortunes: The British in Bengal in the Eighteenth Century, 1st edn. Oxford University Press, Oxford (1976)
32. Megargee, E.I.: The California psychological inventory. In: Butcher, J.N. (ed.) Oxford Handbook of Personality Assessment, 1st edn, pp. 323–335. Oxford University Press, New York (2009)
33. Mitnick, B.M.: Origin of the theory of agency: an account by one of the theory's originators. SSRN Electron. J. (2011). https://doi.org/10.2139/ssrn.1020378
34. Myers, I.B., McCaulley, M.H., Quenk, N.L., Hammer, A.L.: MBTI Manual, 3rd edn. Consulting Psychologists Press, Palo Alto (1998)
35. Pahl-Wostl, C., Ebenhöh, E.: Heuristics to characterise human behaviour in agent based models. In: International Congress on Environmental Modelling and Software, Osnabrück, Germany (2004)
36. Pereira, D., Oliveira, E., Moreira, N.: Formal modelling of emotions in BDI agents. In: Sadri, F., Satoh, K. (eds.) CLIMA 2007. LNCS (LNAI), vol. 5056, pp. 62–81. Springer, Heidelberg (2008). https://doi.org/10.1007/978-3-540-88833-8_4
37. Purvis, M.K., Purvis, M.A., Frantz, C.K.: CKSW: a folk-sociological meta-model for agent-based modelling. In: Social Path Workshop. University of Surrey (2014)
38. Ross, S.A.: The economic theory of agency: the principal's problem. Am. Econ. Rev. **63**(2), 134–139 (1973). https://www.jstor.org/stable/1817064
39. Sedigh, A.H.A., Frantz, C.K., Savarimuthu, B.T.R., Purvis, M.K., Purvis, M.A.: A comparison of two historical trader societies - an agent-based simulation study of English east India company and New-Julfa. In: Davidsson, P., Verhagen, H. (eds.) MABS 2018. LNCS (LNAI), vol. 11463, pp. 17–31. Springer, Cham (2019). https://doi.org/10.1007/978-3-030-22270-3_2
40. Skarlicki, D.P., Folger, R., Tesluk, P.: Personality as a moderator in the relationship between fairness and retaliation. Acad. Manag. J. **42**(1), 100–108 (1999)

41. Spector, P.E., Fox, S.: Counterproductive work behavior and organisational citizenship behavior: are they opposite forms of active behavior? Appl. Psychol. **59**(1), 21–39 (2010)
42. Sunshine, J., Tyler, T.R.: The role of procedural justice and legitimacy in shaping public support for policing. Law Soc. Rev. **37**(3), 513–548 (2003)
43. Tagliacozzo, R.: Smokers' self-categorization and the reduction of cognitive dissonance. Addict. Behav. **4**(4), 393–399 (1979). https://doi.org/10.1016/0306-4603(79)90010-8
44. Wilensky, U.: Netlogo. Technical report, Center for Connected Learning and Computer-Based Modeling, Northwestern University, Evanston, IL (1999)
45. Zhao, H., Seibert, S.E.: The Big Five personality dimensions and entrepreneurial status: a meta-analytical review. J. Appl. Psychol. **91**(2), 259–271 (2006). https://doi.org/10.1037/0021-9010.91.2.259
46. Zhao, H., Seibert, S.E., Lumpkin, G.T.: The relationship of personality to entrepreneurial intentions and performance: a meta-analytic review. J. Manag. **36**(2), 381–404 (2010)

A Norm Emergence Framework for Normative MAS – Position Paper

Andreasa Morris-Martin(✉), Marina De Vos, and Julian Padget

University of Bath, Bath, UK
{a.l.morris.martin,m.d.vos,j.a.padget}@bath.ac.uk

Abstract. Norm emergence is typically studied in the context of multiagent systems (MAS) where norms are implicit, and participating agents use simplistic decision-making mechanisms. These implicit norms are usually unconsciously shared and adopted through agent interaction. A norm is deemed to have emerged when a threshold or predetermined percentage of agents follow the "norm". Conversely, in normative MAS, norms are typically explicit and agents deliberately share norms through communication or are informed about norms by an authority, following which an agent decides whether to adopt the norm or not. The decision to adopt a norm by the agent can happen immediately after recognition or when an applicable situation arises. In this paper, we make the case that, similarly, a norm has emerged in a normative MAS when a percentage of agents adopt the norm. Furthermore, we posit that agents themselves can and should be involved in norm synthesis, and hence influence the norms governing the MAS, in line with Ostrom's eight principles. Consequently, we put forward a framework for the emergence of norms within a normative MAS, that allows participating agents to propose/request changes to the normative system, while special-purpose synthesizer agents formulate new norms or revisions in response to these requests. Synthesizers must collectively agree that the new norm or norm revision should proceed, and then finally be approved by an "Oracle". The normative system is then modified to incorporate the norm.

Keywords: Norm synthesis · Synthesizer agents · Normative MAS · Normative system

1 Introduction

Multiagent systems (MAS) enable participating agents to interact with each other and their environment to accomplish individual goals and collective goals. MAS utilise norms to encourage coordination and cooperation, and to avoid the occurrence of undesirable states. Hollander and Wu [17] define a normative MAS as a system which combines concepts of norms with explicit representations of normative information in order to provide a solution to problems relating to openness in MAS. In contrast, in some MAS norms may not be considered at

A. Aler Tubella et al. (Eds.): COIN 2017/COINE 2020, LNAI 12298, pp. 156–174, 2021.
https://doi.org/10.1007/978-3-030-72376-7_9

all or the concept of norms is present but only as implicit representations of normative information.

The normative system, the set of norms in the MAS, is normally created as a result of the process of norm synthesis. Norm synthesis is the creation and updating of norms to avoid conflict situations – unwanted states in the MAS. Norm synthesis can be offline, which occurs mostly during design time [22] or as a separate process outside the system governed by the norms [30], where norms are determined by the designer or other stakeholders. A normative system resulting from offline synthesis is typically fixed for the lifetime of the system. But, over time, with changing environments, the norms can become partly or wholly irrelevant. Consequently, it becomes necessary to update the normative system leading to the introduction of online norm synthesis.

Online norm synthesis occurs while the system is live, and (new/revised) norms are typically determined by a centralised mechanism with global knowledge and without any input from the participants [1,25]. There exists a subset of decentralised online norm synthesis mechanisms [14,15], that allow agents to submit their personal strategies, then the most popular strategy is incorporated into the normative system; a similar approach is undertaken in [36]. Additionally runtime norm revision approaches [10,11] and dynamic normative systems [18,20,21] present other avenues where normative systems can be changed while the system is live.

On the other hand, the introduction of norms into a MAS without an explicit normative system, is orchestrated by participating agents in simulation models of norm emergence [32,41,44] , where the norms are defined as the preferred action from a set of actions, and the norm is usually learnt through agent interactions. However these norms do not become part of an explicit normative system as with work by [14,15,36] that also involve individual agent strategies as norms.

In this paper, we introduce a framework that allows participating agents to affect the online norm synthesis process. During runtime, participating agents can identify the norms or situations that require normative regulation, as long as there are the necessary affordances [33] for participating agents to propose or request changes to the normative system. We propose synthesizer agents which, upon request from participating agents, synthesise norms for the MAS to meet the identified need. We believe that after we encode the synthesised norm into the normative system, and it is adopted by a sufficient number of agents, we may ultimately observe the emergence of synthesised norm(s).

The rest of the paper is structured as follows. Section 2 which situates the proposed framework by discussing the gap identified in the literature. Section 3 gives a high level description of the framework, after which we discuss the stages of the framework in more detail: Section 4 highlights the main contribution which defines the norm creation stage, Sect. 5 discusses norm propagation, then norm adoption in Sect. 6, finishing in Sect. 7, with norm emergence. The paper concludes in Sect. 8, where we briefly discuss how the framework can facilitate the emergence of norms in open normative MAS and allow for the normative component to be changed in response to issues affecting agents participating in the MAS.

2 Research Context

Norms in the (MAS) literature are looked at from two distinct perspectives: norms as deontic concepts and norms as a preference behaviour. Each perspective implements the life cycle of norms differently, but can broadly be seen to follow similar stages. The norm life cycle defines the stages a norm goes through in its lifetime. The widely accepted norm life cycle [40], based on simulation studies has a three stage process: norm formation/creation, norm propagation and norm emergence. The literature also provides variations to the norm life cycle for example: Hollander and Wu [17] present a ten stage process which is encapsulated into three super-processes, and Savarimuthu and Cranefield [40] and Mahmoud et al. [24] present separate five stage processes. Frantz and Pigozzi [12], after an analysis of existing life cycle models present a refined evolutionary, rather than end to end model, with five stages namely: Creation, Transmission, Identification, Internalization and Forgetting. They consider Evolution and Emergence as phenomena rather than explicit stages in the model [12].

A closer look at the norm life cycle enables us to better understand the different perspectives on norms. We consider the widely accepted three stage process in our analysis.

2.1 The Prescriptive Perspective and the Norm Life Cycle

The first perspective, norms as deontic concepts, views norms as permissions or prohibitions and obligations, or commitments and is referred to as *norms as prescriptions* [7], or the *prescriptive approach* [39]. Here we refer to it as the *prescriptive perspective*. Its literature uses an explicit representation of norms, typically internal as agent beliefs, but can also be external and referenceable.

The norm life cycle in a society with explicit norm representation exhibits the following stages: (i) creation: a norm is introduced into the society, source often unknown, (ii) identification: agents become aware of the norm and update their beliefs, (iii) adoption: agents reason about adopting the norm, (iv) propagation: agents deliberately, or possibly unintentionally, inform others of the norm, (v) emergence: not usually considered, but inferrable when a predetermined threshold of agents have adopted the norm.

The prescriptive perspective branch of the literature presents the norm life cycle with a focus on norm identification and adoption. It also considers the synthesis of norms as an alternative to the norm creation stage, as it defines the norms that will regulate the behaviour of the agents within the MAS. Norm synthesis is geared towards creating norms to avoid conflicts and can occur both online and offline. Recently in normative MAS, online norm synthesis is becoming a popular topic, as it allows for the introduction of norms into the MAS at runtime to meet changing circumstances. Another benefit of online norm synthesis is that it can cater for observed states, or agent capabilities that had not been conceived at the time the MAS was designed [16]. The online norm synthesis mechanisms cited [1,6,25–28] here operate by monitoring the state of the environment and proposing norms to resolve conflicts, that can or have occurred, to prevent their occurrence in the future. For example, [26–28] do so by prohibiting the action of an agent in the timestep before the conflict. The majority of online methods cited above utilise a centralised mechanism with global knowledge, and to the best of our knowledge only AOCMAS [6] employs a decentralised mechanism.

AOCMAS is a two-level distributed MAS architecture that equips an organisation with adaptive capabilities. At one level there are domain agents who are concerned with their individual goals, and above them are assistant agents who are concerned with the organisation's goals and help to facilitate the adaption. Assistants are responsible for or oversee a cluster of domain agents. Assistant agents partially observe the state of the organisation at runtime and propose regulations, rules or legal norms, for problems identified. Before proposing new solutions, assistants check if an existing stored solution is applicable using case-based reasoning (CBR). If none is found, they propose a set of regulations, and each regulation in the set is voted on by all assistants. The regulations with the majority vote become the new set of regulations, that over time are evaluated for effectiveness and may be updated or removed.

Another branch of online norm synthesis mechanisms [14,15,36] incorporates the strategies of individual agents into the normative system through voting, utilising a decentralised mechanism. In [14,15] the most popular strategy becomes part of the normative system, whereas in [36] the most popular strategy and associated sanction is selected, then put to a vote, before it can become part of the normative system. The norms derived here are geared at providing agents with a consistent strategy from among alternatives, presumably operationalised as obligations rather than prohibitions.

We note that the literature on norm synthesis, which is applicable to the norm creation stage of the norm life cycle, fails to investigate the impact of the remainder of the norm life cycle. Instead the focus is on determining an appropriate set of norms, after which it is assumed that either these norms will be adopted by agents or that the norms will be regimented. It is surprising that a disconnect exists within a single perspective of the norm literature, but research in different sections of the literature investigate various processes of the norm life cycle independently, with little attempt to combine or sequence the activities together. This gap, we believe, can readily be filled, by using norm synthesis in lieu of norm creation, while the other stages continue as normal in the prescriptive approach.

2.2 The Emergence Perspective and the Norm Life Cycle

The second perspective of norms is as a preference behaviour. This views norms as a predetermined or computed preference behaviour to execute from among a set of behaviours in a given situation. The preference behaviour perspective is referred to as *norms as conventions* [7] or the *emergence approach* [39], here we refer to it as the *emergence perspective.* Its literature typically uses an implicit norm representation. However it is imperative to note that the deliberate communication of an agent's strategy to another agent would necessitate an explicit representation of the norm. Additionally [8,42] for example, enable agents to make explicit representations of social norms that have been identified via observation.

The norm life cycle in a society with implicit norms usually has these stages: (i) creation: the initial or predetermined strategy for an agent from a set of available actions, (ii) propagation: the sharing of an agent's strategy either unintentionally or deliberately, (iii) emergence: a percentage of agents follow this strategy for every instance of the triggering situation. The norm life cycle with implicit norms is usually seen in simulation models of norm emergence.

The emergence perspective literature is focused primarily on the study of norm emergence. Norm emergence is normally defined as the point in a MAS when a threshold or predetermined percentage of agents adopt a norm. There is generally no discussion of the activities that precede or follow this point in the state of the MAS. In [31] we present the notion that a refinement of norm emergence is needed, as it is difficult to fully understand the emergence of a norm without taking into account the preceding activities of norm creation and propagation. Therefore norm emergence is henceforward what is normally the norm life cycle, but including norm creation and propagation.

Utilising the interactions of agents at runtime as a basis for the creation of norms, as in norm emergence, is another potential solution for the source of norms in the prescriptive perspective, this is similar to the discussion from [12] of a second entry point to the life cycle model. Using norm emergence as a basis for norm creation is not an automatic fix however, as there are disadvantages to using norm emergence alone. Morales et al. [30] suggest that norm emergence is inappropriate to synthesise norms for MAS where there are numerous inter-dependent conflict situations. Additionally, norm emergence does not usually allow for the explicit representations of norms. This can be problematic, because when norms are implicit, there can be confusion among the agents about the prevailing norm, because different subsets of agents may adopt different norms. Additionally agents can have different interpretations about the prevailing norm(s) based on their beliefs [17], whereas [12] consider these different interpretations of norms as a form of norm change.

2.3 Research Opportunity

As we have alluded to earlier, norm emergence in its traditional sense is comparable to online norm synthesis, since both involve the creation of norms at runtime. In norm synthesis the creation of the norms is motivated by a single external entity: external in the sense that it does not involve participating agents, while in norm emergence it is achieved internally by the participating agents' behaviour. The creation of norms in norm emergence is naturally distributed and online, while norm synthesis is usually centralised and often times offline.

We submit that it can be beneficial to use participating agents within the MAS in the norm synthesis process, thereby taking the benefits of the distributed and online approach of norm emergence and adopting it into the norm synthesis process, to produce explicitly represented norms. The final product is an approach that facilitates the emergence of norms in a normative MAS system. Building on the concept of distributed agents having the ability to create norms, we put forward a framework that allows participating agents to request the inclusion/modification of norms in the normative system, based on their experiences within the MAS.

We situate this notion of participating agents contributing to the norms on two of Ostrom's [34] eight principles for governing the commons. Foremost, the need to allow participatory decision making, especially from those who are likely to be affected by the rules/decisions, and secondly the need to ensure the rules in place meet the needs of the local context, that is the participant's needs. We believe these two principles, which are intended to aid proper governance of the commons, are applicable to defining rules for normative MAS with different contexts.

Haynes *et al.* [16] examine how emergent behaviours in a system can be beneficial to the system and should be encouraged and spread, while non-beneficial emergent behaviour should be discouraged. We suggest that beneficial emergent behaviour can further be encoded explicitly as legal norms within the normative MAS. Therefore beneficial emergent behaviours can give rise to the emergence of obligation norms, permission norms and prohibition norms for alternative behaviours. Likewise, non-beneficial emergent behaviours could give rise to the emergence of prohibition norms, obligation norms to avoid certain states and revocation of permission norms.

Frantz et al. [13] examine how agents can derive normative information from their observations and present them as explicit prescriptions with a focus on social norms. In addition, [8,42] show how agents can identify the prevailing norms based on their observations and experiences. The preceding allow us to see the usefulness in equipping agents with the capacity to identify and formulate norms based on their interactions with the system. Therefore the inclusion of agents capable of identifying and formulating norms in a MAS supports the notion of agents that can synthesise different types of norms (for the MAS), a concept we believe presents an opportunity for future research. This is different from the approaches presented in [14,15,36], which allow the synthesis of norms for an action selection strategy from among existing options.

Note however that we do not expect participating agents to be able to properly synthesise norms for the MAS in our approach, because they would need access to domain knowledge and history of the MAS, which a participating agent would not normally have. Additionally, there is a need for higher minimum requirements on the cognitive abilities of participating agents that may make the MAS inaccessible to some agent types. Therefore, we propose agents communicate requests to synthesizer agents, who are responsible for a subset of agents within the MAS. Each synthesizer agent is capable of synthesising norms, based on the request from the participating agents, and their (partial) knowledge of the domain and the environment. We contend that the request for norm change from a participating agent aligns with triggering the initiation of norm synthesis from the bottom up.

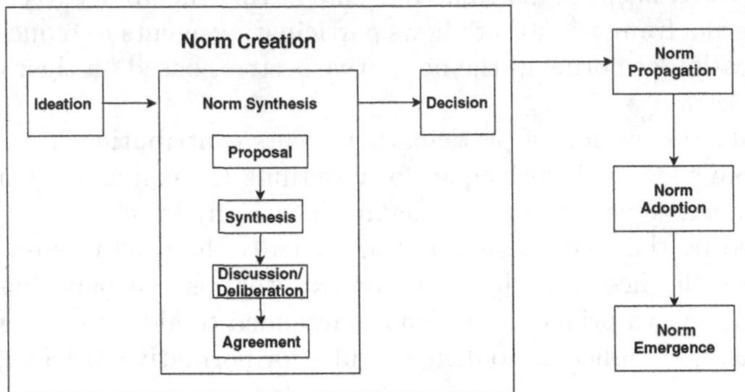

Fig. 1. A conceptualisation of norm emergence for normative MAS

3 Norm Emergence Framework

Agents operating in a MAS, like in human societies, could potentially determine the norms that would better regulate the society. In the emergence perspective literature, it is accepted that agents learn their behaviour from interacting with other agents. This means that the strategy of one agent or a set of agents can become the norm in the society. The usefulness of employing the concept of the agents determining the norm, as a potential answer to the source of the norm in the prescriptive perspective, is worth investigating, thereby allowing the norms of a system to be determined by the agents that participate in the system. [13] show how agents can prescribe social norms based on their observations, but this focuses on an agent's individual norms, rather than incorporating these into the normative system, on the other hand [14,15,36] demonstrate mechanisms to embed the social norm/strategies of agents into the normative system for governing the entire MAS.

The goal of our approach is to explore techniques for developing self-governing systems, in which agents participate in the revision of the norms that affect them. This would preclude the need for direct human intervention to synthesise norms for changing environments, or at the least, require minimal human intervention. The removal of human involvement though useful in this context unearths risks that must be considered in developing MAS. We provide a brief explanation in Sect. 4.3. Decision Stage.

We conceptualise a model that pulls together three research strands, namely: (i) the life cycle of norms in the prescriptive perspective (ii) the life cycle of norms in the emergence perspective, and (iii) the norm synthesis process, in order to construct a framework that facilitates the emergence of norms in a normative MAS. Thereby, we aim to identify the complementary activities – norm creation in emergence and norm identification and adoption in normative MAS and explicitly represented norms from norm synthesis, remove duplicate and unnecessary activities, and sequence them in a way that a new model is revealed. The resulting model enables us to define a norm emergence framework for normative MAS which we sketch in Fig. 2.

The model details the process of norms being synthesised, which begins with the initial recognition of the need for a new norm in the MAS by a participating agent. We conceive of two types of agents operating within the MAS: participant agents and synthesizer agents. The topology of the agents within the MAS will not be considered as we do not consider interactions within the MAS to be influenced by social distance or connections between participating agents. We will however aim for there to be a uniform distribution of agents to synthesizers based on the number of synthesizer agents in use.

Participating Agents. We put forward some assumptions about the agents that may participate in such a MAS, specifically: (i) the agent has an explicit internal representation of norms and some non-trivial cognitive or reasoning abilities, (ii) the agent considers norms in their action-selection and planning processes, and (iii) the agent is capable of perceiving a need for a norm change, either as a new or revised norm.

The agent's perception of the need for a norm change is predicated on agents considering norms when acting, and being able to observe the effect of their actions on the environment via action feedback. The participating agents in our model are inherently *normative agents* and rather *naive* because they assume that the norm(s) they enact are solely responsible for the feedback they receive.

Synthesizer Agents. The framework calls for a distinguished set of agents with partial perception of the MAS, that we refer to as synthesizers. Participating agents are assigned a synthesizer agent upon entry to the MAS. Synthesizer agents are agents designed with knowledge of the domain context: goals, actions, conflicting states, norms. They are capable of perceiving all the actions of the agents for which they are responsible and the environment state at any given time. Synthesizer agents in this model are inspired by the assistant agents in [6], which compute regulations utilising a partial perspective of the MAS, but do so after observing a problem, whereas synthesizer agents here await requests from participating agents. Additionally, assistants [6] vote on the regulations determining which shall be included, and similarly synthesizer agents must vote to decide whether or not to include all the norms proposed after discussions.

We note that synthesizer agents in our model can potentially be proactive as well. They can be proactive by examining traces and identifying when conflicting states occur, then proposing norms to avoid them in the future, without waiting on instruction from the agent to do so. Such an approach echoes elements of [26,

28–30]. Synthesizer agents could also have other functions within a MAS, such as being responsible for the enforcement of sanctions if violation occurs. We have however decided to limit the functions of the synthesizers in this framework to participating in the process of synthesising norms for the normative system only upon receipt of requests from agents. This we believe allows us to demonstrate norm synthesis initiated from the bottom-up which is different from existing research on norm synthesis.

Components of the Framework. The stages of the conceptual model of our framework are: (i) norm creation, (ii) norm propagation, (iii) norm adoption, and (iv) norm emergence as shown in Fig. 1 and Fig. 2.

Of the existing life cycle models, the stages of our conceptual framework are most closely aligned with the life cycle model of norm emergence in [12], with respect to the sequencing of stages but with some differences. Our norm creation stage encapsulates the norm creation activities of [12] that are shown as two entry points to their model at norm creation and identification. Our decision for one entry point is premised on utilising special-purpose synthesizer agents which encode the norms based on requests from individual agents. Therefore, though agent's experiences form the basis for changes to the normative system, these changes are managed by a group of domain agents, synthesizers, and changes must be approved before the rules/norms of the system are changed.

The activities of norm propagation are similar to that of transmission and norm adoption with identification, however norm emergence is represented as a specific stage in our model, while it is viewed as a phenomenon in [12]. Emergence is a specific stage in our framework because we consider it to be an activity that will be realised when a number of agents acting in a particular way exceeds a threshold.

We do not consider the forgetting of norms in our model. Our assumption is that modifications to the normative system could result in additions, modifications or deletions to the norms, which can be viewed as similar to the concept of forgetting being a byproduct of evolving norms in [12], though their lifecycle provides a specific stage to represent it. Additionally [12] discuss evolution as another phenomenon and though we do not consider it in our framework, it can be considered to exist in a similar way in our model, through the actions of the synthesizer agents on the set of norms.

The key difference we claim between our framework and the existing life cycle models, is that it builds a bridge from a theoretical understanding of the norm life cycle to a framework that operationalises the stages to bring about the emergence of norms in a normative MAS, utilising synthesizer agents. We discuss each of the stages of our conceptual model: norm creation, norm propagation, norm adoption, and norm emergence, in the remaining sections of the paper.

4 Norm Creation Stage

The creation stage comprises three sub-processes (i) ideation (ii) norm synthesis, and (iii) decision, depicted in Fig. 2, component 1. In the ideal scenario, at the

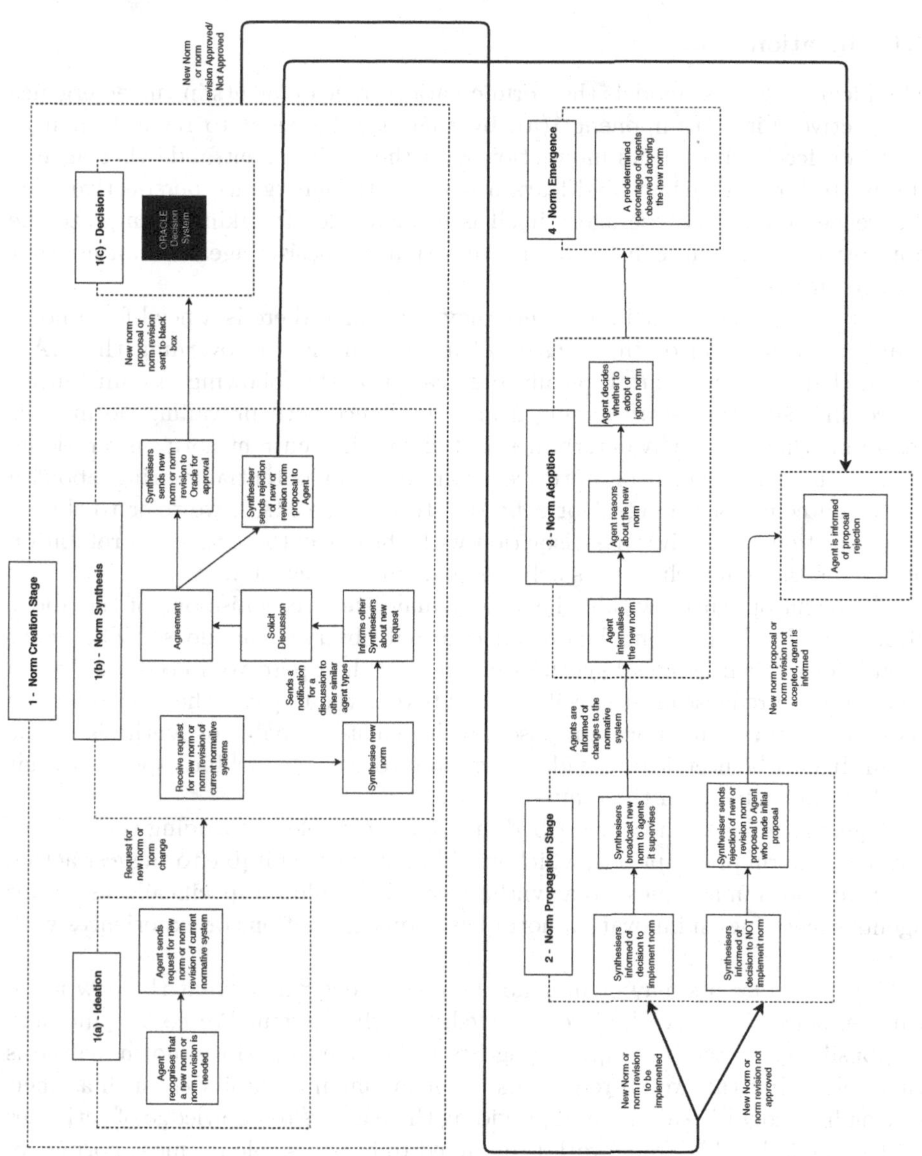

Fig. 2. Conceptual Model for norm emergence in normative MAS

end of creation, there is a norm that must be incorporated into the normative system. If not, the request would not have been approved, and thereafter the synthesizers and the initial requesting agent must be informed.

4.1 Ideation

The ideation process models the norm creation stage of agents in the emergence perspective, Fig. 2, component 1(a), by enabling the agent to request changes based on feedback from its interaction with the environment and other agents, similar to how an agent would learn a norm in the emergence perspective. The difference here is that the agent itself is not capable of making changes to the normative system, but can communicate with a synthesizer agent to initiate that change on their behalf.

A participating agent in a society may determine there is a need for a norm change: a new norm or the revision of an existing norm governing the MAS. Norm change requests are typically predicated on the following circumstances: (i) conflict situation/state arising from compliance with prevailing norms, (ii) reasoning that repeatedly determines that violation of current norms is a rational choice, (ii) a new norm or norm revision that can potentially bring about a better outcome for the agent or a better state in the MAS; we refer to this as an innovation norm, (iv) dissatisfaction with the current norms, e.g. prohibition of actions that can help agents achieve goals more efficiently.

An agent operating within the society may likely recognise one of the above situations developing long before an external observer can do so. The agent then informs their assigned synthesizer agent of their perceived need for a norm change. Each request must specify the context of the request, the reason for the request and the actual norm proposed, if the agent is capable of synthesising the norm. It may be useful to provide a template to the agents which specifies what needs to be included in the request.

Agents similar to those described in [13] are capable of encoding their observations as norm prescriptions, which would make them suitable to suggest actual norm revisions in a request to a synthesizer. This could be specifically useful for agents suggesting an innovation norm based on observations or experiences with the system.

Individual agents may or may not be able to determine what the new norm can be, since they have limited knowledge of the system. We could put more responsibility on the participating agents to be able to perform norm synthesis themselves, but this would require us to set minimum capabilities, such as their having high cognitive ability and providing them access to knowledge of activities within the MAS. The framework is intended to be accessible for most normative agents so we prefer an approach which does not impose significant requirements.

4.2 Norm Synthesis Stage

The norm synthesis process, as depicted in Fig. 2, component 1(b), enables the encoding of the agents' request, which would have been influenced by their behaviour, into an explicit legal norm that can address the issue within the request. Synthesizer agents, upon receipt of a proposal, begin the process of synthesising a new norm to address the proposal, but additionally, the synthesizer agents engage in discussion and the establishment of a consensus about the request. The sub-processes of the norm synthesis stage are: proposal, synthesis, discussion/deliberation, and agreement, each of which we now discuss in more detail.

Proposal. After receiving a proposal, synthesiser agents must parse the request in preparation for synthesising one or more norms. Agents utilise a provided template to make proposals and the synthesizer will be equipped to interpret it. Synthesizers will normally address requests chronologically and will only handle one request at a time; if multiple requests occur over a short space of time, they are queued. It is at this point that synthesisers have to decide which requests warrant action, by applying a filtering mechanism. Synthesizers could employ an automated rejection process, which returns a message to participating agents when their norm requests have been deemed to not warrant action. We note however that a filtering service could potentially be made available to participating agents, whereby an intermediate mechanism processes the complaint, provides feedback and then the agent decides whether to make a request of the synthesizer agent.

Synthesis. The act of synthesising or encoding the norm occurs here. This process utilises the originating agent's request, information about the environment that it can perceive and the domain context. Alternatively, if the participating agent is able to synthesise a norm that will meet the identified need and include it in the request, then this process entails the synthesizer agent determining the validity of the norm.

During synthesis, the synthesizer agent must reason whether the synthesised norm(s) is capable of addressing the need identified by the agent. For example, for a conflict situation, the norm should ensure that once followed, that conflict situation is no longer observed, or for an innovation norm, the norm once adopted ensures that the agents are more efficient in accomplishing their goals, and those of the MAS, or the observation of more acceptable states in the MAS.

Existing literature employs different mechanisms for synthesising norms. SENSE [30] considers the context of the interacting agents in the time-step before the conflict situation and the actions taken by the agents in that time-step. It then synthesises a norm by prohibiting the action of any one of the participating agents. This is similar to IRON [26,28]. Another technique, utilised in [2,23], is built on inductive logic programming and uses the following inputs: a normative system (which could be an empty set), the observation traces and the normative conditions that must hold in the final states. It utilises the proceeding to revise the normative system producing norms (rules) that are compatible with the supplied trace and the condition. Both [2,23] and [30] are offline mechanisms, but can potentially be replicated for online use.

Finally, the proposed new norm is put forward to the other synthesizer agents for discussion and agreement.

Discussion/Deliberation. The synthesising agent informs other synthesizer agents about the new norm and solicits a discussion via a discussion mechanism, which we will call a discussion board, that is visible and accessible only to synthesizer agents. There is potential to have the agents in the system be able to view this discussion board. We considered the possibility of providing *read-only* access to participating agents, but this would require them to have the ability to parse and understand the discussions on the board, erecting further technical barriers to access.

Synthesizers are alerted when there is a new activity on the discussion board and they can engage in the discussion when ready. The presenting synthesizer agent may be required to defend their proposed norm. An argumentation or negotiation scheme may be appropriate here and can be developed based on existing argumentation frameworks such as [3–5,37]. Synthesiser agents will be required to defend the validity of the proposed norm under scrutiny to other synthesizers, not unlike the agents in [3], who have to defend their preferred action or abort.

The resolution of internal norm conflicts and modifications, based on new perspectives highlighted by the other synthesizers, can result in the revision of the proposed norm. It is the responsibility of the synthesizer that proposes the norm to ensure that after any changes made during this process, the modified norm can still meet the needs of the initial request. Therefore, it is possible that the initial proposed norm may be revised, and the actual outcome is a consequence of modifications made as part of this stage.

Agreement. To proceed to the next stage, there needs to be agreement, where, say, a predetermined percentage of synthesisers must agree that the new norm should be introduced into the normative system. Synthesizers can come to agreement using several methods: (i) a clear direction forward can be established based on the outcome(s) of the previous discussion phase, (ii) synthesizers can attempt to reach a consensus on the norm proposal for or against it proceeding, or (iii) synthesizers can utilise a voting mechanism (agreed in advance).

If a decision to allow the norm proposal to proceed cannot be reached, the presenting synthesizer must inform the proposing agent that the norm change was rejected. The synthesizer can provide reasons for the rejection so that the proposing agent can possibly refine and submit a new request/proposal. Once a decision is reached, the agreed norm change is passed on to the decision stage for a final decision on its inclusion in the normative system of the MAS.

4.3 Decision Stage

The decision about whether a norm change will be made is done by a decision making mechanism, which we will refer to as the "Oracle" as depicted in Fig. 2, component 1(c). The Oracle is assumed to have access to the entire state of the MAS. The context and domain of the MAS may require that this decision incorporates human input [35,46]. Human input might be necessary to preclude the risk of destabilisation of the MAS due to repeated norm synthesis or the synthesis of norms that are potentially detrimental to the purpose of the MAS. The domain of the MAS being modelled will determine whether the Oracle's final decision to modify the normative system requires human input, or if an automated decision only can be allowed. For example, in a MAS interacting directly with humans or whose impact can be catastrophic, it may be preferred if a human(s) authorises the changes to the normative system.

A possible solution would be for the mechanism to make a recommendation that needs to be accepted by a human oversight process before implementation. We note that though including a human at this stage can provide human accountability, it raises the challenge of ensuring that the human and the system have the same understanding of the goals of the system. Otherwise we risk a situation where both human and system may need to prove which party is correct. This could necessitate further arbitration mechanisms to avoid stagnation within the MAS.

Though norm conflicts would have been considered in discussions with other synthesizers, there may still be norm conflicts arising from external interaction. This can occur when the MAS may be itself governed by a higher level MAS [19] and the norms of this MAS must not conflict with the norms of the governing MAS. These conflicts, if they exist must be resolved, and this can be achieved utilising techniques similar to [19]. The stability of the normative system within the MAS must also be considered and should be incorporated into the final decision on the modification of the normative system. At the end of this process, the decision to include or reject the norm proposed is communicated to the synthesizer agents.

5 Norm Propagation

At the end of the norm creation stage, a norm has either been accepted for inclusion into the normative system or been rejected. The preceding decision must be communicated to the synthesizer agents by the Oracle. The norm propagation activities are depicted in Fig. 2, component 2. In the case of a modification to the normative system, synthesiser agents are tasked with spreading this information to the agents they are responsible for as it is necessary that all participating agents in the MAS be aware of any changes to the normative system. Synthesizers can choose an appropriate norm propagation mechanism to communicate with their assigned participating agents. Broadcasting is one solution, a common knowledge source, as used in [43] is another, which advises agents when new information is available, or synthesizers can use a distributed sharing mechanism, where they inform some agents, who then inform other agents they are connected to. This latter approach could possibly affect whether all agents become aware of the modifications to the normative system in a timely manner. Alternatively, if the norm change proposal was rejected, the synthesizer needs to communicate this to the agent that made the initial proposal.

6 Norm Adoption

The adoption of the norm requires the agent to internalise and reason about adopting the norm. The norm adoption activities are depicted in Fig. 2, component 3. Internalising the norm means making an internal representation of the norm, while the adoption of the norm is the decision whether to adopt the norm after reasoning about it. The internalisation of the norm is initiated when agents are made aware of modifications to the normative system. As agents are assumed to have an explicit internal representation of norms, see Sect. 3, this internalisation of the norm means agents will have to incorporate the norm as part of their beliefs. We note the potential for misinterpretations and changes to the norms as a result of this internalisation process [12,17], however we consider the inclusion of a centralised, externally referenceable normative system as helping to minimise the effects of this.

Once internalised, agents can reason about the validity and applicability of the norm and decide whether it is useful to adopt it. Some agents will do this once and adopt the norm in every situation that it is applicable going forward, as with the normative agents in [9]. Other agents will reason about it every time a decision to act needs to be made, similar to agents in [4,38] and graded normative agents in [9].

7 Norm Emergence

The norm emergence activities are depicted in Fig. 2, component 4. Once an agent has adopted the norm and complies with it, the percentage of agents doing so may reach the threshold for emergence. At this point it can be said that the norm has emerged within the MAS. If the percentage of agents adopting the norm never reaches the threshold for emergence, it may be useful to see if the opposite prevails. That is, where a large percentage of agents violate the norm. If this is the case then it may be necessary to reevaluate the norm's place within the normative system, which could ultimately lead to its removal.

8 Conclusions

In this paper we present a framework for norm emergence in normative MAS premised on utilising the experiences of participating agents to trigger changes in the normative system. We describe a distinguished population of synthesizer agents, who accept requests from participating agents and synthesise norms in response to these requests. We believe that this is a useful approach for open MAS as there is no need to impose any requirements on the participating agents but can instead provide a set of synthesizer agents that have the requisite capabilities to perform the role. The introduction of synthesisers, that can propose changes to the normative system, provides participating agents with recourse when they are not satisfied with their experience in the MAS. Instead of leaving the MAS, they can potentially initiate changes within the MAS that will not only improve the experience for themselves, but perhaps for other agents. Participating agents will only need to know who their synthesizer agent is and what information should be provided.

We posit that the use of special-purpose synthesizer agents that address the needs of participating agents, equips the MAS to modify its normative system at runtime, thereby facilitating decentralised runtime norm synthesis in the MAS. Furthermore we posit that the inclusion of discussion and agreement phases for synthesizer agents to agree on the inclusion of norms is an important addition to the framework. A synthesizer will synthesise norms based on a partial context, and as a result it could synthesise norms that, though capable of resolving the proposed issue, are not useful for the collective MAS.

The remaining synthesiser agents will be able to assess the proposed norm and determine how it will affect their own view of the MAS. The intention is that only norms that are beneficial to a majority or all agents of the MAS shall achieve consensus to proceed to the final stage of verification in the MAS: the *decision stage*. The goal is that this additional layer will aid the MAS by helping to maintain the stability of the normative system and preventing agents from introducing norms that are detrimental to it. It is also the stage where norms can be checked for compliance with governing external MASs, if they exist and/or non-negotiable MAS norms/rules. This stage can also allow for human input depending on the domain of the MAS.

The normative system is modified if the norm is approved by the Oracle mechanism in the decision stage, and agents within the MAS need to be informed of changes to the normative MAS. Participating agents will then reason about adopting the norm and over time a threshold of agents may choose to adopt the norm. Ultimately we may observe the emergence of the norm in the MAS that was synthesised based on a request by a participating agent.

References

1. Alechina, N., Bulling, N., Dastani, M., Logan, B.: Practical run-time norm enforcement with bounded lookahead. In: Weiss, et al. [45], pp. 443–451
2. Athakravi, D., Corapi, D., Russo, A., De Vos, M., Padget, J., Satoh, K.: Handling change in normative specifications. In: Baldoni, M., Dennis, L., Mascardi, V., Vasconcelos, W. (eds.) DALT 2012. LNCS (LNAI), vol. 7784, pp. 1–19. Springer, Heidelberg (2013). https://doi.org/10.1007/978-3-642-37890-4_1
3. Atkinson, K., Bench-Capon, T.: Practical reasoning as presumptive argumentation using action based alternating transition systems. Artif. Intell. **171**(10–15), 855–874 (2007). https://doi.org/10.1016/j.artint.2007.04.009
4. Bench-Capon, T., Modgil, S.: Norms and value based reasoning: justifying compliance and violation. Artif. Intell. Law **25**(1), 29–64 (2017). https://doi.org/10.1007/s10506-017-9194-9
5. Boella, G., van der Torre, L.: BDI and BOID argumentation. In: Proceedings of IJCAI Workshop on Computational Models of Natural Argument, vol. 3 (2003)
6. Campos, J., Lopez-Sanchez, M., Salamó, M., Avila, P., Rodríguez-Aguilar, J.A.: Robust regulation adaptation in multi-agent systems. ACM Trans. Auton. Adapt. Syst. **8**(3), 1–27 (2013). https://doi.org/10.1145/2517328

7. Conte, R., Castelfranchi, C.: From conventions to prescriptions. Towards an integrated view of norms. Artif. Intell. Law **7**(4), 323–340 (1999)
8. Cranefield, S., Savarimuthu, T., Meneguzzi, F., Oren, N.: A Bayesian approach to norm identification. In: Proceedings of the 2015 International Conference on Autonomous Agents and Multiagent Systems, AAMAS 2015, pp. 1743–1744. International Foundation for Autonomous Agents and Multiagent Systems, Richland, SC (2015)
9. Criado, N., Argente, E., Botti, V.: Normative deliberation in graded BDI agents. In: Dix, J., Witteveen, C. (eds.) MATES 2010. LNCS (LNAI), vol. 6251, pp. 52–63. Springer, Heidelberg (2010). https://doi.org/10.1007/978-3-642-16178-0_7
10. Dell'Anna, D., Dastani, M., Dalpiaz, F.: Runtime norm revision using Bayesian networks. In: Miller, T., Oren, N., Sakurai, Y., Noda, I., Savarimuthu, B.T.R., Cao Son, T. (eds.) PRIMA 2018. LNCS (LNAI), vol. 11224, pp. 279–295. Springer, Cham (2018). https://doi.org/10.1007/978-3-030-03098-8_17
11. Dell'Anna, D., Dastani, M., Dalpiaz, F.: Runtime revision of norms and sanctions based on agent preferences. In: Elkind, E., Veloso, M., Agmon, N., Taylor, M.E. (eds.) Proceedings of the 18th International Conference on Autonomous Agents and MultiAgent Systems, AAMAS 2019, Montreal, QC, Canada, May 13–17, pp. 1609–1617 (2017). International Foundation for Autonomous Agents and Multiagent Systems (2019). http://dl.acm.org/citation.cfm?id=3331881
12. Frantz, C., Pigozzi, G.: Modeling norm dynamics in multiagent systems. FLAP **5**(2), 491–564 (2018). https://www.collegepublications.co.uk/downloads/ifcolog00022.pdf
13. Frantz, C.K., Purvis, M.K., Savarimuthu, B.T.R., Nowostawski, M.: Modelling dynamic normative understanding in agent societies. Scalable Comput. Pract. Exp. **16**(4), 355–380 (2015). http://www.scpe.org/index.php/scpe/article/view/1128
14. Ghorbani, A., Bravo, G.: Managing the commons: a simple model of the emergence of institutions through collective action. Int. J. Commons **10**(1), 200–219 (2016). https://doi.org/10.18352/ijc.606
15. Ghorbani, A., Bravo, G., Frey, U., Theesfeld, I.: Self-organization in the commons: an empirically-tested model. Environ. Modell. Softw. **96**, 30–45 (2017). https://doi.org/10.1016/j.envsoft.2017.06.039
16. Haynes, C., Luck, M., McBurney, P., Mahmoud, S., Ví tek, T., Miles, S.: Engineering the emergence of norms: a review. Knowl. Eng. Rev. **32**, e18 (2017). https://doi.org/10.1017/S0269888917000169
17. Hollander, C.D., Wu, A.S.: The current state of normative agent-based systems. J. Artif. Soc. Soc. Simul. **14**(2) (2011). https://doi.org/10.18564/jasss.1750
18. Huang, X., Ruan, J., Chen, Q., Su, K.: Normative multiagent systems: The dynamic generalization. In: Kambhampati, S. (ed.) Proceedings of the Twenty-Fifth International Joint Conference on Artificial Intelligence, IJCAI 2016, New York, NY, USA, 9–15 July 2016, pp. 1123–1129. IJCAI/AAAI Press (2016). http://www.ijcai.org/Abstract/16/163
19. King, T.C., De Vos, M., Dignum, V., Jonker, C.M., Li, T., Padget, J., van Riemsdijk, M.B.: Automated multi-level governance compliance checking. Auton. Agent. Multi-Agent Syst. **31**(6), 1283–1343 (2017). https://doi.org/10.1007/s10458-017-9363-y
20. Knobbout, M., Dastani, M., Meyer, J.-J.C.: Reasoning about dynamic normative systems. In: Fermé, E., Leite, J. (eds.) JELIA 2014. LNCS (LNAI), vol. 8761, pp. 628–636. Springer, Cham (2014). https://doi.org/10.1007/978-3-319-11558-0_46

21. Knobbout, M., Dastani, M., Meyer, J.C.: A dynamic logic of norm change. In: Kaminka, G.A., et al. (eds.) ECAI 2016–22nd European Conference on Artificial Intelligence, 29 August–2 September 2016, The Hague, The Netherlands - Including Prestigious Applications of Artificial Intelligence (PAIS 2016). Frontiers in Artificial Intelligence and Applications, vol. 285, pp. 886–894. IOS Press (2016). https://doi.org/10.3233/978-1-61499-672-9-886
22. Lee, J.H., Padget, J., Logan, B., Dybalova, D., Alechina, N.: *N-Jason*: run-time norm compliance in AgentSpeak(L). In: Dalpiaz, F., Dix, J., van Riemsdijk, M.B. (eds.) EMAS 2014. LNCS (LNAI), vol. 8758, pp. 367–387. Springer, Cham (2014). https://doi.org/10.1007/978-3-319-14484-9_19
23. Li, T.: Normative Conflict Detection and Resolution in Cooperating Institutions. Ph.D. thesis, University of Bath, July 2014. https://researchportal.bath.ac.uk/files/123040954/Tingting_thesis_final.pdf
24. Mahmoud, M.A., Ahmad, M.S., Mohd Yusoff, M.Z., Mustapha, A.: A review of norms and normative multiagent systems. Sci. World J. (2014). https://doi.org/10.1155/2014/684587. Hindawi Publishing Corporation
25. Mashayekhi, M., Du, H., List, G.F., Singh, M.P.: Silk: a simulation study of regulating open normative multiagent systems. In: Proceedings of the Twenty-Fifth International Joint Conference on Artificial Intelligence, IJCAI 2016, pp. 373–379. AAAI Press (2016)
26. Morales, J., Lopez-Sanchez, M., Rodriguez-Aguilar, J.A., Wooldridge, M., Vasconcelos, W.: Automated synthesis of normative systems. In: Proceedings of the 2013 International Conference on Autonomous Agents and Multi-agent Systems, pp. 483–490. International Foundation for Autonomous Agents and Multiagent Systems (2013)
27. Morales, J., López-Sánchez, M., Rodríguez-Aguilar, J.A., Wooldridge, M.J., Vasconcelos, W.W.: Synthesising liberal normative systems. In: Weiss et al. [45], pp. 433–441
28. Morales, J., López-sánchez, M., Rodriguez-Aguilar, J.A., Vasconcelos, W., Wooldridge, M.: Online automated synthesis of compact normative systems. ACM Trans. Auton. Adapt. Syst. **10**(1), 1–33 (2015). https://doi.org/10.1145/2720024
29. Morales, J., Wooldridge, M., Rodríguez-Aguilar, J.A., López-Sánchez, M.: Evolutionary synthesis of stable normative systems. In: Proceedings of the 16th Conference on Autonomous Agents and MultiAgent Systems, AAMAS 2017, pp. 1646–1648. International Foundation for Autonomous Agents and Multiagent Systems, Richland, SC (2017)
30. Morales, J., Wooldridge, M., Rodríguez-Aguilar, J.A., López-Sánchez, M.: Off-line synthesis of evolutionarily stable normative systems. Auton. Agents Multi-Agent Syst. (2018). https://doi.org/10.1007/s10458-018-9390-3
31. Morris-Martin, A., De Vos, M., Padget, J.: Norm emergence in multiagent systems: a viewpoint paper. Auton. Agent. Multi-Agent Syst. **33**(6), 706–749 (2019). https://doi.org/10.1007/s10458-019-09422-0
32. Mukherjee, P., Sen, S., Airiau, S.: Emergence of norms with biased interactions in heterogeneous agent societies. In: 2007 IEEE/WIC/ACM International Conferences on Web Intelligence and Intelligent Agent Technology Workshops, pp. 512–515. IEEE (2007). https://doi.org/10.1109/WI-IATW.2007.115

33. Noriega, P., Sabater-Mir, J., Verhagen, H., Padget, J., d'Inverno, M.: fIdentifying affordances for modelling second-order emergent phenomena with the $\mathcal{WIT}$ framework. In: Sukthankar, G., Rodriguez-Aguilar, J.A. (eds.) AAMAS 2017. LNCS (LNAI), vol. 10643, pp. 208–227. Springer, Cham (2017). https://doi.org/10.1007/978-3-319-71679-4_14
34. Ostrom, E.: Governing the Commons. The Evolution of Institutions for Collective Action, CUP (1990)
35. Rahwan, I.: Society-in-the-loop: programming the algorithmic social contract. Ethics Inf. Technol. **20**(1), 5–14 (2018). https://doi.org/10.1007/s10676-017-9430-8
36. Riveret, R., Artikis, A., Busquets, D., Pitt, J.: Self-governance by transfiguration: from learning to prescriptions. In: Cariani, F., Grossi, D., Meheus, J., Parent, X. (eds.) DEON 2014. LNCS (LNAI), vol. 8554, pp. 177–191. Springer, Cham (2014). https://doi.org/10.1007/978-3-319-08615-6_14
37. Riveret, R., Rotolo, A., Sartor, G.: Probabilistic rule-based argumentation for norm-governed learning agents. Artif. Intell. Law **20**(4), 383–420 (2012). https://doi.org/10.1007/s10506-012-9134-7
38. dos Santos Neto, B.F., da Silva, V.T., de Lucena, C.J.P.: Developing goal-oriented normative agents: the NBDI architecture. In: Filipe, J., Fred, A. (eds.) ICAART 2011. CCIS, vol. 271, pp. 176–191. Springer, Heidelberg (2013). https://doi.org/10.1007/978-3-642-29966-7_12
39. Savarimuthu, B.T.R., Arulanandam, R., Savarimuthu, S.: Emergence of a sharing norm in a simulated hunter-gatherer society. In: Proceedings of the 2011 IEEE/WIC/ACM International Conference on Intelligent Agent Technology, IAT 2011, Campus Scientifique de la Doua, Lyon, France, 22–27 August 2011, pp. 34–37 (2011). https://doi.org/10.1109/WI-IAT.2011.141
40. Savarimuthu, B.T.R., Cranefield, S.: Norm creation, spreading and emergence: a survey of simulation models of norms in multi-agent systems. Multiagent Grid Syst. **7**(1), 21–54 (2011). https://doi.org/10.3233/MGS-2011-0167
41. Savarimuthu, B.T.R., Cranefield, S., Purvis, M.K., Purvis, M.A.: Norm emergence in agent societies formed by dynamically changing networks. Web Intell. Agent Syst. Int. J. **7**(3), 223–232 (2009). https://doi.org/10.3233/WIA-2009-0164
42. Savarimuthu, B.T.R., Cranefield, S., Purvis, M., Purvis, M.K.: Identifying prohibition norms in agent societies. Artif. Intell. Law **21**(1), 1–46 (2013). https://doi.org/10.1007/s10506-012-9126-7
43. Savarimuthu, B.T.R., Purvis, M., Purvis, M., Cranefield, S.: Social norm emergence in virtual agent societies. In: Baldoni, M., Son, T.C., van Riemsdijk, M.B., Winikoff, M. (eds.) DALT 2008. LNCS (LNAI), vol. 5397, pp. 18–28. Springer, Heidelberg (2009). https://doi.org/10.1007/978-3-540-93920-7_2
44. Villatoro, D., Sen, S., Sabater-Mir, J.: Topology and memory effect on convention emergence, pp. 233–240. IEEE (2009). https://doi.org/10.1109/WI-IAT.2009.155
45. Weiss, G., Yolum, P., Bordini, R.H., Elkind, E. (eds.) Proceedings of the 2015 International Conference on Autonomous Agents and Multiagent Systems, AAMAS 2015, Istanbul, Turkey, 4–8 May 2015. ACM (2015)
46. Zanzotto, F.M.: Viewpoint: human-in-the-loop artificial intelligence. J. Artif. Int. Res. **64**(1), 243–252 (2019). https://doi.org/10.1613/jair.1.11345

Social Rules for Agent Systems

René Mellema([✉]), Maarten Jensen, and Frank Dignum

Umeå University, Umeå, Sweden
{rene.mellema,maarten.jensen,dignum}@cs.umu.se

Abstract. When creating (open) agent systems it has become common practice to use social concepts such as social practices, norms and conventions to model the way the interactions between the agents are regulated. However, in the literature most papers concentrate on only one of these aspects at the time. Therefore there is hardly any research on how these social concepts relate. It is also unclear whether something like a norm evolves from a social practice or convention or whether they are complete independent entities. In this paper we investigate some of the conceptual differences between these concepts. Whether they are fundamentally stemming from a single social object or should be seen as different types of objects altogether. And finally, when one should which type of concept in an implementation or a combination of them.

1 Introduction

In the last twenty years several social rules such as conventions, norms and recently also social practices, rituals and habits have been used to model agent behaviour in multi-agent systems. The main intuition behind the use of these rules is that agents are at least partially autonomous and thus their behaviour cannot just be constrained through some hard constraints. Moreover, the social rules have not only a constraining character, but also have a motivational component in that they are part of the deliberation process. E.g. a norm to keep to the traffic rules as a bicyclist can lead to a plan to leave home early for a meeting in order to have enough time to navigate the traffic in a legal manner. The fact that the social rules have different aspects and consequences makes them difficult to implement in a uniform way as that implementation depends on what kind of internal mechanisms are available in the agents as well as in the environment. Thus different applications have concentrated on different aspects of the social rules, while most applications only use one of the social rule types.

In this paper we will discuss the different types of social rules. In particular we will look at social practices, conventions, social norms, moral norms, legal norms, rituals and habits. In a later stage we will also include the more complex social concepts such as institutions and organizations that are built in top of these social rules. See e.g. [12]. We will give a short overview of all the selected

This research was partially supported by the Wallenberg AI, Autonomous Systems and Software Program (WASP) funded by the Knut and Alice Wallenberg Foundation.

A. Aler Tubella et al. (Eds.): COIN 2017/COINE 2020, LNAI 12298, pp. 175–180, 2021.
https://doi.org/10.1007/978-3-030-72376-7_10

social rules in Sect. 2. These social rules are then compared in Sect. 3. In Sect. 4, we will go over some implications for implementation and in the last section we give some preliminary conclusions.

A more detailed version of this article can be found at: https://arxiv.org/abs/2004.12797.

2 Social Rules

In this section we briefly discuss the different social rule types and indicate their main characteristics.

Social Practices come from social practice theory [3,4,9–11], which claims that human life is best understood as constellations of interacting persons. Within this theory, social practices are a kind of interaction pattern that can be triggered in certain contexts. As mentioned in [9,11], a social practice consists of three parts:

- *resources*: the time, place, objects, and *actors* used in the practice
- *activities*: the (type of) actions involved and their ordering
- *meaning*: the social interpretations that are linked with the social practice, such as kinship and familiarity

In [8] we have shown how a formal definition of social practices can be given geared towards its use in computer science. E.g. for activities we defined ways to specify plan patterns and actions that will fit in them and can be used by the participants in the practice. We have insufficient space to give the complete formal description, but it is important to mention that social practices exist only through their regular execution by individuals in physical contexts. Good examples are handshakes as greetings or soccer games as played in a park by a group of friends.

Conventions are patterns of behaviour that are not connected to an intrinsic value by themselves, but that aid coordination since most people know about and follow them. The standard formalization for conventions comes from [7] and are formulated in game theory, as an equilibrium in a so called cooperation game. The utility of conventions comes from the fact that following a convention gives a simple rule to act in an interaction situation which otherwise would give no clue what to do. E.g. if a Skype or Zoom connection breaks the convention is that the host of the meeting will try to reconnect. As one can see this rule does not promote a specific value and thus cannot be seen as a norm. It just is a functional way to smooth the coordination.

Norms have been studied for a long time, but so far, no unique definition or classification has been given that all people agree upon. We view norms as rules that prohibit or oblige certain situations or actions, where violation of these rules can lead to sanctions by other people or institutions. For our purposes, we use the following simplified classification:

- *Social norms* describe standard patterns of behaviour within a group of people, deviation of which is seen as wrong because it is different from what is normal.
- *Moral norms* are more individual based rules based on what people value, but do not have to be bound to specific behaviour.
- *Formal (or legal) norms* are institutionalized rules that are not enforced by the society directly, but by an appointed authority.

Norms are tied to values such as *conformity, environment and safety.*

Rituals, similar to social practices, describe interactions between people. However, unlike social practices, these interactions put little focus on the actual effect [5], but more on the social meaning. They tend to be characterized by formalism, tradition, invariance, rule-governance, (sacred) symbolism, and performance [2]. Examples are the wedding ritual, baptism and initiation for sororities.

Habits are individual behavioral rules. In fact, they are "a more or less fixed way of thinking, willing or feeling acquired through previous repetition of a mental experience" [1]. While they are individual, they can be used to anticipate others' behaviour, and can in that way aid in planning for coordination.

3 Comparison of Social Rules

Social practices can be seen as the basis of the other social rules. They are emerging patterns of interactions that are attached to the specific people practicing them. From social practices, other rules can emerge such as norms, conventions, rituals and even habits.

Conventions and habits do not have any specific social meaning associated with them. Rituals do have a specific meaning, but there the functional effect is not very important. Thus the actual actions performed in a ritual are there to recognize that the ritual is performed and the social effect is achieved. In that sense a ritual can be seen as a degenerated social practice where only a social meaning is left and no practical effect, while the plan pattern is solidified to a strict protocol. Habits can be seen as social practices that are tied to just one person.

Beside the above points, social practices are more situated and bound to specific situations and contexts than the other rules. Whereas a social practice can be between two people, both conventions and norms only work if they are applied within societies, and rituals are specific to groups of people. The exception to this rule are habits, who are completely personal, and require no interaction at all.

The different social rules also have different effects. There is little social effect from conventions and habits. This is different for norms, where someone who consistently follows the norms will be seen as an upstanding member of society. This effect is even stronger for social practices and rituals, where someone that follows them is seen as promoting the attached meaning. For rituals it is even stronger, since they can make someone part of the in-group.

Violations of the various social rules also have different effects. Here, the norms tend to be a bit different from the other social rules, in that violation of a norm normally leads to sanctions, whereas for all the other social rules, violation normally either leads to discontinuation of the behaviour (habits, rituals) or to a change in the interaction (practices, conventions). The latter case is the main driver behind change in social practices.

Figure 1 visualizes the general relations between the different social rules along the two dimensions of functional/social effects and based on whether individuals can uphold the rule or groups are needed. We place habits as purely individual and social practices as group interactions. While social practices have a slightly more social meaning, habits are usually more functional. On the other axis we can see rituals and conventions, they are both less individual. However they differ in the sense that rituals are very social meaning focused, while conventions are very functionally driven. Norms are for the most part in the social meaning realm, with social norms being the most social. The moral norms are more individual and legal norms are very individual. They are indeed created by a society, however upholding these norms does not depend on the group but is up to each individual. Following these norms is very individual as well as one does not need people around to abide to the law.

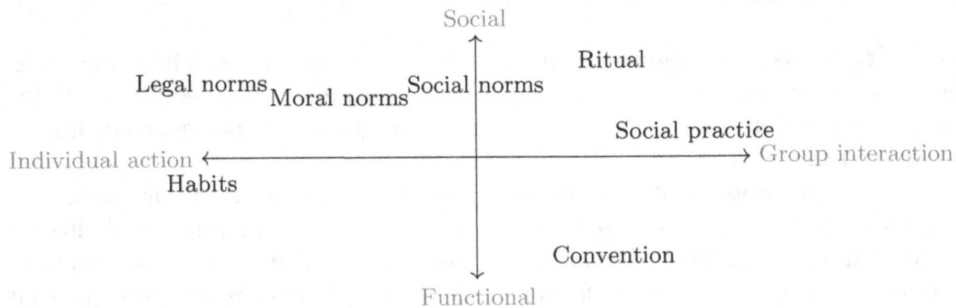

Fig. 1. Representation of relation between the discussed social rules.

4 Implementing Social Rules

While social practices can be seen as the basis for all social rules, this does not make them the easiest to implement. In fact, their generality makes them one of the hardest to implement, since there are hardly any constraints on them. It is mainly a repeating behaviour affecting two or more parties, meaning their usefulness depends on their frequency. This points in the direction that some learning mechanism is needed. However, if the social practice is supposed to be readily available to all agents, then they could also be included as plan patterns for all agents. Another aspect of social practices that is important is that they are context dependent, so this would also require a system for recognising contexts.

Conventions are normally formalized in game theory, so for an implementation it is easiest to also work with preferences over actions. However, when doing so it is important to keep in mind that what makes a convention is not necessarily the behaviour itself, but the fact that everyone does the same. So, for example, whether or not all agents walk on the right or the left is not relevant, as long as they all stick to the same side.

Norms can be implemented in various ways, from simple to complex. In the simple case, they can be used as constraints on the behaviour, disallowing agents to take certain actions. In the more complex implementations there are two things to keep in mind: who does the sanctioning, and how the norms are taken into account in the deliberation. For the former, a centeralized system is easiest to implement. This is because in a decentralized system the agents also have to take into account who punishes violating agents. For the latter, it is important that the agents are aware of the norm, and what effect it would have to follow or break it.

Habits can be implemented as plans for an agent, without a need to consider the actions of others. However, it is also known that as actions are repeated, they become more habitual [6]. Therefore, also habits can benefit from a learning component.

Similarly to habits, rituals can be implemented as plans. While there is interaction in rituals, this interaction can be implemented as preconditions on the next step in the plan. Rituals are also more static than habits, so they would not necessarily require a learning mechanism.

5 Conclusion

We discussed a number of types of social rules and compared them on a conceptual level. We created some meta theories on how the social rules could be related. Comparing their properties in terms of what is alike and what is different sharpens the initial definitions of the social rules. For example comparing social practices with habits forced us to think about whether a social practice is only social or could also be individual. We do not claim that these definitions are set in stone, this is rather a starting point for comparison and will be further defined in the future.

This work will be used as foundation for a methodology, to analyze and formalize the social rules, and for an implementation of a framework to be used for social simulations, social robotics and socially aware AI. Following up on this work, our next focus will be the context in which the rules are used, as it seems to be very important for habits, social practices and rituals to allow agents to know the context they are situated in, which allows for proper action selection.

References

1. Andrews, B.R.: Habit. Am. J. Psychol. **14**(2), 121–149 (1903)

2. Bell, C.: Ritual: Perspectives and Dimensions. Oxford University Press, Oxford (1997)
3. Bourdieu, P.T.R.N.: Outline of a Theory of Practice. Cambridge University Press, Cambridge (1972)
4. Giddens, A.: Central problems in social theory: action, structure and contradiction in social analysis. University of California Press (1979)
5. Kyriakidis, E.: The archaeology of ritual (2007)
6. Lally, P., van Jaarsveld, C.H.M., Potts, H.W.W., Wardle, J.: How are habits formed: modelling habit formation in the real world. Eur. J. Soc. Psychol. **40**(6), 998–1009 (2010)
7. Lewis, D.: Convention: A Philosophical Study. Blackwell Publishing, Hoboken (1969)
8. Miller, T., Dignum, V., Dignum, F.: Planning for human-agent collaboration using social practices. In: First International Workshop on Socio-cognitive Systems at IJCAI 2018 (2018)
9. Reckwitz, A.: Toward a theory of social practices. Eur. J. Soc. Theory **5**(2), 243–263 (2002)
10. Schatzki, T.R.: A Primer on Practices. In: Practice-Based Education: Perspectives and Strategies, pp. 13–26. SensePublishers, Rotterdam (2012)
11. Shove, E., Pantzar, M., Watson, M.: The Dynamics of Social Practice. Sage, London (2012)
12. Vazquez-Salceda, J., Dignum, V., Dignum, F.: Organizing multiagent systems. JAAMAS **11**(3), 307–360 (2005)

Author Index

Author Index

Printed in the United States
by Baker & Taylor Publisher Services